Praxis 0089
Middle School
Social Studies
Teacher Certification Exam

By: Sharon Wynne, M.S.

XAMonline, INC.
Boston

XAMonline, Inc.
25 First Street, Suite 106
Cambridge, MA 02141
Toll Free 1-800-301-4647
Email: info@xamonline.com
Web www.xamonline.com
Fax: 1-617-583-5552

Library of Congress Cataloging-in-Publication Data

Wynne, Sharon A.
Middle School Social Studies 0089: Teacher Certification / Sharon A. Wynne. -3rd ed.
ISBN 978-1-60787-344-0

1. Middle School Social Studies 0089.   2. Study Guides.   3. Praxis
4. Teachers' Certification & Licensure.   5. Careers

Disclaimer:
The opinions expressed in this publication are the sole works of XAMonline and were created independently from the National Education Association, Educational Testing Service, or any State Department of Education, National Evaluation Systems or other testing affiliates. Between the time of publication and printing, state specific standards as well as testing formats and web site information may change that is not included in part or in whole within this product. Sample test questions are developed by XAMonline and reflect similar content as on real tests; however, they are not former tests. XAMonline assembles content that aligns with state standards but makes no claims or guarantees teacher candidates a passing score. Numerical scores are determined by testing companies such as NES or ETS and then are compared with individual state standards. A passing score varies from state to state.

Printed in the United States of America   œ-1

PRAXIS: Middle School Social Studies 0089
ISBN: 978-1-60787-344-0

About the Subject Assessments

Praxis™: Subject Assessment in Social Studies 5-9 examination

Purpose: The assessments are designed to test the knowledge and competencies of prospective secondary-level teachers. The question bank from which the assessment is drawn is undergoing constant revision. As a result, your test may include questions that will not count towards your score.

Test Version: There are two versions of subject assessments for social studies tests for Praxis. Although both versions of the test emphasize conceptual comprehension, synthesis, and analysis of the principles of social studies, the major difference between versions lies in the *degree* to which the examinee's knowledge is tested.

Version 1: **Social Studies 6–12** This version requires a greater depth of comprehension in U.S. history, world history, economics, geography, political science, anthropology, and psychology. The social science 6-12 guide is based on a typical knowledge level of persons who have completed a *bachelor's degree program* in social science.

Version 2: **Social Studies 5–9** This version tests the examinee's knowledge level in less detail than the first version does. The degree of knowledge required is typically based on completion of *introductory-level course work* in the same areas mentioned above. Although U.S. history remains the focus of both tests, fewer questions on that topic are included in Social Studies 5–9.

Taking the Correct Version of the Subject Assessment: While some states offer just one test called a social studies test, Praxis breaks out those topics into two tests. You would take the 5–9 test to become a middle school teacher and the 6-12 test if you plan on teaching at the high school level. However, as licensure requirements change, it's highly recommended that you consult your educational institution's teaching preparation counselor or your state board of education's teacher licensure division to verify which version of the assessment you should take. We have not mentioned a history test. If you plan on applying for a position in another state, consider a history option. Visit the XAMonline.com Web site for information about becoming certified in a particular state.

Time Allowance, Format, and Length: The time allowance and format for both versions are identical. You will have 2 hours to complete the test; there are 90 multiple-choice questions worth 75 percent of the total score and three constructed-response questions worth 25 percent of the total score.

Content Areas: Both versions of the subject assessments share a degree of commonality in that the test content categories are divided into 6 broad areas that roughly overlap between test versions. Version 1 has a narrower focus on specific disciplines than does Version 2.

	Content Category	Number of Questions	Percentage of Total Score
I.	United States History	22-24	18-20%
II.	World History	16-19	14-16%
III.	Government/Civics	13-15	11-13%
IV.	Geography	14-16	11-14%
V.	Economics	12-14	10-12%
VI.	Sociology and Anthropology	0-6	0-5%
VII.	Short Content Essays	3	25%

Test Taxonomy: Both versions of the subject assessments are constructed on the comprehension, synthesis, and analysis levels of Bloom's Taxonomy. In many questions, the candidate must apply knowledge of more than one discipline in order to answer the questions correctly.

Additional Information about the Praxis Assessments: The Praxis™ series subject assessments are developed by the Educational Testing Service (ETS). The ETS provides additional information on the Praxis series assessments, including registration, preparation and testing procedures, and such study materials as topical guides—about 30 pages of information including approximately 25 additional sample questions.

Table of Contents

Great Study and Testing Tips!

What to study in order to prepare for the subject assessments is the focus of this study guide, but equally important is *how* you study.

You can increase your chances of truly mastering the information by taking some simple, but effective, steps.

Study Tips:

1. Some foods aid the learning process. Foods such as milk, nuts, seeds, rice, and oats help your study efforts by releasing natural memory enhancers called CCKs (*cholecystokinin*) composed of *tryptophan*, *choline*, and *phenylalanine*. All of these chemicals enhance the neurotransmitters associated with memory. Before studying, try a light, protein-rich meal of eggs, turkey, and fish. All of these foods release the memory-enhancing chemicals. The better the connections, the more you comprehend.

Likewise, before you take a test, stick to a light snack of energy-boosting and relaxing foods. A glass of milk, a piece of fruit, or some peanuts all release various memory-boosting chemicals and help you relax and focus on the subject at hand.

2. Learn to take great notes. A by-product of our modern culture is that we have grown accustomed to getting our information in short doses (e.g., TV news sound bites or *USA Today*-style newspaper articles.)

Consequently, we've subconsciously trained ourselves to assimilate information better in neat little packages. Scrawling your notes all over the paper fragments the flow of the information. Strive for clarity. Newspapers use a standard format to achieve clarity. Your notes can be much clearer through use of proper formatting. A very effective format is called the Cornell Method.

Take a sheet of lined loose-leaf notebook paper and draw a line all the way down the paper about 1–2 inches from the left-hand edge.

Draw another line across the width of the paper about 1–2 inches from the bottom. Repeat this process on the reverse side of the page.

Look at the highly effective result. You have ample room for notes, a left hand margin for special emphasis items or inserting supplementary data from the textbook, a large area at the bottom for a brief summary, and a little rectangular space for just about anything you want.

3. Get the concept then the details. Too often, we focus on the details and don't gather an understanding of the concept. However, if you simply memorize only dates, places, or names, you may well miss the whole point of the subject.

A key way to understand material is to put it in your own words. If you are working from a textbook, automatically summarize each paragraph in your mind. If you are outlining text, don't simply copy the author's words.

Rephrase them in your own words. You remember your own thoughts and words much better than someone else's and subconsciously tend to associate the important details to the core concepts.

4. Ask Why. Pull apart written material paragraph by paragraph and don't forget the captions under the illustrations.

Example: If the heading is "Stream Erosion," flip it around to read "Why do streams erode?" Then answer the questions.

If you train your mind to think in a series of questions and answers, not only will you learn more, you will reduce test anxiety because you are used to answering questions.

5. Read for reinforcement and future needs. Even if you only have ten minutes, put your notes or a book in your hand. Your mind is similar to a computer; you have to input data in order to have it processed. *By reading, you are creating the neural connections for future retrieval.* The more times you read something, the more you reinforce the learning of ideas.

Even if you don't fully understand something on the first pass, *your mind stores much of the material for later recall.*

6. Relax to learn, so go into exile. Our bodies respond to an inner clock called biorhythms. Burning the midnight oil works well for some people, but not everyone.

If possible, set aside a particular place to study that is free of distractions. Shut off the television, cell phone, and pager and exile your friends and family during your study period.

If you really are bothered by silence, try background music. Light classical music at a low volume has been shown to aid in concentration better than other types. Instrumental music that evokes pleasant emotions is highly recommended. Try just about anything by Mozart. It relaxes you.

7. <u>Use arrows, not highlighters</u>. At best, it's difficult to read a page full of yellow, pink, blue, and green streaks. Try staring at a neon sign for a while and you'll soon see that the rainbow of colors obscures the message.

A quick note, a brief dash of color, an underline, and an arrow pointing to a particular passage are much clearer than too many highlighted words.

8. <u>Budget your study time</u>. Although you shouldn't ignore any of the material, *allocate your available study time in the same ratio that topics may appear on the test.*

Testing Tips:

1. Get smart; play dumb. **Don't read anything into the question.** Don't make an assumption that the test writer is looking for something other than what is asked. Stick to the question as written and don't read extra things into it.

2. Read the question and all the choices *twice* **before answering the question.** You may miss something by not carefully reading and then re-reading both the question and the answers.

If you really don't have a clue as to the right answer, leave it blank on the first time through. Go on to the other questions; they may provide a clue about how to answer the skipped questions.

If later on, you still can't answer the skipped ones . . . *Guess.* The only penalty for guessing is that you *might* get it wrong. Only one thing is certain; if you don't put anything down, you *will* get it wrong!

3. Turn the question into a statement. Look at the way the questions are worded. The syntax of the question usually provides a clue. Does it seem more familiar as a statement than as a question? Does it sound strange?

By turning a question into a statement, you may be able to spot if an answer sounds right, and it may also trigger memories of material you have read.

4. Look for hidden clues. It's actually very difficult to compose multiple-foil (choice) questions without giving away part of the answer in the options presented.

In most multiple-choice questions, you can often readily eliminate one or two of the potential answers. This leaves you with only two real possibilities and automatically your odds go to fifty-fifty for very little work.

5. Trust your instincts. For every fact that you have read, you subconsciously retain something of that knowledge. On questions that you aren't really certain about, go with your basic instincts. **Your first impression about how to answer a question is usually correct.**

6. Mark your answers directly on the test booklet. Don't bother trying to fill in the optical scan sheet on the first pass through the test.

Just mark your answers very carefully when you eventually transcribe them to the scan sheet.

7. Watch the clock! You have a set amount of time to answer the questions. Don't get bogged down trying to answer a single question at the expense of ten questions you can more readily answer

DOMAIN I.   **UNITED STATES HISTORY**

COMPETENCY 1.1   PHYSICAL GEOGRAPHY OF NORTH AMERICA

Skill 1.1a   Demonstrate knowledge of North America's location in the world and of the continent's rivers, lakes, and important land features

North America consists of Canada, the United States of America, and Mexico. Some geographers also include the Caribbean island nations of the West Indies including Cuba, Jamaica, Haiti, and the Dominican Republic; and the land bridge of Central America, including Panama, Honduras, El Salvador, Nicaragua, Guatemala, and others.

At the most northern extreme of the continent, Alaska and Canada border the Arctic Ocean. At the most southern extreme, the Isthmus of Panama borders Colombia. The west coast borders the Pacific Ocean, while the east coast borders the Atlantic Ocean, the Caribbean Sea, and the Gulf of Mexico, further southeast.

The major freshwater bodies are the Great Lakes—Huron, Ontario, Michigan, Erie and Superior—which lie between Canada and the United States. The Mississippi River is the longest North American river, extending from the U.S.-Canada border to the Gulf of Mexico, draining the Ohio River from the east and the Missouri River to the west. Other significant rivers are the St. Lawrence, which connects Lake Erie to the Atlantic Ocean, and the Rio Grande, which forms much of the border between Mexico and the United States.

The three most significant North American mountain ranges are the Appalachian Mountains, which extend south along the eastern seaboard from the Canadian Maritime Provinces to Georgia in the United States; the Rocky Mountains, which extend from west-central Canada through the United States to Mexico; and the Sierra Nevada cordillera, which extends from Alaska in the United States, through Canada, through the west coast of the United States, and through Mexico and Mesoamerica to South America.

Skill 1.1b   Demonstrate knowledge of broad climate patterns and physiographic regions

Climate
Climate is the average weather that a specific region or location experiences over an extended period of time. Studying the climate of an area includes learning information such as the area's regular temperatures and levels of precipitation. Climate also relates to factors such as wind and barometric pressure, and it may determine regional characteristic such as the length of the growing season.

Four reasons for the different climate regions on Earth are variations in the following:

- latitude,
- amount of moisture,
- temperatures in land and water, and
- land surface.

Earth has many different climates. Some countries, particularly relatively small ones, may contain just one kind of climate. Many countries span climate regions, however. Regions of climates are divided according to latitude.

Although geographers do not agree on the exact boundaries of each zone, the latitudes may be broken out roughly as follows:

- From the equator (0°) to 30° are the **low latitudes**.
- From 30° to 65° are the **middle latitudes**.
- From 65° to the poles are the **high latitudes**.

Low latitudes

The **low latitudes** contain rainforest, savanna, and desert climates. The tropical rainforest climate is found in equatorial lowlands and is hot and wet. There is sun, extreme heat, and frequent rainfall. Although daily temperatures rarely rise above 90 degrees Fahrenheit, the daily humidity is always high, leaving everything sticky and damp. North and south of the tropical rainforests are the tropical grasslands called savannas, the "lands of two seasons"—a winter dry season and a summer wet season. Further north and south of the tropical grasslands, or savannas, are the deserts. These areas are the hottest and driest parts of Earth, receiving less than ten inches of annual rainfall. These areas have extreme temperatures both night and day. After the sun sets, the land cools quickly, dropping the temperature as much as 50 degrees Fahrenheit. In North America, the area from the southern tip of Mexico to the Gulf coast of the United States is in the low latitudes.

Middle latitudes

The **middle latitudes** contain the Mediterranean, the humid-subtropical, the humid-continental, the marine, the steppe, and the desert climates. The Mediterranean climate is located mostly between 30° and 40° north and south latitude. Summers are hot and dry and winters are mild. The growing season usually lasts all year, and what little rain the region gets falls during the winter months. In North America, the Mediterranean climate exists mainly in southern California.

The humid-subtropical climate is found north and south of the tropics. These moist areas are found on the eastern side of their continents. One feature of these locations is their proximity to warm ocean currents. The winds that blow across these currents bring in warm, moist air all year round. Because of the long, warm summers and short, mild winters, these regions have a long growing season, which means that different crops can be grown several times a year. All these factors contribute to the productivity of this climate type, which supports more people than any of the other climates. In North America, this climate occurs on the southeastern coast of the United States.

The North American marine climate is found in the U.S. Pacific Northwest and the western coast of Canada. The ocean winds are wet and warm, bringing a mild, rainy climate to these areas. In the summer, the daily temperatures average at or below 70 degrees Fahrenheit. The temperatures rarely fall below freezing during the winter because of the warming effect of the ocean waters.

The humid-continental climate of the northern and central United States and south-central and southeastern Canada is the "climate of four seasons": spring, summer, fall, and winter. Cold winters, hot summers, and enough rainfall to grow a variety of crops are the major characteristics of this climate. In areas with the humid-continental climate, some of the world's best farmlands and important activities such as trading and mining are found. Differences in temperatures throughout the year are determined by how far inland a place is.

The steppe, or prairie, climate is located in the interior of the North American continent. Called the Great Plains in Canada and the United States, these dry flatlands are far from ocean breezes. Although the summers are similar to those of the humid-continental climate, the big difference is in the amount of annual rainfall. In the prairie (steppe) climate, rainfall is light and uncertain; ten to twenty inches a year, mainly in spring and summer, is considered normal. Where rain is more plentiful, grass grows; in areas of less rain, the prairies gradually become deserts. The middle-latitude deserts of North America are in the southwestern United States and northern Mexico.

High latitudes
The two major climates found in the high latitudes are **tundra** and **taiga**. The word "tundra," meaning marshy plain, aptly describes the climatic conditions in the extreme northern areas of Canada and the state of Alaska. Winters are extremely cold and very long. For most of the year, the ground is frozen, but it becomes rather mushy during the very short summer months. Surprisingly, less snow falls in the area of the tundra than in the eastern part of the United States. The tundra is home to rich plant and animal life. However, because of the harshness of the extreme cold, very few people live there and no crops can be raised.

The taiga is the northern forest region south of the tundra. The world's largest forestlands are here, along with vast mineral wealth and fur- bearing animals. The winter temperatures are colder and the summer temperatures are hotter than those in the tundra because the taiga climate region, with most of its lands covered with marshes and swamps, is farther from the waters of the Arctic Ocean. The climate is so extreme that very few people live here; they are not able to grow crops because of the extremely short growing season.

Vertical climate

In areas of high mountains, there exists a unique type of climate, usually different from that of the general area. This climate is called a "vertical climate" because the temperatures, crops, vegetation, and human activities change with increasing elevation. At the foot of the mountain, one may find a hot, rainy climate and the cultivation of many lowland crops. As one climbs higher, the air becomes cooler, the climate changes sharply, and economic activities change to such endeavors as grazing sheep and growing corn. At the top of many mountains, snow is found year-round.

COMPETENCY 1.2   NATIVE AMERICANS

Skill 1.2a   Demonstrate knowledge of Native American tribes living in the various regions of North America

Strong archaeological evidence supports the contention that most ancestors of the Americas' native peoples crossed what is now the Bering Strait from Asia to Alaska several thousand years ago, eventually settling in all parts of the Americas. Evidence also suggests that some may have arrived from Asia and the Pacific islands via a more southerly transoceanic route.

Anthropologists and ethnologists have traditionally divided the indigenous peoples of North America into the following groups according to language family.

- Inuit—in the north, from western Arctic Alaska, across Arctic Canada to the Canadian Maritimes;
- Dineh—from interior Alaska to the Sonoran Desert in Mexico (Athapaskan, Apache, Navajo, etc.);
- Anishinabe (Algonquian)—eastern woodlands United States and Canada (Ojibwe, Mohican, Abenaki);
- Siouan—midwestern and western Great Plains of the United States and Canada (Lakota, Dakota, Nakota);
- Iroquoian—northeastern United States and southeastern Canada woodlands (Seneca, Oneida, Mohawk, Onondaga, Cayuga);
- Nahuatl—central Mexico (Aztec);
- Mayan—southern Mexico and Mesoamerica; and
- Northwest Indian—southern Alaska panhandle through Pacific-coastal Canada to the Oregon coast (Tlingit, Haida, Tsimshian, Nitnat).

Skill 1.2b   Demonstrate understanding of the political, economic, social, and cultural life of Native American peoples

Native American tribes lived throughout what we now call the United States in varying degrees of togetherness. They adopted different customs, pursued different methods of agriculture and food gathering, and made slightly different weapons. They fought among themselves and with other peoples. They had established varying degrees of culture long before Columbus or any other European explorer arrived on the scene.

Northeast

One of the best-known Native American tribes was the **Algonquian**. We know so much about this tribe because they were one of the first to interact with the newly arrived English settlers in Plymouth, Massachusetts, and elsewhere. The Algonquians lived in wigwams and wore clothing made from animal skins. They were proficient hunters, gatherers, and trappers who also knew quite a bit about farming. To the overall Native American culture, they contributed wampum and dream catchers.

Algonquians such as the English speaker Squanto shared this agricultural knowledge, including how to plant and cultivate corn, pumpkins, and squash, with the English settlers. Algonquian groups stretched through many of the colonies. In Virginia, famous Algonquians included Pocahontas and her father, Powhatan, both of whom are immortalized in English literature. In the West, Tecumseh and Black Hawk, became known for their fierce fighting abilities.

Another tribe who lived in the Northeast was the **Iroquois**. They lived in longhouses and wore clothes made of buckskin. They, too, were expert farmers, growing the "three sisters" (corn, squash, and beans). Five of the Iroquois tribes formed a confederacy, a shared form of government. This confederacy allowed chosen tribal representatives to vote on issues affecting all members of the group, and it has been considered an influence on the later American forms of representative government. The Iroquois also formed the False Face Society, a group of medicine men who shared their medical knowledge with others but kept their identities secret while doing so. These masks are one of the enduring symbols of the Native American era.

Southeast
Living in the Southeast were the **Seminoles** and the **Creeks**, a huge collection of people who lived in chickees (open, bark-covered houses) and wore clothes made from plant fibers. They were expert planters and hunters and were proficient at paddling the dugout canoes they made. The bead necklaces they created were some of the most beautiful on the continent. They are best known, however, for their struggle, especially the one led by the great Osceola, against Spanish and English settlers.

The **Cherokee** also lived in the Southeast. They were one of the most advanced tribes, living in domed houses and wearing deerskin and rabbit fur. Accomplished hunters, farmers, and fishermen, the Cherokee were known the continent over for their intricate and beautiful basketry and clay pottery. They also played a game called lacrosse, which survives to this day in countries around the world.

Great Plains
In the middle of the continent lived the Plains tribes, such as the **Sioux**, the **Cheyenne**, the **Blackfeet**, the **Comanche**, and the **Pawnee**. These peoples lived in teepees and wore buffalo skins and feather headdresses. They hunted wild animals on the plains, especially the buffalo, on which they relied for most of the necessities of life. They were well known for their many ceremonies, including the sun dance and for the peace pipes that they smoked. Famous Plains people include Crazy Horse and Sitting Bull, who strenuously fought U.S. expansion into western Native American lands; Sacagawea, member of the Lewis and Clark expedition; and Chief Joseph, the famous Nez Perce leader.

Southwest

Dotting the deserts of the Southwest were a handful of tribes, including the famous **Pueblo**, who lived in structures that bear their name. They wore clothes made of wool and woven cotton, farmed crops in the middle of desert land, created exquisite pottery and Kachina dolls, and had one of the most complex religions of all the tribes. They are perhaps best known for the challenging vista-based villages that they constructed in large openings in the sheer faces of cliffs and for their **adobes**, mudbrick buildings that housed their living and meeting quarters. The Pueblos chose their own chiefs. Their government was perhaps one of the oldest representative governments in the world.

Another well-known Southwestern tribe was the **Apache,** whose most famous leader was **Geronimo**. The Apache lived in homes called wickiups, which were made of bark, grass, and branches. They wore cotton clothing and were excellent hunters and gatherers. Adept at basketry, the Apache believed that everything in Nature had special powers and that they were honored just to be part of it all.

The **Navajo**, also residents of the Southwest, lived in hogans (round homes built with forked sticks) and wore clothes of rabbit skin. Their major contributions to the overall culture of the continent were in sand painting, weapon making, silversmithing, and weaving. Navajo hands crafted some of the most beautiful woven rugs.

Northwest

Living in the Northwest were the **Inuit**, who lived in tents made from animal skins or, in some cases, igloos. They wore clothes made of animal skins, usually from seals or caribou. They were excellent fishermen and hunters. They crafted efficient kayaks and umiaks to take them through waterways, and harpoons with which to hunt animals. The Inuit are perhaps best known for their great carvings of ivory figures and tall totem poles.

COMPETENCY 1.3   EUROPEAN EXPLORATION AND COLONIZATION

Skill 1.3a   Identify the major explorers and the reasons for European exploration

The first Europeans in the New World were Norsemen led by Eric the Red and later, his son Leif the Lucky. The first documented contact between Europeans and Native Americans that has archaeological evidence to support it was the Viking settlement of eastern Canada in 1000 CE. Under the leadership of Leif Eriksson, the Norse immigrants first encountered hostile Inuit in what is now northeastern Quebec and ventured south to Inland, what is now L'ans aux Meadows, to establish a permanent settlement. Again, their encounter with the Native Americans was hostile. Eventually the incessant warfare between the Viking immigrants and the Native Americans, fought under conditions of relative parity of weapons, compelled the Vikings to abandon the Inland settlement, never to return. Several centuries passed between these early efforts and the beginning of the Age of Exploration.

A number of individuals and events led to the time of exploration and discoveries in the 1500s. The Vivaldo brothers and Marco Polo wrote of their travels and experiences, which signaled the early beginnings. Survivors from the Crusades made their way home to different places in Europe, bringing new information about exotic lands, people, and customs, as well as desirable foods and goods such as spices and silks.

The Renaissance ushered in a time of curiosity, learning, and incredible energy that sparked the desire for trade to procure these new, exotic products and to find better, faster, and cheaper trade routes to get to them. The work of geographers, astronomers, and mapmakers made important contributions; many studied and applied the work of such men as Hipparchus of Greece, Ptolemy of Egypt, Tycho Brahe of Denmark, and Fra Mauro of Italy.

Portugal made the start under the encouragement, support, and financing of Prince Henry the Navigator. The better known explorers who sailed under the flag of Portugal included Cabral, Diaz, and Vasco da Gama, who successfully sailed all the way from Portugal, around the southern tip of Africa, to Calcutta, India.

Christopher Columbus, sailing for Spain, is credited with the discovery of America although he never set foot on its soil. Columbus visited the Bahamas in 1492 but never landed on either Bermuda or Florida. Magellan is credited with the first circumnavigation of Earth. Other Spanish explorers made their marks in parts of what are now the United States, Mexico, and South America. These Spanish explorers included the *conquistadores,* such as Cortez and Pizarro, who conquered native Mesoamerican empires to establish Spanish supremacy. Ponce de Leon and Cabeza de Vaca investigated parts of what is now the southern United States such as Florida and Texas on behalf of Spain, hoping to find gold and riches.

The reasons for Spanish involvement in the Americas included

- the spirit of adventure;
- the desire for land;
- the expansion of Spanish power, influence, and empire;
- the desire for great wealth;
- the expansion of Roman Catholic influence; and
- the conversion of native peoples to Christianity.

For France, claims to various parts of North America were the result of the efforts of such men as Verrazano, Champlain, Cartier, LaSalle, Father Marquette and Joliet. Dutch claims were based on the work of Henry Hudson. John Cabot gave England its stake in North America, along with John Hawkins, Sir Francis Drake, and the half-brothers Sir Walter Raleigh and Sir Humphrey Gilbert.

Skill 1.3b   Demonstrate understanding of the consequences of early contacts between Europeans and Native Americans

The arrival of Christopher Columbus in the New World in 1492 CE marked the beginning of a period of immense change. Columbus, a Genoese adventurer commanding a squadron of Spanish ships, landed on what is now believed to be the island of Hispaniola, which is now Haiti and the Dominican Republic. Although the Native American inhabitants were initially curious and welcomed the newcomers, hostilities quickly ensued as the Spaniards raided indigenous villages for gold and slaves. Unlike the Vikings of five centuries earlier, the Spaniards had an advantage in arms. They had firearms; however, many of the Native Americans perished as a result of contracting diseases for which they had no immunity. The European and African immigrants brought such diseases as smallpox, measles, shingles, cholera, and influenza. As successive Spanish expeditions established landfalls along the Gulf Coast in Florida, Mesoamerica and other locations, a similar pattern of the search for gold, the taking of native populations for slaves, and the introduction of new diseases spelled disaster for the Native Americans.

The Columbian Exchange was the transfer of crops, animals, people, and diseases between Europe and the New World. The Indians who came in contact with the Spaniards were introduced to never-before-seen animals, plants, and seeds from the Old World. The animals included horses, cattle, donkeys, pigs, sheep, goats, and poultry.

Barrels were cut in half and filled with earth to transport and transplant trees bearing the following:

Apples	Oranges	Limes	Cherries
Pears	Walnuts	Olives	Lemons
Figs	Apricots	Almonds	

Even sugar cane and flowers made it to America, along with bags bringing seeds of wheat, barley, rye, flax, lentils, rice, and peas.

Skill 1.3c Demonstrate knowledge of colonization by various European powers

Spain

Spanish settlement had its beginnings in the Caribbean with the establishment of colonies on Hispaniola (at Santo Domingo, which became the capital of the West Indies), Puerto Rico, and Cuba. The first permanent settlement in what is now the United States was established in 1565 at St. Augustine, Florida. A later permanent settlement in the southwestern United States was founded in 1609 at Santa Fe, New Mexico. At the peak of Spanish power, the area in the United States claimed, settled, and controlled by Spain included Florida and all land west of the Mississippi River. Of course, France and England also laid claim to the same areas.

All Spanish colonies belonged to the king of Spain. He was considered an absolute monarch with complete, or absolute, power and he claimed to rule by divine right—the belief that God had given him the right to rule and he answered only to God for his actions. His word was final and the law. The people had no voice in government. The land, the people, and the wealth all belonged to him to use as he pleased. He appointed personal representatives, or viceroys, to rule for him in his colonies. They ruled in his name with complete authority. Since the majority of them were the king's friends and advisers, they were richly rewarded with land grants, gold and silver, trading privileges, and the right to operate the gold and silver mines.

Spain's control over its New World colonies lasted more than 300 years, longer than that of England or France. To this day, Spanish influence remains in names of places, art, architecture, music, literature, law, and cuisine. The Spanish settlements in North America were not commercial enterprises; they were there to protect and defend trading and wealth from Spain's colonies in Mexico and South America. Consequently, the Spanish settlements in what is now the United States never really prospered.

France

The part of North America claimed by France was called New France. It consisted of the land west of the Appalachian Mountains. This area of claim and settlement included the St. Lawrence Valley, the Great Lakes, the Mississippi Valley, and the entire region of land westward to the Rocky Mountains. The French established the permanent settlements of Montreal and New Orleans, thus giving them control of the two major gateways into the heart of North America: its vast, rich interior. The St. Lawrence River, the Great Lakes, and the Mississippi River, along with its tributaries, made it possible for the French explorers and traders to roam at will, virtually unhindered in exploring, trapping, trading, and furthering the interests of France.

Most of the French settlements were in Canada along the St. Lawrence River. Only scattered forts and trading posts were established in the upper Mississippi Valley and the Great Lakes region. The rulers of France originally intended New France to have vast estates owned by nobles and worked by peasants who would live on the estates in compact farming villages—the New World version of the Old World's medieval system of feudalism. However, it didn't work out that way. Each of the nobles wanted his estate to be on the river for ease of transportation. The peasants working the estates also wanted the prime waterfront location. The result of all this real estate squabbling was that New France's settled areas wound up mostly as a string of farmhouses stretching from Quebec to Montreal along the St. Lawrence and Richelieu Rivers. As a result, France failed to develop the same kinds of large-scale settlements in their colonies that the English did in theirs.

In the nonsettled areas of the interior the French fur traders operated. They made alliances with the friendly tribes of Indians, spending the winters with them and getting the furs needed for trade. In the spring, they would return to Montreal in time to trade their furs for the products brought from France, which usually arrived at about the same time. Most of the wealth for New France and its mother country came from the fur trade, which provided a livelihood for many, many people. Manufacturers and workmen back in France, ship-owners and merchants, as well as the fur traders and their Indian allies, all benefited. However, the freedom of roaming and trapping in the interior was a strong enticement for the younger, stronger men and, as a result, the French did not strengthen the areas they had settled along the St. Lawrence.

England

Before 1763, when England was rapidly on the way to becoming the most powerful of the three major Western European powers, its thirteen colonies, located between the Atlantic and the Appalachian Mountains, physically occupied the least amount of land. Early English attempts at colonization in Roanoke and Jamestown faced great difficulties at first, with Roanoke failing completely and Jamestown barely surviving until the beginnings of its cash-crop tobacco agriculture. Nonetheless, the thirteen English colonies were successful and, by the time they had gained their independence from Britain, were more than able to govern themselves. They had a rich historical heritage of law, tradition, and documents leading the way to a constitutional government conducted according to laws and customs. The settlers in the British colonies highly valued individual freedom, democratic government, and getting ahead through hard work.

Skill 1.3d   Demonstrate knowledge of the establishment and growth of the English colonies, including their political, economic, social, and cultural organization and institutions

The English colonies were mostly considered commercial ventures to make a profit for the Crown or the company or whoever financed its beginnings. One colony was strictly a philanthropic enterprise and three others were formed primarily for religious reasons, but the other nine were started for economic reasons. Settlers in these unique colonies came for different reasons:

- religious freedom,
- political freedom,
- economic prosperity, and
- land ownership.

The colonies were divided generally into the three regions of **New England, Middle Atlantic, and Southern**. The culture of each was distinct and affected attitude and ideas towards politics, religion, and economic activities. The geography of each region also contributed to its unique characteristics.

New England
The **New England colonies** consisted of Massachusetts, Rhode Island, Connecticut, and New Hampshire; Maine was part of Massachusetts, and Vermont was part of New Hampshire. Religious motives led to the creation of most of these colonies. Puritans seeking religious freedom settled Massachusetts, and exiled religious dissidents Anne Hutchinson and Roger Williams began Rhode Island and Connecticut, respectively.

Life in the New England colonies was centered on towns. Each family farmed its own plot of land, but a short summer growing season and a limited amount of good soil gave rise to other economic activities such as manufacturing, fishing, shipbuilding, and trade. The vast majority of the settlers shared similar origins in England and Scotland. Towns were carefully planned and laid out the same way. The form of government was the town meeting, where all adult males met to make the laws. The legislative body, the General Court, consisted of an upper and a lower house.

Middle Atlantic
The **Middle, or Middle Atlantic, colonies** included New York, New Jersey, Pennsylvania, Delaware, and Maryland. New York and New Jersey were previously the Dutch colony of New Netherlands, and Delaware had been, at one time, New Sweden. These five colonies from their beginnings were considered "melting pots," with settlers from many different nations and backgrounds.

Because the soil was very fertile, the land was gently rolling, and a mild climate provided a long growing season, the main economic activity was farming, with settlers scattered over the countryside cultivating rather large farms.

The farms in the Middle Colonies produced a large surplus of food, not only for the colonists themselves but also for sale. This colonial region became known as the "breadbasket" of the New World. The New York and Philadelphia seaports were constantly filled with ships being loaded with meat, flour, and other foodstuffs for the West Indies and England. There were other economic activities such as shipbuilding, iron mines, and factories producing paper, glass, and textiles. The legislative body in Pennsylvania consisted of one house. In the other four colonies, the legislative body had two houses. Also, units of local government were in counties and towns.

Southern

The **Southern colonies** were Virginia, North and South Carolina, and Georgia. Virginia was the first successful permanent English colony, and Georgia was the last. The year 1619 was very important in the history of Virginia and the United States, with three very significant events occurring. First, sixty women were sent to Virginia to marry and establish families. Second, twenty Africans, the first of thousands, arrived. Third, and most important, the Virginia colonists were granted the right to self-government, and they began by electing their own representatives to their own legislative body, the House of Burgesses.

The major economic activity in this region was farming. Here the soil was very fertile and the climate was very mild with an even longer growing season than in the Middle colonies. The large plantations that eventually required large numbers of slaves were located in the coastal or tidewater areas. Although the wealthy slave-owning planters set the pattern of life in this region, most of the people lived inland, away from coastal areas. They were small farmers; and very few, if any, owned slaves.

The daily life of the colonists differed greatly according to whether they lived in the coastal settlements or the inland ones. The planters and the people living in the coastal cities and towns had a way of life similar to that in towns in England. The influence was seen and heard in how people dressed and talked. The architectural styles of houses and public buildings and the social divisions or levels of society mimicked that of England. Both the planters and city dwellers enjoyed an active social life and had strong emotional ties to England.

On the other hand, life inland on the frontier had marked differences. All facets of daily living—clothing, food, housing, economic and social activities—were connected to what was needed to sustain life and survive in the wilderness. The settlers produced everything themselves. They were self-sufficient, extremely individualistic, and independent. Few, if any, levels of society or class distinctions existed because people considered themselves to be the equal to all others, regardless of their station in life. The roots of equality, independence, and individual rights and freedoms were extremely strong and well developed. People were not judged by their fancy dress, expensive houses, eloquent language, or the titles following their names.

COMPETENCY 1.4   ESTABLISHING A NEW NATION (1776–1791)

Skill 1.4a   Demonstrate understanding of the American Revolution, including its causes, leaders, events, and results

One historian explained that the British were interested only in raising money to pay war debts, regulating the trade and commerce of the colonies, and looking after business and financial interests between England and the rest of her empire. The establishment of overseas colonies was, first and foremost, a commercial enterprise, not a political one. The political aspect was secondary and assumed. The British took it for granted that Parliament was supreme and was recognized as such by the colonists; they were very resentful of the colonial challenge to the British Parliament's authority. They were contemptuously indifferent to politics in America and had no wish to exert any control over it. As resistance and disobedience swelled and increased in America, the British increased their efforts to punish the Americans and put them in their place.

The British had been extremely lax and totally inconsistent in enforcing the mercantile or trade laws passed in the years before 1754. The government itself was not particularly stable, so actions against the colonies occurred in anger and the attitude was one of moral superiority: that they knew how to manage America better than the Americans did themselves. This, of course, points to a lack of sufficient knowledge of conditions and opinions in America. The colonists had been left on their own for nearly 150 years; and by the time the Revolutionary War began, they were quite adept at self-government and adequately handling the affairs of their daily lives. The Americans equated ownership of land or property with the right to vote. Property was considered the foundation of life and liberty and, in the colonial mind and tradition, these went together.

American colonists in the English colonies had always considered themselves to be citizens of Great Britain and loyal subjects of the British Crown (with all the traditional rights and privileges pursuant to that status). They had lived their lives as free men and developed their own town governments and colonial legislatures based on beliefs and principles that traced back through English history to the time of Magna Carta. They had always been vocal participants in their own social, cultural, and political development. It may have been unique, but they considered it to be British in its essence.

The British incurred a great deal of debt fighting the French and Indian War in the colonies, and the resulting economic measures intended to recoup its costs created immense tension between the British and the American colonists. Therefore, when an indirect tax on tea was imposed, the British felt it was warranted. The colonists viewed any tax, direct or indirect, as an attack on their property. They felt that, as a representative body, the British Parliament should protect British citizens, including the colonists, from arbitrary taxation. Since they felt they were not represented in Parliament, they had no protection.

The colonists had their own tradition of publishing the views and sentiments of individuals regarding issues of parochial interest and matters of concern that crossed colonial boundaries. In print—through newspapers and pamphlets—dialogue and debate over matters quite trivial or quite significant became common public practice in the American colonies. As strains with the mother country began to develop and increase—especially after the French and Indian War—the resulting issues became increasingly focused in print throughout the colonies. No doubt the discussions and debates published carried their sentiments over to the homes, taverns, and other places where the people met to discuss events of the day.

An important result of this was a growing "Americanism" in the sentiments of those writers published, and a sense of connection among American people transcended colonial boundaries.

From the initial Stamp Act in 1765, through the Boston Massacre in 1770, to the time of the Tea Act in 1773, which resulted in the Boston Tea Party, and beyond, colonial presses were rife with discussion and debate about what they considered to be an unacceptable situation. Parliament intended to assert its right to tax and legislatively control the colonies of Great Britain in whatever manner it saw as prudent and appropriate. Most American colonists, believing themselves to be full British subjects, would deny Parliament's assertions so long as they were not provided with full and equal representation within Parliament.

One of the most notable spokesmen for the American cause was, in fact, an Englishman. Thomas Paine (1737-1809) came to America in November 1774. He was immediately taken up by the social issues and politics in the American colonies and insinuated himself into the dialogue of current issues, which was ongoing and conducted through newspapers and pamphlets. Within months of his arrival, he published his first article in America.

Paine is best remembered for *Common Sense*. In a number of publications, spanning the war years (from 1776 through 1783), Thomas Paine wrote a series of addresses, inspiring the American people and reprimanding British authorities. One of his most famous publications, produced at a time of ill fortune for the American cause and disenchantment for many members of the fledgling American Army, began,

> *These are the times that try men's souls. The summer soldier and the sunshine patriot will, in this crisis, shrink from the service of their country; but he that stands it now, deserves the love and thanks of man and woman. Tyranny, like hell, is not easily conquered; yet we have this consolation with us, that the harder the conflict, the more glorious the triumph.*

The writings of Thomas Paine and the impact of the publication of *Common Sense* were credited with influencing Congress and the populace at large to declare independence.

On August 23, 1775, George III declared that the colonies were in rebellion and warned them to stop. By 1776, the colonists and their representatives in the Second Continental Congress realized that things were past the point of no return. The Declaration of Independence was drafted and later declared on July 4, 1776. Thomas Jefferson authored the Declaration of Independence with assistance from Benjamin Franklin and John Adams. After a long string of inequities imposed by the British government without the consent of the American colonists, taxation by Parliament, and impositions such as the quartering of British troops without recompense to the hosts, the Continental Congress resolved to address these grievances by a unanimous declaration to break away from the Crown.

As leader of the Continental Army, George Washington labored against tremendous odds to wage a victorious war. The turning point in the Americans' favor occurred in 1777 with the American victory at Saratoga. Because of this victory, the French decided to align themselves with the Americans against the British. With the aid of French warships blocking the entrance to Chesapeake Bay, British General Cornwallis trapped at Yorktown, Virginia, surrendered in 1781 and the fighting was over. The Treaty of Paris officially ending the war was signed in 1783.

After independence was declared and during the war, the former colonies now found themselves as independent states. The Second Continental Congress was conducting a war with representation by delegates from thirteen separate states. The Congress had no power to act for the states or to require them to accept and follow its wishes. A permanent united government was desperately needed. On November 15, 1777, the Articles of Confederation were adopted, creating a league of free and independent states.

Skill 1.4b   Demonstrate knowledge of the Declaration of Independence and other revolutionary documents

The Declaration of Independence was the founding document of the United States of America. The Articles of Confederation were the first attempt that the newly independent states made to reach a new understanding among themselves with regard to self-governance. The Declaration was intended to demonstrate the reasons the colonies were seeking separation from Great Britain. For the most part conceived and written by Thomas Jefferson, the Declaration is not only important for what it says but also for how it says it. The Declaration is, in many respects, a poetic document. Instead of a simple recitation of the colonists' grievances, it set out clearly the reasons for the colonists' seeking their freedom from Great Britain. They had tried all means to resolve the dispute peacefully. It was the right of a people, when all other methods of addressing their grievances had been tried and failed, to separate themselves from that power that was keeping them from fully expressing their rights to "**life, liberty, and the pursuit of happiness.**"

The Declaration of Independence can be divided into three main parts:

- Statements of the general state of humanity and the natural rights inherent in all civil societies. Jefferson talks about "self-evident" truths, unalienable rights of people to "Life, Liberty and the Pursuit of Happiness" which show considerable influence from primarily French thinkers of the Enlightenment during the seventeenth and eighteenth centuries. He also clearly states that a government that no longer respects these inherent rights loses its legitimacy and has become despotic, and the governed have the right to throw off such a government (a call for insurrection against the sovereign).
- An enumeration of specific and detailed grievances which point out why the current sovereign has lost the right to govern. It also lists how the king even subverted English common law and legal traditions dating back to antiquity.
- The last part of the text states that the colonists had exhausted all civil and legal means of having their grievances addressed by the British government and now had the right and duty to break with the Crown and be a free and independent nation.

The final section of the Declaration contains the signatures of the representatives of the colonies to the Continental Congress in Philadelphia. Realizing that they had committed an act of treason, punishable by death by hanging, Benjamin Franklin counseled unity, lest they "all hang separately."

Other authors, printers, publishers, and factions were also active in promoting the new American attitude toward independence. Of significant note was the **Virginia Declaration of Rights**, drafted by George Mason in May 1776 and amended by Thomas Ludwell Lee and the Virginia Convention. Thomas Jefferson was influenced by it when he drafted the Declaration of Independence only a month later. This document would also influence James Madison when drawing up the Bill of Rights (1789) and Marquis de Lafayette when he drafted the French Declaration of the Rights of Man and Citizen (1789).

Skill 1.4c   Demonstrate knowledge of the first government of the United States under the Articles of Confederation

The **Articles of Confederation** outlined the first political system under which the newly independent colonies tried to organize themselves. It was drafted in 1776 after the Declaration of Independence; passed by the Continental Congress on

November 15, 1777; ratified by the thirteen states; and took effect on March 1, 1781.

The newly independent states were unwilling to give too much power to a national government. They had struggled against the perceived tyrannical rule of Great Britain and did not want to replace one harsh ruler with another. After many debates, the form of the Articles was accepted. The central government of the new United States of America consisted of a Congress of two to seven delegates from each state with each state having just one vote. The Articles gave Congress the power to declare war, appoint military officers, and coin money. The Congress was also responsible for foreign affairs. The Articles of Confederation limited the powers of the Congress by giving the states final authority. Although Congress could pass laws, at least nine of the thirteen states had to approve a law before it went into effect. Congress could not pass any laws regarding taxes. To get money, Congress had to ask each state for it; no state could be forced to pay.

Some of Congress's powers included borrowing and coining money, directing foreign affairs, declaring war and making peace, building and equipping a navy, regulating weights and measures, and asking the states to supply men and money for an army. The delegates to Congress had no real authority as each state carefully and jealously guarded its own interests and limited powers under the Articles. Also, the delegates to Congress were paid by their states and had to vote as directed by their state legislatures.

Thus, the Articles created a loose alliance among the thirteen states. The national government was weak, in part, because it didn't have a strong chief executive to carry out laws passed by the legislature. This weak national government might have worked if the states had been able to get along with each other. The serious weakness was the lack of certain powers. Congress could not regulate finances, interstate trade, or foreign trade and could not enforce treaties and retain military power.Something better and more efficient was needed.

In May 1787, delegates from all the states except Rhode Island began meeting in Philadelphia. At first, they met to revise the Articles of Confederation as instructed by Congress; but they soon realized that much more was needed. Abandoning the instructions, they set out to write a new constitution, the foundation of all government in the United States and a model for representative government throughout the world.

Skill 1.4d Demonstrate understanding of the process of writing and adopting the Constitution and the Bill of Rights

The beginnings of civil liberties and the idea of civil rights in the United States go back to the democratic ideas of the ancient Greeks. The early struggles for civil rights and the very philosophies that led people to come to the New World in the first place—religious freedom, political freedom, and the right to live one's life as one sees fit—are basic to the American ideal. These ideas are embodied in the Declaration of Independence and the Constitution.

The first order of business was the agreement among all the delegates that the convention would be kept secret. No discussion of the convention outside of the meeting room would be allowed. They wanted to be able to discuss, argue, and agree among themselves before presenting the completed document to the American people.

The delegates were afraid that if the people were aware of what was taking place before it was completed, the entire country would be plunged into argument and dissension. It would be extremely difficult, if not impossible, to settle differences and come to an agreement. Between the official notes kept and the complete notes of future President James Madison, an accurate picture of the events of the Convention is part of the historical record.

The delegates went to Philadelphia representing different areas and different interests. They all agreed on a strong central government but not one with unlimited powers. They also agreed that no one part of government could control the rest. It would be a republican form of government (sometimes referred to as representative democracy) in which the supreme power was in the hands of the voters who would elect the men who would govern for them.

One of the first serious controversies involved equal representation in Congress. Vehement disagreement arose between the small states and the large states. Virginia's Governor Edmund Randolph's proposal that state population determine the number of representatives sent to Congress was known as the Virginia Plan. New Jersey delegate William Paterson countered with the proposal known as the New Jersey Plan, that each state have equal representation.

After much argument and debate, they devised the **Great Compromise** also known as the Connecticut Compromise, proposed by Roger Sherman. It was agreed that Congress would have two houses. A Senate would consist of two Senators from each state, giving equal representation. The number of members elected to the House of Representatives would be based on each state's population. Both houses could draft bills to debate and vote on with the exception of bills pertaining to money, which must originate in the House of Representatives.

Another major controversy involved economic differences between the North and the South. One issue concerned the counting of African slaves when determining representation in the House of Representatives. The southern delegates wanted slaves counted for representation but did not want the number of slaves to determine the amount of taxes to be paid. The northern delegates argued the opposite: count the slaves for taxation but not for representation. The resulting agreement was known as the "three-fifths" compromise. Three-fifths of the slaves would be counted for both taxes and for determining representation in the House.

The last major compromise, also between the North and the South, was the **Commerce Compromise**. The economic interests of the northern part of the country were ones of industry and business whereas the South's economic interests were primarily agricultural. The northern merchants wanted the government to regulate and control commerce with foreign nations and with the states. Of course, southern planters opposed this idea because they felt that any tariff laws passed would be unfavorable to them. The acceptable compromise to this dispute was that Congress was given the power to regulate commerce with other nations and the states, including levying tariffs on imports. However, Congress did not have the power to levy tariffs on any exports. This increased southern concern about the effect tariffs would have on the slave trade. The delegates finally agreed that the importation of slaves would continue for twenty more years with no interference from Congress. Any import tax could not exceed ten dollars per person. After 1808, Congress would be able to decide whether to prohibit or regulate any further slave importation.

Of course, when work was completed and the document was presented, nine states had to approve it before it could go into effect. There was no little amount of discussion, arguing, debating, and haranguing. The opposition had the following three major objections:

- The states seemed as if they were being asked to surrender too much power to the national government.
- The voters did not have enough control and influence over the men who would be elected by them to run the government.
- The document lacked a "bill of rights" guaranteeing hard-won individual freedoms and liberties.

Those who wanted to see a strong central government, such as Alexander Hamilton and John Jay, were called Federalists. Hamilton and Jay, along with James Madison, wrote a series of letters to the New York newspapers, urging that state to ratify the Constitution. These letters became known as the Federalist Papers.

In the Anti-Federalist camp were Thomas Jefferson and Patrick Henry. These men and many like them were worried that a strong national government would descend into the kind of tyranny that they had just abolished. They, too, wrote a series of arguments to the New York newspapers; however, they argued against the Constitution and thus those letters were called the Anti-Federalist Papers.

In the end, both sides got most of what they wanted. The Federalists got their strong national government, which was held in place by the famous "checks and balances." The Anti-Federalists got the Bill of Rights, the first ten amendments to the Constitution that protect some of the most basic of human rights. The states that were in doubt about ratification of the Constitution signed on when the Bill of Rights was promised.

In 1789, the first Congress passed these amendments and by December 1791 three-fourths of the states at that time had ratified them. The Bill of Rights protects certain liberties and basic rights, such as freedom of speech and religion, and the right to a fair trial. James Madison, who wrote the amendments, said that the Bill of Rights does not give Americans these rights. According to Madison, people already have these rights. They are natural rights that belong to all human beings. The Bill of Rights simply prevents the government from taking away these rights.

Eleven states finally ratified the document and the new national government went into effect. It was no small feat that the delegates were able to produce a workable document that satisfied all opinions, feelings, and viewpoints. The separation of powers of the three branches of government and the built-in system of checks and balances to keep power balanced were a stroke of genius. It provided for the individuals and the states and an organized central authority to keep a new, inexperienced nation on track. The framers of the U.S. Constitution created a system of government so flexible that it has continued in its basic form to this day. In 1789, the Electoral College unanimously elected George Washington as the first president and the new nation was on its way.

COMPETENCY 1.5   EARLY YEARS OF THE NEW NATION (1791–1829)

Skill 1.5a   **Demonstrate understanding of political development, including early presidential administrations, establishment of the federal judiciary, and inception and growth of political parties**

Early presidents and the birth of the two-party system

The early presidential administrations established much of the form and many of the procedures still present today, including the development of the party system. George Washington, the first U.S. president, established the first Cabinet form. In the Cabinet, individual advisors oversee the various functions of the executive branch and advise the President, who makes the final decisions. Divisions within Washington's cabinet and within Congress during his administration eventually led to the development of political parties, which Washington opposed.

The two parties that developed through the early 1790s were led by Thomas Jefferson as the Secretary of State and Alexander Hamilton as the Secretary of the Treasury. Jefferson and Hamilton were different in many ways—not the least of which were their views on what should be the proper form of government of the United States. This difference helped to shape the parties that formed around them.

Hamilton wanted the federal government to be stronger than the state governments. Jefferson believed that the state governments should be stronger. Hamilton supported the creation of the first Bank of the United States while Jefferson opposed it because he felt that it gave too much power to wealthy investors who would help run it. Jefferson interpreted the Constitution strictly and argued that it does not grant the federal government the power to create a national bank. Hamilton interpreted the Constitution much more loosely. He pointed out that the Constitution gave Congress the power to make all laws "necessary and proper" to carry out its duties. He reasoned that, since Congress had the right to collect taxes, Congress had the right to create the bank.

Hamilton wanted the government to encourage economic growth. He favored the growth of trade and manufacturing, and the rise of cities as the necessary parts of economic growth. He favored the business leaders and mistrusted the common people. Jefferson believed that the common people, especially the farmers, were the backbone of the nation. He thought that the rise of big cities and manufacturing would corrupt American life.

Finally, Hamilton and Jefferson had their disagreements only in private. But when Congress began to pass many of Hamilton's ideas and programs, Jefferson and his friend James Madison decided to organize support for their own views. They moved quietly and very cautiously in the beginning.

In 1791 they went to New York, telling people that they were going to study its wildlife. Actually, Jefferson was more interested in meeting with several important New York politicians such as its governor, George Clinton, and Aaron Burr, a strong critic of Hamilton. Jefferson asked Clinton and Burr to help defeat Hamilton's program by getting New Yorkers to vote for Jefferson's supporters in the next election.

Before long, leaders in other states began to organize support for either Jefferson or Hamilton. Jefferson's supporters called themselves Democratic-Republicans (often this was shortened just to Republicans, though in actuality it was the forerunner of today's Democratic Party). Meanwhile, Hamilton and his supporters were known as Federalists, because they favored a strong federal government. The Federalists had the support of the merchants and ship owners in the Northeast and some planters in the South. Small farmers, craft workers, and some of the wealthier landowners supported Jefferson and the Democratic-Republicans.

Washington's vice-president, John Adams, was elected to succeed him. Adams's administration was marked by the new nation's first entanglement in international affairs. With Britain and France at war, Adams's Federalist Party supported the British and Vice-President Thomas Jefferson's Republican Party supported the French. The nation was nearly brought to the brink of war with France, but Adams managed to negotiate a treaty that avoided full conflict. In the process, however, he lost the support of his party and was defeated after one term by Thomas Jefferson.

The federal court system

Article III of the U.S. Constitution created a Supreme Court and authorized Congress to create other federal courts as it deemed necessary. In 1789, Congress passed the **Judiciary Act**, which set the number of Supreme Court justices at six, with one Chief Justice and five associates. The Judiciary Act also created thirteen judicial districts, each with one district judge who was authorized to hear maritime and other types of cases. Most federal trial cases were heard by circuit courts, which were originally made up of two Supreme Court justices and the local district judge. In 1793, Congress changed the circuit court to one Supreme Court justice and the local district judge.

In 1801, the Federalist majority in Congress sought to place more power in the district courts and removed the requirement that a Supreme Court justice preside over circuit courts. The following year, however, Jeffersonian Republicans took the majority in Congress and reversed this decision. As the demands of the growing nation increased in the following decades, the federal judiciary system was expanded by adding Supreme Court justices and enlarging the district and circuit systems.

Skill 1.5b   Demonstrate understanding of foreign policy issues, including the Louisiana Purchase, the War of 1812, and the Monroe Doctrine

Louisiana Purchase

The new nation's greatest territorial gain happened under President Thomas Jefferson in 1803. In 1800, Napoleon Bonaparte of France secured the Louisiana Territory from Spain, which had held it since 1792. The vast area stretched westward from the Mississippi River to the Rocky Mountains and northward to Canada. An effort was made to keep the transaction a secret, but the news reached the U.S. State Department. The United States did not have a particular problem with Spanish control of the territory since Spain was weak and was not a threat to America. However, the relationship with France was different. Though not the world power that Great Britain was, France was still strong and, under Napoleon's leadership, was again acquiring an empire. President Jefferson had three major reasons for concern.

- With the French controlling New Orleans at the mouth of the Mississippi River, westerners would lose their *right of deposit*, which would greatly affect their ability to trade. This right was very important to the Americans who were living in the area between the Mississippi and the Appalachians. They were unable to get heavy products to eastern markets but could float them on rafts down the Ohio and Mississippi Rivers to New Orleans to ships heading to Europe or the Atlantic coast ports. If France prohibited this, it would be a financial disaster for the Americans.

- President Jefferson also worried that, if the French possessed the Louisiana Territory, America would be extremely limited in its expansion into the interior of the continent.

- Under Napoleon Bonaparte, France was becoming more powerful and aggressive. This increase in power would be a constant worry and threat to the western border of the United States. President Jefferson was very interested in the western part of the country and firmly believed that it was both necessary and desirable to strengthen western lands. So Jefferson wrote to the American minister to France, Robert R. Livingston, to offer Napoleon up to $10 million for New Orleans and West Florida. Napoleon countered the offer with the question of how much the United States would be willing to pay for all of Louisiana. After some discussion, it was agreed to pay $15 million, and the largest land transaction in history was negotiated in 1803, resulting in the eventual formation of fifteen states.

After the United States purchased the Louisiana Territory, Jefferson appointed Captains Meriwether Lewis and William Clark to explore the new territory and find out exactly what had been bought. The expedition extended beyond the Louisiana Territory to the Pacific Ocean. Lewis and Clark returned two years later with maps, journals, and artifacts from their expedition. This led the way for future explorers to make more knowledge about the territory available and resulted in the westward movement and the later belief in the doctrine of Manifest Destiny.

Foreign policy

In 1804, the United States engaged in the first of a series of armed conflicts with the Barbary pirates of North Africa. The rulers of Morocco, Algiers, Tunis, and Tripoli—the Barbary States of North Africa—had long been seizing ships of foreign nations and demanding ransoms for the crews. The nations of Europe decided it was cheaper and easier to pay an annual tribute or bribe. The United States had been doing this since 1783, when trade between the Mediterranean countries and the newly independent nation began. When the rulers in Tripoli demanded a ridiculously high bribe and chopped down the flagpole of the American consulate there, Jefferson had had enough. The first skirmish against Tripoli in 1804 and 1805 was successful. In 1815, the payment of bribes to the rulers ceased. U.S. ships could trade and sail freely in the Mediterranean.

War of 1812

The United States' involvement in the **War of 1812** came about largely because of the political and economic struggles between France and Great Britain. Other incentives for war with Great Britain included

- the expansion of settlers westward and the resulting need for more land,
- the agitation of Indians by Canadian fur traders,
- the impressment of U.S. sailors onto British ships, and
- the agitation of War Hawks in Congress.

Napoleon's goal was complete conquest and control of Europe, including (and especially) Great Britain. Although British troops were temporarily driven off the mainland of Europe, the Royal Navy still controlled the seas across which France had to bring the products needed. America traded with both nations, especially with France and its colonies. The British decided to destroy the American trade with France, mainly for the following two reasons: products and goods from the United States gave Napoleon what he needed to keep up his struggle with Britain. Napoleon and France were the enemy, and it was felt that the Americans were aiding the Mother Country's enemy. (b) Britain felt threatened by the increasing strength and success of the U.S. merchant fleet. They were becoming major competitors with the ship owners and merchants in Britain.

The British issued the Orders in Council, a series of measures prohibiting American ships from entering any French ports, not only in Europe, but also in India and the West Indies. At the same time, Napoleon began efforts for a coastal blockade of the British Isles. He issued a series of orders prohibiting all nations, including the United States, from trading with the British. And he didn't stop there. He threatened seizure of every ship entering any French port after it had stopped at any British port or British colony, even threatening to seize every ship inspected by British cruisers or that paid any duties to their government. Adding to all of this, the British were stopping American ships and seizing, or impressing, American seamen into service on British ships. Americans were outraged.

In 1807, Congress passed the **Embargo Act,** forbidding American ships from sailing to foreign ports. This embargo could not be completely enforced, and it greatly hurt business and trade in the United States. The unpopular act was repealed in 1809. Two additional acts passed by Congress after James Madison became president attempted to regulate trade with other nations and to have Britain and France remove the restrictions they had put on American shipping. The catch was that, whichever nation removed restrictions, the U.S. agreed not to trade with the other one. Napoleon was clever and was the first to agree, prompting Madison to issue orders prohibiting trade with Britain, ignoring warnings from the British not to do so. Of course, this did not work either, and although Britain eventually rescinded the Orders in Council, war came in June 1812 and ended Christmas Eve, 1814, with the signing of the Treaty of Ghent.

During the War of 1812, Americans were divided over not only whether it was necessary to fight but also what territories they should fight for and take. The nation was still young and not adequately prepared to fight another war. The primary American objective was to conquer Canada, but it failed.

Two naval victories and one military victory stood out for the United States. Oliver Perry gained control of Lake Erie, and Thomas MacDonough fought on Lake Champlain.   Both of these naval battles successfully prevented the British invasion of the United States from Canada. Nevertheless, British troops landed on the Potomac,below Washington D.C., marched into the city, and burned the public buildings, including the White House. Andrew Jackson's victory at New Orleans helped bring him to national attention and damaged the antiwar stance of the waning Federalists. However, the battle actually took place after Britain and the United States had reached an agreement, and it had no impact on the war's outcome. The peace treaty did little for the United States' territorial expansion, but it brought peace, released prisoners of war, restored all occupied territory, and set up a commission to settle boundary disputes with Canada. The war proved to be a turning point in U.S. history. Since then, European events have profoundly shaped U.S. policies, especially foreign policies. The United States also again asserted itself as an entity fully independent of Great Britain.

Monroe Doctrine
In his message to Congress on December 2, 1823, President James Monroe delivered the Monroe Doctrine. The United States was informing the powers of

the Old World that the American continents were no longer open to European colonization and that any effort to extend European political influence into the New World would be considered by the United States "as dangerous to our peace and safety." The United States would not interfere in European wars or internal affairs and expected Europe to stay out of American affairs.

Skill 1.5c Demonstrate understanding of economic development, including Hamilton's economic plan, tariffs, and changes in agriculture, commerce, and industry

Hamilton's economic plan

In the domestic affairs of the new nation, the first problems dealt with finances—paying for the war debts of the Revolutionary War and other financial needs. Secretary of the Treasury Alexander Hamilton wanted the government to increase tariffs and put taxes on certain products made in the United States, for example, liquor. This money in turn would be used to pay war debts of the federal government and the states. Money would be available for expenses and necessary internal improvements.

To provide for this, Hamilton favored a national bank. Secretary of State Thomas Jefferson, along with southern supporters, opposed many of Hamilton's suggested plans. Later, Jefferson relented and gave support to some proposals. In return, Hamilton and his northern supporters agreed to locate the nation's capital in the South. Jefferson continued to oppose a national bank, but Congress set up the first one in 1791, chartered for the next twenty years.

Hamilton's plans and the creation of the bank had an immediate effect on the economics of the new nation. With the creation of paper securities, finance became more liquid, allowing for the creation of a stock market fueled by speculation. These securities could be used as collateral for loans to provide for expansion in industry and the creation of infrastructure such as roads, canals, and bridges, which in turn expanded the market for agricultural products. Foreign investment was also stimulated, and exports increased.

Advances in agriculture

Advances in U.S. agriculture were a direct result of the advances in technological development and the new political awareness about the power of organization and shared information and education.

Eli Whitney was born in Massachusetts during the colonial period and, as a citizen of the recently formed United States, graduated from Yale College in 1792. Early in 1793, he designed and constructed the first cotton gin ("gin" for engine). This machine automated the process for separating cottonseed from the short-cotton fiber—previously, a long and laborious process. Whitney may have been a bit ahead of his time and failed to profit from his invention.

However, others soon copied his cotton gin and were more successful in reaching the appropriate markets.

Once Whitney's cotton gin was accepted by the planters of the South and established on the plantations, cotton would become a king crop in southern agriculture. The "peculiar institution" of slavery would become even more profitable and remain institutionalized for many years to come. The advent of the cotton gin and the resulting increase in the production of cotton for the world's markets meant vast increases in wealth and political power for the South. Other agricultural areas of the country that were not part of the plantation system also experienced growth and change during these years. In the 1820s, agricultural periodicals became commonplace, providing shared information about agriculture and discussing issues of concern to farmers. From 1825 on, some schools and colleges started offering courses in agriculture or in sciences useful in agriculture.

Skill 1.5d   Demonstrate understanding of social and cultural development in this period, including immigration and the frontier, family life and the role of women, religious life, and nationalism and regionalism

Social and cultural development
During the years from 1791 to 1829, Americans were gradually becoming a new and distinct people. The heritage of European colonialism had provided the colonies with many traditions and social practices that were gradually abandoned. Some of the more common customs and traditions that blended well with the changing attitudes of the American people continued to be practiced for several decades to come. This was true of many common business practices and traditional mores regarding proper and appropriate social interactions. Concern over European intrigues and a second war against Great Britain served to help the American people distance themselves more and more from any reliance on—and old connections with—the European nations.

Immigration increased during this period, especially as new territories opened for exploration and settlement. Most of the new arrivals came from the same Western European countries as the original colonists. The major exception to the ethnicity of most immigrants to the United States through much of this period continued to be African slaves, imported against their will to provide a chattel labor force.

Because of compromises made by the federal government with certain states, Congress was unable to act against the importation of slaves and the slave trade until January 1, 1808. At that time, a bill was unanimously passed forbidding the importation of slaves. However, since smuggling slaves was lucrative and difficult for the government to control, the illicit trade continued for more than a decade. During this time, tens of thousands of additional African slaves were brought into the United States. Finally, in 1819 Congress declared this practice to be piracy. We have no record that any of the practitioners were ever condemned as pirates, but the effort by the federal government seemed to have the desired effect. Of course, the internal trade and sale of slaves continued to flourish until the Civil War, becoming far more lucrative when importation ceased.

Role of women

Abigail Adams was a unique individual, but not necessarily an unusual woman for her time. Women of this period lived lives—and had attitudes about life— which might seem quite alien to American people today. Most people of the time believed there were definite distinctions regarding what it meant to be a woman and what it meant to be a man. They were aware of these distinctions in the natural world and saw them reinforced in the religious doctrine of their faiths.

Social customs, traditions, and the practices of lawmaking institutions adopted these distinctions or were adapted to conform to socially acceptable conventions. These conditions were generally accepted by women and men alike: there were roles for men and there were roles for women—just as there were garments appropriate to each sex.

Some women during this period had the right to vote and participated in the election process. These women were usually residents of new territories, which did not adhere to the restrictions of the various states. When these territories eventually became states, however, these women were excluded from this process. Women did enjoy the right to vote in one state—New Jersey. This right was granted to women in the adoption of the constitution of New Jersey in 1776, but the right was revoked in 1807.

While most women were excluded from the franchise (they were not allowed to vote), many men were excluded as well. Slaves of either sex could not vote. Freedmen were often prevented from voting. And in various jurisdictions— federal, state, county, municipal elections, etc., a man could be prohibited from voting because of poverty, lack of property ownership, inability to write, or any one of many restrictions intended to limit the franchise.

But women did have spheres of influence. Their influences were in the home and family as well as in the social, rather than the political, aspects of the community. During the early national period particularly, the notion of "Republican motherhood" helped define women's roles. This idea suggested that women played an important part in defining the national character by instilling important republican values in their sons.

Women also organized for the betterment of their community and the society in which they lived. As individuals and in groups, they influenced the development and maintenance of religious and educational institutions and those establishments that provided for the sick and the indigent. For example, the Troy

Female Seminary was opened in New York by Emma Willard in 1821 to provide an exemplary curriculum for girls. In 1825, Frances Wright established her own Utopian community in Nashoba, Tennessee.

Through their families and, specifically, the male members in their role as voters, women influenced the political life of the community as well. It would be an unwise political candidate who proposed a platform that the women of the community would not support.

In this new country there was a sense of youthful vigor and a view to new opportunities and new ideas. For many, these ideals held true as much in their spiritual life as in any other aspect of life. Many Americans seemed to be seeking something new and meaningful.

Religious life

The Second Great Awakening was an evangelical Protestant revival that preached personal responsibility for one's actions, both individually and socially. This movement was led by preachers, including Charles Finney, who traveled the country preaching the gospel of social responsibility. This point of view was taken up by the mainline Protestant denominations (Episcopal, Methodist, Presbyterian, Lutheran, Congregational, etc.). Part of the later social reform movement that led to an end to child labor, to better working conditions, and to other changes in social attitudes arose from this new recognition that the Christian faith should be expressed for the good of society.

Closely allied with the Second Great Awakening was the **temperance movement**. This movement to end the sale and consumption of alcohol arose from religious beliefs, the violence many women and children experienced from heavy drinkers, and from the effect of alcohol consumption on the work force. The Society for the Promotion of Temperance was organized in Boston in 1826.

Rise of regionalism and sectionalism

As the new country began to stretch its boundaries physically, new territories and opportunities were opened up to new and old Americans, alike. During the Era of Good Feelings in the early 1800s, **nationalism** held great importance in U.S. society and culture. Americans believed strongly in the values and goals of their new nation and, as a result, economic, political, and cultural nationalism grew. New concepts such as regionalism and sectionalism also began to take on more meaning.

Regionalism is the political division of an area into partially autonomous regions or loyalty to the interests of a particular region. **Sectionalism** is generally defined as excessive devotion to local interests and customs. When the United States declared independence from England, the founding fathers created a political point of view that created national unity while respecting the uniqueness and individual rights of each of the thirteen colonies or states. The colonies had been populated and governed by England and other countries. Some colonists came to America in search of religious freedom, others for a fresh start, and others for economic opportunity. Each colony had a particular culture and identity.

As the young nation grew, territories came to be defined as states. The states began to acquire their own particular cultures and identities. In time, regional interests and cultures also began to take shape. Religious interests, economic life, and geography began to be understood as definitive of particular regions. The northeast tended toward industrial development. The south tended to rely upon agriculture. The west was an area of untamed open spaces where people settled and practiced agriculture and animal husbandry.

Each of these regions came to be defined, at least to some extent, by way people made their living and the economic and social institutions that supported them. In the industrialized North, the factory system tended to create a division between the business and industry tycoons and the poor industrial workers. The conditions in which the labor force worked were far from ideal—long work days, poor conditions, and minimal pay.

The South was characterized by cities that were centers of social and commercial life. The agriculture that supported the region was practiced on plantations which were owned by the wealthy and worked by slaves or indentured servants.

The West was a vast expanse to be explored and tamed. Life on a western ranch was distinctly different from life in either the industrial North or the agricultural South. The challenges of each region were also distinctly different. For example, the roles of women and children in the Northern and Southern economies were different, as was the importance of trade. Religion was called upon to support each unique regional lifestyle.

As the nation extended its borders into the lands west of the Mississippi, thousands of settlers streamed into this part of the country, bringing with them ideas and concepts and adapting them to the development of the unique characteristics of the region. Equality for everyone, as stated in the Declaration of Independence, did not yet apply to minority groups such as African-Americans or American Indians. Voting rights and the right to hold public office were restricted in varying degrees in each state. All of these factors decidedly affected the political, economic, and social life of the country, and all three were focused in the attitudes of the three sections of the country towards slavery.

COMPETENCY 1.6 CONTINUED NATIONAL DEVELOPMENT (1829–1850S)

Skill 1.6a **Demonstrate understanding of political development, including Jacksonian democracy, the nullification crisis, Manifest Destiny, the Mexican War and Cession, and the Oregon Territory**

Jacksonian democracy

The election of Andrew Jackson as president signaled a swing of the political pendulum from government influenced by the wealthy, aristocratic Easterners to the interests of the western farmers and pioneers and the era of the "common man." Jacksonian Democracy was a policy of equal political power for all. After the War of 1812, Henry Clay and his supporters favored economic measures that came to be known as the American System. These measures involved using tariffs to protect American farmers and manufacturers from having to compete with foreign products, thus stimulating industrial growth and employment. With more people working, more farm products would be consumed, prosperous farmers would be able to buy more manufactured goods, and the additional money from tariffs would make it possible for the government to make needed internal improvements such as transportation and infrastructure.

To get the process going, Congress had not only passed a high tariff in 1816 but had also chartered a second Bank of the United States. Upon becoming president, Jackson fought to get rid of the bank. One of the many duties of the bank was to regulate the supply of money for the nation. The president believed that the bank was a monopoly that favored the wealthy. Congress voted in 1832 to renew the bank's charter, but after Jackson vetoed the bill and withdrew the government's money, the bank finally collapsed.

Nullification crisis

Jackson also faced the nullification issue raised by South Carolina. In 1828, Congress passed a law placing high tariffs on goods imported into the United States. Southerners, led by John C. Calhoun, South Carolina's then vice-president of the United States, felt that the tariff favored the manufacturing interests of New England. Calhoun denounced it as an abomination and claimed that any state could nullify any of the federal laws that it considered unconstitutional.

The tariff was reduced in 1832 but not enough to satisfy South Carolina, which promptly threatened to secede from the Union. Although Jackson agreed with the rights of states, he also believed in preservation of the Union. He held firm in his stance that the federal government was sovereign over the states. A year later, the tariffs were lowered and the crisis was averted.

Manifest Destiny

It was the belief of many that the United States was destined to control all of the land between the two oceans. One newspaper editor coined the term "Manifest Destiny" to describe it. The mass migration westward put the U.S. government on a collision course with the Native Americans, Great Britain, Spain, and Mexico. In the Northwest, the fur traders and the missionaries ran up against the Native Americans and the claims of Great Britain for the Oregon country.

Mexican War

Spain had claimed the American Southwest since the 1540s. Spanish settlers had spread northward from Mexico City and in the 1700s, had established missions, forts, villages, towns, and very large ranches. After the purchase of the Louisiana Territory in 1803, Americans began moving into Spanish territory. A few hundred American families in what is now Texas were allowed to live there but had to agree to become loyal subjects of Spain. In 1821, Mexico successfully revolted against Spanish rule, won independence, and chose to be more tolerant towards the American settlers and traders. The Mexican government encouraged and allowed extensive trade and settlement, especially in Texas. Many of the new settlers were southerners who brought their slaves. Slavery was outlawed in Mexico and technically illegal in Texas, although the Mexican government looked the other way.

With the influx of so many Americans and the liberal policies of the Mexican government, concern over the possible growth and development of an American state within Mexico grew. Settlement restrictions, cancellation of land grants, the forbidding of slavery and increased military activity brought everything to a head. The order of events included the fight for Texas independence, the brief Republic of Texas, the eventual annexation of Texas by the United States, statehood, and finally, war with Mexico.

The Texas controversy was not the sole reason for war. Since American settlers had begun pouring into the Southwest, the cultural differences played a prominent part. Friction increased between land-hungry Americans swarming into western lands and the Mexican government, which controlled these lands. A clash was bound to occur.

The clash was not only political but also cultural and economic. The Spanish influence permeated all parts of southwestern life—law, language, architecture, religion, and customs. By this time, the doctrine of Manifest Destiny was in the hearts and on the lips of those seeking new areas of settlement and a new life.

Skill 1.6b   Demonstrate knowledge of geographic expansion, including the development of the transportation network and the displacement of Native Americans

During the early nineteenth century, the United States continued its steady westward movement. Encouraged by the notion of Manifest Destiny, settlers pushed into the frontier. Under President James Monroe, the United States officially acquired land in Florida and set a new boundary line between U.S. and British territory in the Pacific Northwest.

The nationalism of the era also encouraged the development of internal transportation systems and other infrastructure. The National Road connected parts of the east with the Midwest, and a growing system of canals allowed goods to be shipped via water at a relatively low cost. In the 1830s, the first railroads began to be built with the first lines laid primarily in the North.

U.S. expansion came at the expense of Native American sovereignty. In 1830, Congress passed the Indian Removal Act to force from their lands the native peoples living east of the Mississippi River. Many tribes resisted, including the Cherokee in Georgia. This group sued in the U.S. court system to protect their rights to their land. The Supreme Court ultimately found in their favor, but President Andrew Jackson disregarded the ruling and sent federal troops to evict the Cherokee. The Cherokee traveled west on **Trail of Tears.** During this grueling journey, thousands of Cherokees died from cold, illness, or starvation.

See also Skill 1.6a, Skill 1.6c

Skill 1.6c   Demonstrate knowledge of industrialization, including technological and agricultural innovations, and the early labor movement

Technological innovations
The **Industrial Revolution** had spread from Great Britain to the United States. Before 1800, most manufacturing activities were done in small shops or in homes. However, starting in the early 1800s, factories with contemporary machines were built, making it easier to produce goods faster. The eastern part of the country became a major industrial area, although some industry developed in the West. At about the same time, improvements began to be made in building roads, railroads, canals, and steamboats. The increased ease of travel facilitated the westward expansion and boosted the economy with faster and cheaper shipment of goods and products, covering larger and larger areas. An example of one of the innovations is the Erie Canal, connecting the interior and Great Lakes with the Hudson River and the coastal port of New York. Canals to facilitate travel connected many other natural waterways.

Robert Fulton's *Clermont* the first commercially successful steamboat, led the way as the fastest method to ship goods, making steamboats the most important way to do so. Later, steam-powered railroads soon became the biggest rival of the steamboat as a means of shipping, eventually becoming the most important transportation method in the opening of the West. With expansion into the interior of the country, the United States became the leading agricultural nation in the world.

Agricultural innovations

In 1830, it took approximately 250 to 300 labor hours to produce 100 bushels (5 acres) of wheat using the walking plow, the brush harrow, the hand broadcast of seed, the sickle, and the flail. This effort was cut dramatically as new technological advances became available for implementation on the farm. Examples of new technology were Cyrus McCormick's reaper, patented in 1834, and John Lane's plows faced with steel blades, first manufactured in the same year. Many other innovations greatly changed the means of agriculture and the lives of farmers in the United States, from the manufacturing partnership of John Deere and Leonard Andrus in 1837 to the development of the first grain elevator in Buffalo, New York, in 1842.

With the aid of these new inventions, the hardy pioneer farmers produced a vast surplus, and emphasis went to producing products with a high sale value. Travel and shipping were greatly helped by the railroad and by new or improved roads such as the **National Road** in the East and the **Oregon and Santa Fe Trails** in the West.

Early labor movement

More industries and factories required more labor. Women, children, and at times, entire families worked long hours and days until the 1830s. By then, the factories were getting larger and employers began hiring immigrants who were coming to America in huge numbers. Factory workers often worked for the lowest wages and in the worst conditions. Some have compared the "wage slavery" of the factories and mills of the time to the chattel slavery in the plantation South. During the 1830s, efforts were made to organize a labor movement to improve working conditions and increase wages. The movement never caught on until after the Civil War, but the seed had been sown.

One of the most significant issues for labor, during this period, was the struggle for the ten-hour work day. Organizers and activists were able to achieve success in the legislatures of several states. But the laws always contained a loophole that allowed workers to contract for longer hours. The ability to remove any employee who was unwilling to agree to such a contract meant that these loopholes allowed employers to retain the upper hand. Some of the more notable events in labor history were the following:

- 1833—The Workingmen's Ticket was formed as a political party to promote labor ideology.

- 1834—The National Trades Union, the first attempt at a national labor federation, was formed in New York City. The Factory Girls' Association was formed in Lowell, Massachusetts, and a strike was called over working conditions and wages. In Dover, New Hampshire, 800 women went out on strike over the right to organize and in opposition to wage reductions.

- 1836—The first national union for a specific trade, the National Cooperative Association of Cordwainers, was founded in New York City. The Equal Rights Party was formed in Utica, New York. The result was a convention of mechanics, farmers, and workingmen who wrote a Declaration of Rights in opposition to bank notes, paper money, and arbitrary power of the courts. They called for legislation to guarantee labor the right to organize. The Factory Girls' Association in Lowell went out on strike again over working conditions and wages.

- 1837—The Panic of 1837 meant an end to the National Trades Union and most other unions. President Jackson declared a ten-hour work day for the Philadelphia Navy Yard to quell discontent caused by Panic of 1837.

- 1838—One-third of the nation's workers were unemployed because of the economic situation.

- 1840—The ten-hour work day without reduction in pay was proclaimed by President Van Buren for all federal employees on public works.

- 1842—In *Commonwealth* v. *Hunt*, the Massachusetts Supreme Court ruled that labor unions are not illegal conspiracies. Legislation was passed in Connecticut and Massachusetts prohibiting children from working more than ten hours per day.

- 1844—The New England Workingmen's Association was formed, with more than 200 delegates, to fight for the ten-hour day for nonfederal workers.

- 1845—Female workers in five cotton mills in Allegheny, Pennsylvania, struck for the ten-hour day. They were supported by workers in Lowell, Massachusetts, and Manchester, New Hampshire. The first professional teacher's association was created in Massachusetts. The Female Labor Reform Association was formed as an auxiliary of the New England Workingmen's Association in Lowell, Massachusetts, to fight for the ten-hour day.

- 1847—New Hampshire was the first state to make the ten-hour day the legal workday.

- 1848—A new child-labor law in Pennsylvania established twelve years old as the minimum age for workers in commercial occupations. Pennsylvania passed a ten-hour day law. When employers violated it, women mill workers rioted and attacked the factory gates with axes.

Skill 1.6d Demonstrate understanding of social and cultural developments, such as changes in the role of women in society, and reform movements

People were exposed to literature, art, newspapers, drama, live entertainment, and political rallies. With better communication and travel, more information was desired about previously unknown areas of the country, especially the West. The discovery of gold and other mineral wealth resulted in a literal surge of settlers and even more interest.

Public schools were established in many of the states with more children being educated. With more literacy and participation in literature and the arts, the young nation was developing its own unique culture and becoming less influenced by and dependent on the culture of Europe.

Reform movements
Other social issues were also addressed. It was during this period that efforts were made to transform the prison system and its emphasis on punishment into a penitentiary system that attempted rehabilitation. It was also during this period that Dorothea Dix led a struggle in the North and the South to establish hospitals for the insane.

Utopianism is the dream of or the desire to create the perfect society. However, by the nineteenth century, few believed this was possible. One of the major "causes" of utopianism is the desire for moral clarity. Against the backdrop of the efforts of a young nation to define itself and to ensure the rights and freedoms of its citizens and within the context of the second great awakening, it is quite easy to see how the reform movements, the religious sentiment, and the gathering national storm would lead to the rise of expressions of desire to create the perfect society.

The following is a partial list of well-known Americans who contributed their leadership and talents to reforms in various fields:

- **Lucretia Mott** and **Elizabeth Cady Stanton** for women's rights;

- **Emma Hart Willard, Catharine Esther Beecher,** and **Mary Lyon** for education for women;

- **Dr. Elizabeth Blackwell**, the first woman doctor in the United States;

- **Antoinette Louisa Blackwell**, the first female minister in the United States;

- **Dorothea Lynde Dix** for reforms in prisons and insane asylums;

- **Elihu Burritt** and **William Ladd** for peace movements;

- **Robert Owen** for a Utopian society;

- **Horace Mann, Henry Barmard, Calvin E. Stowe, Caleb Mills**, and **John Swett** for public education; and

- **Benjamin Lundy, David Walker, William Lloyd Garrison, Isaac Hooper, Arthur and Lewis Tappan, Theodore Weld, Frederick Douglass, Harriet Tubman, James G. Birney, Henry Highland Garnet, James Forten, Robert Purvis, Harriet Beecher Stowe, Wendell Phillips, and John Brown** for abolition of slavery and the Underground Railroad.

Other contributors to American culture in the first half of the nineteenth centure were

- authors **Louisa Mae Alcott, James Fenimore Cooper, Washington Irving, Walt Whitman, Henry David Thoreau, Ralph Waldo Emerson, Herman Melville, Richard Henry Dana, Nathaniel Hawthorne, Henry Wadsworth Longfellow, John Greenleaf Whittier, Edgar Allan Poe, Oliver Wendell Holmes;**

- explorers **John C. Fremont, Zebulon Pike, Kit Carson;**

- American statesmen **Henry Clay, Daniel Webster, Stephen Douglas, John C. Calhoun;**

- inventors **Robert Fulton, Cyrus McCormick, Eli Whitney;** and

- lexicographer **Noah Webster**.

See also Skill 1.5d

COMPETENCY 1.7   CIVIL WAR ERA (1850–1870s)

Skill 1.7a   Demonstrate knowledge of the growth of sectionalism (North, South, and West), and of attempts at political compromise

The character of the North and the South was quite distinct in the years leading up to the Civil War. From the earliest settlement of the colonies, the South had been more dependent on the cultivation of cash crops such as tobacco for its economic success. During the early nineteenth century, this division between North and South was furthered by the rise of "King Cotton" in the South and the beginnings of industrialization in the North. The Southern economy became even more dependent on the free labor provided by enslaved people to meet high demand for cotton exports while Northern economies instead began to transform into ones based on manufacturing.

The growth of the United States also increased sectional tensions. As new states entered the Union, Southerners worried that the delicate balance of slave and free states maintained in the Senate would tip in favor of Northern interests, possibly endangering the continuation of the institution of slavery. Political solutions such as the Missouri Compromise and Compromise of 1850 attempted to correct the problem, but they succeeded only in delaying the conflagration. Antislavery feeling rose in the North even as Southerners fought to maintain their way of life. When Abraham Lincoln won the presidency in the election of 1860, Southern leaders believed that division was inevitable and states began seceding from the Union.

Missouri Compromise
The first serious clash between North and South had occurred during 1819–20 when James Monroe was in office as president, and it concerned Missouri's admittance to the Union. The Missouri Territory allowed slavery and, if admitted, Missouri would cause an imbalance in the number of U.S. Senators. Alabama had already been admitted as a slave state and that had balanced the Senate with the North and South each having 22 senators. The first Missouri Compromise resolved the conflict by admitting Maine as a free state along with Missouri as a slave state, thus continuing to keep a balance of power in the Senate with the same number of free and slave states.

An additional provision of this compromise was that, with the admission of Missouri, slavery would not be allowed in the rest of the Louisiana Purchase territory north of latitude 36°30'. This was acceptable to the Southern congressmen since it was not profitable to grow cotton on land north of this latitude line anyway. It was thought that the crisis had been resolved, but in the next year it was discovered that, in its state constitution, Missouri discriminated against free blacks. Antislavery supporters in Congress went into an uproar, determined to exclude Missouri from the Union.

Henry Clay, known as the Great Compromiser, then proposed a second Missouri Compromise, which was acceptable to everyone. His proposal stated that the Constitution of the United States guaranteed protections and privileges to citizens of states and Missouri's proposed constitution could not deny these protections to any of its citizens. The acceptance in 1820 of this second compromise opened the way for Missouri's statehood—a temporary reprieve only.

Congress took up consideration of new territories between Missouri and present-day Idaho. Again, heated debate over permitting slavery in these areas flared up. Those opposed to slavery used the Missouri Compromise to prove their point showing that the land being considered for territories was part of the area where slavery was banned. On May 25, 1854, Congress passed the infamous Kansas-Nebraska Act, which nullified the provision creating the territories of Kansas and Nebraska. This act gave the people of these two territories the ability to decide for themselves whether or not to permit slavery. Feelings were so deep and divided that any further attempts to compromise would end with little, if any, success. Political and social turmoil swirled everywhere. Kansas became known as "Bleeding Kansas" because of the extreme violence and bloodshed that occurred throughout the territory as a result of the two governments that existed there, one proslavery and the other antislavery.

Sectional tensions grow

The rise of the abolitionist movement in the North, the publication of *Uncle Tom's Cabin*, and issues of trade and efforts by the national government to control trade for the regions coalesced around the issue of slavery in a nation that was founded on the principle of the inalienable right of every person to be free. As the South defended its lifestyle and its economy and the right of the states to be self-determining, the North became stronger in its criticism of slavery. The result was a growing sectionalism between the North and the South throughout the 1850s.

In 1857 the Supreme Court handed down a pivotal decision in *Dred Scott v Sanford*. **Dred Scott** was a slave whose owner had taken him from slave state Missouri to free state Illinois into the Minnesota Territory, free under the provisions of the Missouri Compromise, then finally back to slave state Missouri. Abolitionists pursued the dilemma by presenting a court case, stating that since Scott had lived in a free state and a free territory, he was in actuality a free man. Two lower courts had ruled before the Supreme Court became involved, one ruling in favor of the abolitionists and one against. The Supreme Court decided that residing in a free state and a free territory did not make Scott a free man because Scott (and all other slaves) was neither a U.S. citizen nor a state citizen of Missouri. Therefore, he did not have the right to sue in state or federal courts. The Court went a step further and ruled that the old Missouri Compromise was now unconstitutional because Congress did not have the power to prohibit slavery in the Territories.

Antislavery supporters were stunned. They had just recently formed the new Republican Party, and one of its platforms was keeping slavery out of the territories. Now, according to the *Dred Scott* decision, this basic party principle was unconstitutional. The only way to ban slavery in new areas was by a constitutional amendment requiring ratification by three-fourths of all states. At that time, such an amendment was out of the question; its supporters would be unable to get a majority because of Southern opposition.

In 1858, Abraham Lincoln and Stephen A. Douglas were running for the office of U.S. Senator from Illinois. They participated in a series of debates that directly affected the outcome of the 1860 presidential election. Lincoln, a Republican, was not an abolitionist, but he believed that slavery was morally wrong and he firmly believed in and supported the Republican Party principle that slavery must not be allowed to extend any further.

On the other hand, Douglas, a Democrat, was up for reelection and knew that if he won this race, he had a good chance of becoming president in 1860. He coined the doctrine of "popular sovereignty" and was responsible for supporting the inflammatory **Kansas-Nebraska Act,** helping its passage through Congress. In the course of the debates, Lincoln challenged Douglas to show that popular sovereignty reconciled with the *Dred Scott* decision. Either way he answered Lincoln, Douglas would lose crucial support from one group or the other. If he supported the *Dred Scott* decision, Southerners would support him but he would lose Northern support. If he stayed with popular sovereignty, Northern support would be his but Southern support would be lost. His reply to Lincoln, stating that territorial legislatures could exclude slavery by refusing to pass laws supporting it, gave him enough support and approval to be reelected to the Senate but it cost him the Democratic nomination for president in 1860.

Southerners came to the realization that Douglas supported and was devoted to popular sovereignty but not necessarily to the expansion of slavery. On the other hand, two years later, Lincoln received the nomination of the Republican Party for president.

See also Skill 1.7c

Skill 1.7b   **Demonstrate knowledge of the abolitionist movement, including the roles of African-Americans and women in the movement**

Abolitionist movement
While there had always been individuals opposed to slavery and the slave trade, during the colonial period in America the Society of Friends (the Quakers) were the only prominent group to denounce slave holding as incompatible with Christian moral values. Perhaps influenced by humanistic values put forth during the Age of Enlightenment and during the American War for Independence, more

American communities became like-minded in their disdain for slavery. As new areas were added to the country (such as the Northwest Territory in 1787) prohibition of slavery in these lands became a major issue. Some protesters were assuaged when Congress banned the transatlantic slave trade in 1808. Others were convinced that the system must exist in order to keep the Southern economy viable. Distance from the "peculiar institution" gave many Northerners cause to ignore the situation as inconsequential to their own lives. The African Colonization Society, founded in 1816, was the major channel for antislavery activity during this period. The goal of this society was to resettle former slaves back in Africa.

The **Second Great Awakening** seemed to also reawaken a moral revulsion to slavery among many Americans. Revivalist preaching created abolitionists out of congregations who came to believe that slave holding was the product of personal sin and the emancipation of slaves was the only means of redemption. Inactivity in the cause of abolition was tantamount to compliance in the sin in the rhetoric of some activists. In the 1830s, newly founded abolitionist groups—most prominently, the American Antislavery Society, founded in 1833—lobbied to change racially discriminatory practices, recognizing that these existing sanctions based on race reinforced the argument for the acceptability and necessity of keeping black people in bondage.

The American Antislavery Society grew very quickly and claimed a membership of tens of thousands. This alone would have been enough to draw great interest to their cause and curious listeners to their rallies. But they were activists, publishing widely and organizing petition drives to change existing laws and sanctions that supported slavery and reinforced racist attitudes. Through their lecturing agents, they provided the public with brilliant and provocative speakers. Several Northern audiences—having had little or no contact with slavery themselves and having only the justifications of the planters and the denunciations of white abolitionists by which to draw their conclusions—were moved by the personal testimony of runaway slaves.

Frederick Douglass
Foremost among these speakers, and a genuine celebrity in his own time, was a man who combined all of the qualities that appealed to the audiences at abolitionist meetings and rallies, Frederick Douglass. Douglass was the son of a white planter and a slave mother and, under the laws of that time, was thus born a slave. Douglass later ran away and became one of the leading figures of the abolition movement.

Douglass became the most recognized spokesman for abolition and civil rights for Negroes in his time. He impressed, conferred with, and influenced the thoughts and actions of such men as William Lloyd Garrison, the committed, hard-line abolition activist from Boston, and President Abraham Lincoln, the man who would ultimately do the most to abolish slavery.

Women and the abolitionist movement

Women were a large portion of the abolitionist movement from its inception. While it was common and considered acceptable for women to be concerned about and involved in issues of morality and humanity, their activism (sometimes extreme) for abolition often brought about more criticism than support from men and women who were neutral about the cause. For whatever reasons, the American Antislavery Society originally banned women from its membership. But activist abolitionist women formed their own organizations which met in national conventions in 1837, 1838, and 1839. Women became an undeniable asset for the cause, their activism and fundraising underpinning the national effort.

William Lloyd Garrison and his followers had a broader platform than many at the time were willing to support, including the extension of women's rights, temperance, and pacifism. In 1840, opponents of the election of a woman officer to the American Antislavery Society quit their membership, allowing the Garrisonians to gain control of the society. Thereafter, women became more prominent in the society. Many, including Lucy Stone, Elizabeth Cady Stanton, and the former slave Sojourner Truth, tolerated insult and risked physical harm to spread the doctrine in lecture halls and to organize supporters.

Underground Railroad

One of the most famous abolitionists of the period was Harriet Tubman, called the "Moses of Her People." She ran away from slavery and spoke and worked as an activist in the movement. She also personally returned to Maryland several times to aid other escaping slaves in their transit through the Underground Railroad.

The Underground Railroad was not a conveyance but rather a system for the escape of slaves, ultimately to Canada. The "railroad" consisted of information, resources (money, food, clothing, etc.,), guides, and safe houses to aid the runaways in escaping their masters and eluding the law, which was bound to return them to the slave holders.

Because of the great risks involved, it was impossible to provide for the aid of slaves consistently, in the same manner and through the same channels, but the process know as the Underground Railroad was instrumental in helping thousands upon thousands of escaped slaves achieve freedom.

John Brown

Many radical and militant abolitionists philosophically opposed the Garrisonians. Mostly, they acted as individuals, apparently impatient with the methods of the larger organizations. The most prominent of these radicals was John Brown. In 1859, Brown and his followers seized the federal arsenal at Harper's Ferry in what is now West Virginia. His purpose was to take the guns stored in the arsenal, give them to slaves nearby, and lead them in a widespread rebellion. He and his men were captured by Colonel Robert E. Lee of the United States Army and after a trial with a guilty verdict, he was hanged. Most Southerners felt that the majority of Northerners approved of Brown's actions, but in actuality most of them were stunned and shocked. Southern newspapers took great pains to quote a small but well-known minority of abolitionists who applauded and supported Brown's actions, which merely served to widen the gap between the two sections.

Skill 1.7c   Demonstrate understanding of the failure of political institutions in the 1850s

In the decade leading up to the Civil War, tensions between the northern and southern states intensified over the issue of slavery. The United States had acquired new territories in the southwest as a result of the Mexican-American War in the late 1840s. In 1850, as the nation was poised to expand, Congress took up the question of whether slavery would be allowed in the new territories.

California was admitted as a "free" state. Texas, a slave state, agreed to alter its border and was compensated for its loss of territory. In the New Mexico Territory, which included the area that is now New Mexico, Arizona, and Utah, no specific prohibition on slavery was implemented. In addition, the Fugitive Slave Law was passed, which required all citizens to assist in the return of runaway slaves to their owners. Faced with two opposite choices, Congress opted to compromise. This group of acts is called the **Compromise of 1850**. It was aimed at balancing the competing claims of the slave-owning southern states and the free northern states.

Rather than creating a quiet balance, this series of compromises actually increased political tension. The **Kansas-Nebraska Act** was one of the primary campaign issues in the famous Lincoln-Douglas debates, as Stephen Douglas had been the architect of the act. Congress's intention to balance the interests of the nation's states only served to accentuate them and draw them into the political arena, contributing directly to the secession of the Confederate States and the Civil War.

The final straw came with the election of Lincoln to the Presidency the next year. Because of a split in the Democratic Party, there were four candidates from four political parties. Lincoln received a minority of the popular vote and a majority of electoral votes. In response, the southern states, one by one, voted to secede from the Union as they had promised they would do if Lincoln and the Republicans were victorious.

See also Skill 1.7a

Skill 1.7d   Demonstrate knowledge of the Civil War (1861–1865), including its causes, leaders, and major events

Relative advantages and goals

South Carolina was the first state to secede from the Union and the first shots of the war were fired on Fort Sumter in Charleston Harbor. Both sides quickly prepared for war. The North had more in its favor, including a larger population, superior economic and transportation systems, and vast industrial, agricultural, and natural resources. The North possessed most of the nation's gold, had about 92 percent of all industries, and almost all known supplies of copper, coal, iron, and various other minerals.

Since most of the nation's railroads were in the North and the Midwest, men and supplies could be easily moved wherever needed. Food could be transported from the farms of the Midwest to workers in the East and to soldiers on the battlefields. International trade could continue unabated due to the North's control of the navy and the merchant fleet. The Union states numbered twenty-four and included western (California and Oregon) and border (Maryland, Delaware, Kentucky, Missouri, and West Virginia) states.

The eleven southern states, South Carolina, Georgia, Florida, Alabama, Mississippi, Louisiana, Texas, Virginia, North Carolina, Tennessee, and Arkansas, made up the Confederacy. Although outnumbered in population, the South was completely confident of victory. Military leaders knew that all they had to do was fight a defensive war and protect their own territory. The North had to invade and defeat an area almost the size of Western Europe. They figured the North would get tired of the struggle and give up.

Another advantage the South had was that a number of its best officers had graduated from the U.S. Military Academy at West Point and had had long years of army experience. Many had exercised varying degrees of command in the Indian Wars and the war with Mexico. Men from the South were conditioned to living outdoors and were more familiar with horses and firearms than men from northeastern cities. Since cotton was such an important crop, Southerners felt that British and French textile mills were so dependent on raw cotton that they would be forced to help the Confederacy in the war.

The South had specific reasons and goals for fighting the war, more so than the North. The major aim of the Confederacy never wavered: to win independence and the right to govern itself as it wished and to preserve slavery. The Northerners were not as clear in their reasons for conducting war. In the beginning, most believed, along with Lincoln, that preservation of the Union was paramount. Only a few extremely fanatical abolitionists looked on the war as a way to end slavery. However, by war's end, more and more northerners had come to believe that freeing the slaves was just as important as restoring the Union.

Strategies and decisive battles

The war strategies for both sides were relatively clear and simple. The South planned a defensive war, wearing down the North until it agreed to peace on Southern terms. The only exception to this defensive strategy was an aggressive plain to gain control of Washington, D.C., go north through the Shenandoah Valley into Maryland and Pennsylvania in order to drive a wedge between the Northeast and the Midwest, interrupt the lines of communication, and end the war quickly. The North had three basic strategies:

- Blockade the Confederate coastline in order to cripple the South;
- Seize control of the Mississippi River and interior railroad lines to split the
  Confederacy in two; and
- Seize the Confederate capital of Richmond, Virginia, driving southward to join up with Union forces coming east from the Mississippi Valley.

Until the Battle of Gettysburg (July 1–3, 1863), the South had won clear victories in battle against the North. Lincoln's commanders—McDowell, McClellan, Burnside, and Hooker—had failed to demonstrate any great military prowess. Lee, on the other hand, had many able officers; he especially depended on "Stonewall" Jackson and Stuart. However, Jackson died at Chancellorsville and was replaced by Longstreet. Lee decided to invade the North; he depended on J.E.B. Stuart and his cavalry to inform him of the Union's troop locations and strengths. Four things worked against Lee at Gettysburg:

- The Union troops gained the best positions and the best ground first, making it easier to make a stand.

- Lee's move into Northern territory put him and his army a long way from food and supply lines. They were more or less on their own.

- Lee thought that his Army of Northern Virginia was invincible and could fight and win under any conditions or circumstances.

- Stuart and his men did not arrive at Gettysburg until the end of the second day of fighting, and, by then, it was too little too late. He and his men had had to detour around Union soldiers, and he was delayed getting the information Lee needed.

Consequently, Lee made the mistake of failing to take Longstreet's advice to regroup back into Southern territory to the supply lines. Lee felt that regrouping was retreating and almost an admission of defeat.

He was convinced the army would be victorious. Longstreet was concerned about the Union troops occupying the best positions and felt that regrouping to a better position would be an advantage. He was also very concerned about the distance from supply lines.

Neither side had intended to fight there, but the fighting began when a Confederate brigade, looking for shoes, stumbled into a Union cavalry unit. On the third and last day, Lee launched a final attempt to break the Union lines. General George Pickett sent his division of three brigades under Generals Garnet, Kemper, and Armistead against Union troops on Cemetery Ridge under the command of General Winfield Scott Hancock. Union lines held, and Lee and the defeated Army of Northern Virginia made their way back to Virginia. Although Lincoln's commander, George Meade, successfully turned back a Confederate charge, he and the Union troops failed to pursue Lee and the Confederates. This battle was the turning point for the North. After Gettysburg, Lee never again had the troop strength to launch a major offensive.

The day after Gettysburg, on July 4, Vicksburg, Mississippi, surrendered to Union General Ulysses Grant, thus severing the western Confederacy from the eastern part. In September 1863, the Confederacy won its last important victory at Chickamauga. In November, the Union victory at Chattanooga made it possible for Union troops to go into Alabama and Georgia and split the eastern Confederacy in two. Lincoln gave Grant command of all Northern armies in March 1864. Grant led his armies into battles in Virginia while Phil Sheridan and his cavalry did as much damage as possible. In a skirmish at a place called Yellow Tavern, Virginia, Sheridan's and Stuart's forces met. Stuart was fatally wounded.

The Union won the Battle of Mobile Bay, and in May 1864, William Tecumseh Sherman began his march to successfully demolish Atlanta, then on to Savannah. He and his troops turned northward through the Carolinas to meet Grant in Virginia. On April 9, 1865, Lee formally surrendered to Grant at the Appomattox Courthouse in Virginia.

Aftermath
The Civil War took more American lives than any other war in history. The South lost one-third of its soldiers in battle, while the North lost about one-sixth of its troops. More than half of the total deaths were caused by disease and the rudimentary conditions of field hospitals. Both sides paid a tremendous economic price, but the South suffered more severely from direct damages, particularly in those areas affected by Sherman's devastating March to the Sea. Destruction was pervasive, with towns, farms, trade, industry, lives, and the homes of men, women, and children all destroyed. For the South, an entire way of life was lost. Deep resentment emerged, and it took the South decades to rebuild its infrastructure and economy.

The effects of the Civil War were tremendous. It changed the methods of waging war and has been called the first modern war. It introduced weapons and tactics that, when improved later, were used extensively in wars of the late 1800s and early1900s. Civil War soldiers were the first to fight in trenches, to fight under a unified command, and to use defenses called "major cordon defenses" (a strategy of advance on all fronts). They were also the first to use repeating and breech-loading weapons. Observation balloons were first used during the Civil War, as were submarines, ironclad ships, and mines. Telegraphy and railroads were first put to military use in the Civil War. It was considered a modern war because of the vast destruction and was "total war," involving the use of all resources of the opposing sides.

See also Skill 1.7a, Skill 1.7c

Skill 1.7e   Demonstrate knowledge of the Reconstruction period, including the various plans for Reconstruction, the new amendments to the Constitution, and the Compromise of 1877

Reconstruction in theory
Following the Civil War, the nation was faced with repairing the torn Union and readmitting the Confederate states. **Reconstruction** refers to the period between 1865 and 1877 when the federal and state governments debated and implemented plans to provide civil rights to freed slaves and to set the terms under which the former Confederate states might once again join the Union.

Planning for Reconstruction began in 1861. Abraham Lincoln's Republican Party favored the extension of voting rights to black men, and Radical Republicans eventually sent the Fifteenth Amendment guaranteeing African-American male suffrage to the states for ratification. In the case of former Confederate soldiers, moderates wanted to allow all but former leaders to vote, while the radicals wanted to require an oath from all eligible voters that they had never borne arms against the Union, which would have excluded all former rebels. Regarding readmission into the Union, moderates favored a much lower standard, with the Radicals demanding nearly impossible conditions for rebel states to return.

Lincoln's moderate plan for Reconstruction was actually part of his effort to win the war. He and the moderates felt that, if it remained easy for states to return to the Union, Confederate states involved in the hostilities might be swayed to rejoin the Union rather than to continue fighting. The radical plan was to ensure that Reconstruction did not actually start until after the war was over.

By executive proclamation and constitutional amendment, slavery was officially ended, although deep prejudice and racism remained. The Union was preserved and the states were finally and truly united. Sectionalism remained strong, especially politically, but not to the degree and with as much violence as had existed before the Civil War. It has been noted that the Civil War may have been American democracy's greatest failure; after all, from 1861 to 1865, calm reason, which is fundamental for democracy, gave way to human passion. Yet, democracy survived.

The Northern victory established that no state has the right to end or leave the Union. Because of its unity, the United States became a major global power. Lincoln never proposed to punish the South; rather, he was most concerned with restoring it to the Union in a program that was flexible and practical rather than rigid and unrealistic. In fact, he never really felt that the states had seceded in leaving the Union; they had simply left the circle for a short time. His presidential Reconstruction plans consisted of two major steps:

- All Southerners taking an oath of allegiance to the Union, promising to accept all federal laws and proclamations dealing with slavery, would receive a full pardon. The only ones excluded from this step were men who had resigned from civil and military positions in the federal government to serve in the Confederacy, those who were part of the Confederate government, those in the Confederate army above the rank of lieutenant, and Confederates who were guilty of mistreating prisoners of war and blacks.

- A state would be able to write a new constitution, elect new officials, and return to the Union, fully equal to all other states, on the condition that at least 10 percent of those who were qualified voters in their states before secession from the Union, and who had voted in the 1860 election, must take an oath of allegiance.

Lincoln's Emancipation Proclamation in 1863 and the Thirteenth Amendment to the U.S. Constitution in 1865 ended slavery in the United States. But these measures did not erase the centuries of racial prejudices that held blacks to be second-class citizens. Those prejudices, along with fear of economic competition from newly freed slaves, led to a series of state laws that permitted or required businesses, landlords, school boards, and others to physically segregate blacks and whites in their everyday lives.

In 1865, Abraham Lincoln was assassinated leaving his vice–president, Andrew Johnson, to oversee the beginning of Reconstruction. A Southern Democrat who became Lincoln's vice-president in 1864, Johnson struck a moderate pose and was willing to allow former confederates to keep control of their state governments. These governments quickly enacted Black Codes that denied the vote to blacks and granted them only limited civil rights.

Postwar amendments
The **Thirteenth Amendment** abolished slavery and involuntary servitude, except as punishment for a crime. The amendment was proposed on January 31, 1865. It was declared ratified by the necessary number of states on December 18, 1865.

The Emancipation Proclamation of 1863 had freed slaves held in states that were considered to be in rebellion. This amendment freed slaves in states and territories controlled by the Union. The Supreme Court has ruled that this amendment does not bar mandatory military service.

The **Fourteenth Amendment** provides for due process and equal protection under the law. It was proposed on June 13, 1866, and ratified on July 28, 1868. The drafters of the amendment took a broad view of national citizenship. The law requires that states provide equal protection under the law to all persons (not just all citizens). This amendment also came to be interpreted as overturning the Dred Scott case (which said that blacks were not, and could not become, citizens of the United States).

The second section of the amendment establishes the "one man, one vote" apportionment of congressional representation. This ended the counting of blacks as 3/5 of a person. Section Three prohibits electing anyone who has engaged in insurrection, rebellion, or treason to Congress or to the Electoral College. Section Four stipulates that the government will not pay "damages" for the loss of slaves or for debts incurred by the Confederate government (e.g., to English or French banks).

The **Fifteenth Amendment** grants voting rights regardless of race, color, or previous condition of servitude. It was ratified on February 3, 1870.

All three of these Constitutional Amendments were part of the Reconstruction effort to create stability and rule of law to provide, protect, and enforce the rights of former slaves throughout the nation.

Reconstruction in practice
After the Civil War, many Southern states passed laws that attempted to restrict the movements of blacks and prevent them from bringing lawsuits or testifying in court. In the *Slaughterhouse Cases* (1871), the Supreme Court ruled that the Fourteenth Amendment applies only to rights granted by the federal government. In the *Civil Rights Cases*, the Court held that the guarantee of rights did not outlaw racial discrimination by individuals and organizations. In the next few decades the Court overturned several laws barring blacks from serving on juries or discriminating against the Chinese immigrants in regulating laundry businesses.

The economic and social chaos in the postwar South was unbelievable, with starvation and disease rampant, especially in the cities. The U.S. Army provided some relief, giving food and clothing to both whites and blacks, but the major responsibility fell to the **Freedmen's Bureau**. Though, to a certain extent, the bureau agents helped southern whites, their main responsibility was to the freed slaves. They tried to assist the freedmen to become self-supporting and to protect them from being taken advantage of by others. Northerners looked on it as a true, honest effort to help the South out of the chaos it was in. Most white Southerners charged the bureau with causing racial frictio by, deliberately encouraging the freedmen to consider former owners as enemies.

In 1866, radical Republicans won control of Congress and passed the Reconstruction Acts, which placed the governments of the southern states under the control of the federal military. With this backing, the Republicans began to implement such radical policies as granting all black men the vote and denying the vote to former confederate soldiers. Congress had passed the 13th, 14th, and Fifteenth Amendments, granting citizenship and civil rights to blacks, and made ratification of these amendments a condition of readmission into the Union by the rebel states. The Republicans found support in the South among freedmen (freed slaves), **scalawags** (white southerners who had not supported the Confederacy), and **carpetbaggers** (northerners who had moved to the South).

Military control of the South continued throughout Grant's administration, despite growing conflict both inside and outside the Republican Party. Conservatives in Congress and in the states opposed the liberal policies of the Republicans. Some Republicans became concerned over corruption issues among Grant's appointees and dropped support for him.

Segregation laws were foreshadowed in the Black Codes. These strict laws proposed by some southern states during Reconstruction sought to recreate the conditions of prewar servitude. Under these codes, blacks were to remain subservient to their white employers and were subject to fines and beatings if they failed to work. Freedmen were afforded some civil rights protection during the Reconstruction period, but beginning around 1876 so called redeemer governments began to take office in southern states after the removal of federal troops. The redeemer-state legislatures began passing segregation laws that came to be known as Jim Crow laws.

Jim Crow laws varied from state to state, but the most significant required separate school systems and libraries for blacks and whites and separate ticket windows, waiting rooms, and seating areas on trains and, later, other public transportation. Restaurant owners were permitted or sometimes required to provide separate entrances, tables, and counters for blacks and whites, so that the two races could not see one another while dining. Public parks and playgrounds were constructed for each race. Landlords were not allowed to mix black and white tenants in apartment houses in some states.

Paralleling the development of segregation legislation in the mid-nineteenth century was the appearance of organized groups opposed to any integration of blacks into white society. The most notable of these was the Ku Klux Klan.

First organized in the South during Reconstruction, the KKK was a loose group made up mainly of former Confederate soldiers who opposed the Reconstruction government and espoused a doctrine of white supremacy. KKK members intimidated and sometimes killed their enemies. The first KKK was never completely organized, despite having nominal leadership. In 1871, President Grant took action to use federal troops to halt the activities of the KKK, and actively prosecuted them in federal court. Klan activity waned, and the organization disappeared.

The **Compromise of 1877** marked the end of Reconstruction. Although no formal records exist to prove a deal was made, historians generally accept that Republican leaders agreed to remove federal troops from the South in exchange for Republican candidate Rutherford B. Hayes receiving the presidency in the disputed 1876 election. Certainly, Hayes did remove federal troops after his inauguration.

COMPETENCY 1.8   EMERGENCE OF THE MODERN UNITED STATES (1877–1900)

Skill 1.8a   Demonstrate understanding of United States expansion and imperialism, including the displacement of Native Americans, the development of the West, and international involvement

Westward expansion

The post-Reconstruction era represents a period of great transformation and expansion for the United States, both economically and geographically. These changes were particularly strong for the South, which was still recovering from the devastation of the Civil War and migration west of the Mississippi River. Great numbers of freedmen moved west, away from their former masters, lured by the promise of land. White migration was also spurred by similar desires for land and resources, leading to boom economies of cotton, cattle, and grain starting in Kansas and spreading westward.

During this period, industrial production grew fastest in the South. However, the South was still predominantly agricultural, featuring land tenancy and sharecropping. This system did not really advance the remaining freed slaves economically since most of the land still belonged to the large plantation owners who retained their holdings from before the Civil War. The economic chasm dividing white landowners and black freedmen only widened as the tenants sank further into debt to their landlords.

Westward movement of significant numbers from the eastern United States had originated with the discovery of gold in the West in the 1840s, and it picked up greater momentum after the Civil War. Settlers were lured by what they perceived as unpopulated places with land for the taking. Migration and settlement were not easy. When settlers arrived, they found that the lands were populated by earlier settlers of Spanish descent and by Native Americans. The Spanish and Native American inhabitants frequently clashed with those who were moving west. Resentment of the new settlers was particularly strong among the tribes that had been ordered to relocate to "Indian Country" prior to 1860.

Displacement of Native Americans

Despite having signed treaties with the United States government years earlier, Native Americans found that virtually all the treaties were ignored and broken as westward settlement accelerated and the government was called upon to protect settlers en route and those that had reached their destinations. Increasing encroachment by white settlers led to a series of wars between the United States and the various Native American nations that were deemed hostile.

Conflict was intense and frequent until 1867, when the federal government established two large tracts of land called reservations in Oklahoma and the Dakotas to which all tribes would be confined. With the Civil War over, troops were sent west to enforce the relocation and reservation-containment policies.Although the bloodshed during these wars was great, it paled in comparison to the number of Native Americans who died from epidemics of deadly diseases for which they had no resistance.

Eventually, the government sought to relocate Native Americans to Indian reservations and to Oklahoma, which lacked necessary resources and was geographically remote from their homelands. The justification for this westward expansion, at the expense of the previous inhabitants, was America's "Manifest Destiny" to tame and settle the continent from coast-to-coast.

Continuing conflict led to passage of the Dawes Act of 1887. This was recognition that confinement to reservations was not working. The law was intended to break up the Indian communities and bring about assimilation into white culture by deeding portions of the reservation lands to individual Indians who were expected to farm their land. The policy continued until 1934.

Armed resistance essentially came to an end by 1890, the same year in which the western frontier was declared by the U.S. Census Bureau to be closed. The surrender of Geronimo and the massacre at Wounded Knee led to a change of strategy by the Indians. Thereafter, the resistance strategy was to preserve their culture and traditions.

Transcontinental railroad

Another major factor contributing to the opening of the West to migration of Americans and the displacement of native peoples was the expansion of the railroad. The transcontinental railroad was completed in 1869, joining the west coast with the existing rail infrastructure terminating at Omaha, Nebraska, its westernmost point. This occurrence not only enabled unprecedented movement of people and goods, it also hastened the near extinction of the buffalo, which the Indians of the Great Plains depended on for their survival.

The completion of the nation's transcontinental railroad contributed greatly to the nation's economic and industrial growth. Some benefits of using the railroads included fast shipping of raw materials by the mining companies and wide dispersion of products to all parts of the country. Many wealthy industrialists and railroad owners saw tremendous profits steadily increasing because of this improved method of transportation. Another impact of interstate railroad expansion was the standardization of time zones in order to maintain the reliability and accuracy of train schedules across vast east-west routes.

American imperialism

Once the American West was subdued and firmly under U.S. control, the United States started looking beyond its shores. Overseas markets were becoming important as American industry produced goods more efficiently and manufacturing capacity grew. Out of concern for the protection of shipping, the

United States modernized and built up its navy, which by 1900 ranked third in the world and provided the means for America to become an imperial power.

The first overseas possessions were Midway Island and Alaska, purchased back in 1867 as championed by William Henry Seward. By the 1880s, Secretary of State James G. Blaine pushed for expanding U.S. trade and influence to Central and South America. In the 1890s, President Grover Cleveland invoked the Monroe Doctrine to intercede in Latin American affairs when it looked like Great Britain was going to exert its influence and power in the Western Hemisphere. In the Pacific, the United States lent its support to American sugar planters who overthrew the Kingdom of Hawaii and eventually annexed it as U.S. territory.

The turning point in American international affairs was the Spanish-American War in 1898. Urged on by the yellow press, the United States used the explosion of the USS Maine as a pretext to invade Cuba. The underlying reason for the conflict, however, was the ambition for empire and economic gain. The war with Spain also triggered the dispatch of the fleet under Admiral George Dewey to the Philippines, followed up by sending Army troops. Victory over the Spanish proved fruitful for American territorial ambitions. Although, in a rare moment of idealism, Congress passed legislation renouncing claims to annex Cuba, the United States did gain control of the island of Puerto Rico; a permanent deep-water naval harbor at Guantanamo Bay, Cuba; the Philippines; and various other Pacific islands formerly possessed by Spain. The occupation of the Philippines led to a guerrilla war, the "Philippines Insurrection," which lasted until 1902. United States rule over the Philippines lasted until 1942, but unlike during the guerrilla war years, later U.S. rule was relatively benign.

Skill 1.8b   Understand the process of industrialization and the political, economic, and social changes associated with industrialization in this period

There was a marked degree of industrialization before and during the Civil War, but at war's end, industry in the United States remained relatively small and concentrated in the industrial hubs of the Northeast. After the war, dramatic changes took place. Mechanization replaced hand labor and extensive nationwide railroad service made possible the wider distribution of goods. New products were invented and made available in large quantities, and large amounts of money from bankers and investors were available for expansion of business operations.

The **Second Industrial Revolution** (1830—1910) resulted in vast improvements in a number of industries that had already been mechanized through such inventions as the Bessemer steel process and the invention of steamships. As a result, new industries, utilizing photography, electricity, and chemical processes, arose. New sources of power were harnessed and applied, including petroleum and hydroelectric power. Precision instruments were developed and engineering was launched.

The direct results of the Second Industrial Revolution, particularly as they affected industry, commerce, and agriculture, included

- enormous increase in productivity;
- significant increase in world trade;
- specialization and division of labor;
- standardization of parts and mass production;
- growth of giant business conglomerates and monopolies; and
- a new revolution in agriculture facilitated by the steam engine, machinery, chemical fertilizers, processing, canning, and refrigeration.

The social results of the Industrial Revolution include

- increase of population, especially in industrial centers;
- advances in science applied to agriculture, sanitation and medicine;
- growth of great cities;
- disappearance of the differences between city dwellers and farmers; and
- faster lifestyles and greater stress from the monotony of the work routine.

This phenomenal industrial growth reshaped U.S. life. Cities became the centers of new business activity, resulting in mass population movements and tremendous growth. This new boom in business resulted in huge fortunes for some Americans and extreme poverty for many others. The discontent this disparity caused resulted in a number of new reform movements from which came measures to control the power and size of big business and to help the poor.

The use of machines in industry enabled workers to produce larger quantities of goods much faster than they could by hand. With the increase in business, hundreds of workers were hired and assigned to perform specific jobs in the production process. This method of organization was called "division of labor." Because of the increasing rate of production, businesses could lower prices for their products and make them affordable for more people. As a result, sales and businesses were increasingly successful and profitable.

Innovations in new industrial processes and technology grew at a pace unmatched at any other time in U.S. history. A great variety of new products or inventions became available such as the typewriter, the telephone, barbed wire, the electric light, and the phonograph. One invention of the era that went on to have a large effect on the U.S. economy was the automobile. Automobiles captured American" imagination during the 1890s although they were not widely available until a few decades later. Thomas Edison was the most prolific inventor of that time. He used a systematic and efficient method to invent and improve on current technology in a profitable manner.

The increase in business and industry was greatly affected by the many rich natural resources found throughout the nation. The industrial machines were powered by the abundant water supply. The construction industry, as well as products made from wood, depended heavily on lumber from the forests. An abundance of coal and iron ore were needed for the steel industry, which profited and grew from the use of steel in such things as skyscrapers, automobiles, bridges, railroad tracks, and machines. Other minerals such as silver, copper, and petroleum played a large role in industrial growth, especially petroleum, from which gasoline was refined as fuel for the increasingly popular automobile.

Skill 1.8c   Understand the causes and consequences of urban development in this period

Between 1870 and 1916 more than 25 million immigrants came into the United States, adding to the phenomenal population growth taking place. This tremendous growth aided business and industry in two ways:

- The number of consumers increased creating a greater demand for products, thus enlarging the markets for the products.
- With increased production and expanding business, more workers were available for newly created jobs.

The abundance of resources, together with growth of industry and the pace of capital investments led to the growth of cities. Populations were shifting from rural agricultural areas to urban industrial areas, and by the early 1900s a third of the nation's population lived in cities. Industry needed workers in its factories, mills, and plants, and rural workers were being displaced by advances in farm machinery.

The dramatic growth of population in cities was fueled by growing industries, more efficient transportation of goods and resources, and the people who migrated to those new industrial jobs, either from rural areas of the United States or from foreign lands. Increased urban populations, often packed into dense tenements, frequently without adequate sanitation or clean water, led to public-health challenges that required cities to establish sanitation, water, and public health departments to cope with and prevent epidemics. Political organizations, seeing the advantage of mobilizing the new industrial working class, created vast patronage programs that sometimes became notorious for corruption in big-city machine politics such as Tammany Hall in New York City.

As business grew, methods of sales and promotion were developed. Salespersons went to all parts of the country promoting the various products, opening large department stores in the growing cities, offering the varied products at affordable prices. People who lived too far from the cities had the advantage of using a mail-order service, buying what they needed from catalogs furnished by the companies.

Developments in communication, such as the telephone and the telegraph, increased the efficiency and prosperity of big business.

Skill 1.8d   Understand political, cultural, and social movements

Rapid urbanization and industrialization led to changes in government, business, and society. The labor movement enjoyed particular growth, despite challenges from business and political leaders.In 1866, the National Labor Union was formed, pushing such issues as the eight-hour workday and new policies of immigration. This organization gave rise to the Knights of Labor and eventually to the American Federation of Labor (AFL) in the 1890s and the Industrial Workers of the World (1905). Skilled laborers, particularly, joined the **American Federation of Labor (AFL)** in an effort to gain better working conditions and wages for its members.

Farmers joined organizations such as the National Grange and Farmers Alliances. Farmers were producing more food than people could afford to buy because of new farmlands rapidly sprouting on the plains and prairies and the development and availability of new farm machinery and newer and better methods of farming. They tried selling their surplus abroad but faced stiff competition from other nations selling the same farm products. Other problems contributed significantly to their situation. Items they needed for daily life were priced exorbitantly high. Having to borrow money to carry on farming activities kept them constantly in debt. Higher interest rates, shortage of money, falling farm prices, dealing with the so-called middlemen, and the increasingly high charges by the railroads to haul farm products to large markets all contributed to the desperate need for reform to relieve the plight of American farmers.

American women began actively campaigning for the right to vote. In 1869, Elizabeth Cady Stanton and Susan B. Anthony founded the organization called **National Woman Suffrage Association**, the same year that the Wyoming Territory gave women the right to vote. Soon after, a few states followed by giving women the right to vote in local elections only.

Governmental reform began with the passage of the **Civil Service Act**, also known as the Pendleton Act. It provided for the Civil Service Commission, a federal agency responsible for giving jobs based on merit rather than as political rewards or favors. By the late nineteenth century, business practices that limited competition had drawn the attention of the government in a shift from its earlier support for purely laissez-faire capitalism. Laws such as the Sherman Antitrust Act worked to break up monopolies and limit the power of huge corporations.

After 1890, more and more attention was called to needs and problems through the efforts of social workers and clergy and the writings of people such as Lincoln Steffens, Ida M. Tarbell, and Upton Sinclair. Civil rights remained at stake, especially in the South. Jim Crow laws were given credibility in 1896 when the Supreme Court handed down its decision in the case *Plessy* v. *Ferguson.* In 1890, Louisiana had passed a law requiring separate train cars for blacks and whites. In 1892, to challenge this law, Homer Plessy, a man who had a black great-grandparent and so was considered legally "black" in that state, purchased a ticket in the white section and took his seat. Upon informing the conductor that he was black, he was told to move to the black car. He refused and was arrested. His case was eventually elevated to the Supreme Court.

The Court ruled against Plessy, thereby ensuring that the Jim Crow laws would continue to proliferate and be enforced. The Court held that segregating races was not unconstitutional as long as the facilities for each were identical. This became known as the "separate but equal" principle. In practice, facilities were seldom equal. Black schools were not funded at the same level, for instance. Streets and parks in black neighborhoods were not maintained.

A number of presidents supported reformist legislation. In 1884, President Grover Cleveland did much to see that the Civil Service Act was enforced. After 1880, a number of political "third" parties were formed and, although they were unsuccessful in getting their presidential candidates elected, Congress passed into law significant reform legislation, including constitutional amendments, because of their efforts.

See also Skill 1.9a

COMPETENCY 1.9   PROGRESSIVE ERA THROUGH THE NEW DEAL (1900–1939)

Skill 1.9a   Demonstrate knowledge of political, economic, and social developments

The late 1800s and early 1900s were a period of the efforts of many to make significant reforms and changes in the areas of politics, society, and the economy. There was a need to reduce the level of poverty and to improve the living conditions of those affected by it. Regulating big business, ridding government of corruption, and making it more responsive to the needs of the people were also on the list of reforms to be accomplished. Until 1890, there was very little success, but from then on the reformers gained increasing public support and were able to achieve some influence in government. Since some of these individuals referred to themselves as "progressives," the period of 1890 to 1917 is referred to by historians as the **Progressive Era.**

Presidents Theodore Roosevelt, William Howard Taft, and Woodrow Wilson supported many of the reform laws in the twentieth century. Some of this legislation was aimed at the unfair business practices of large corporations. Such legislation included the Sherman Antitrust Act of 1890, the Clayton Antitrust Act of 1914, the Underwood Tariff of 1913, and the establishment of the Federal Trade Commission in 1914.

Another successful reform was the adoption of the secret ballot in voting, as were such measures as the direct primary, the referendum, the recall, and the passage of the Seventeenth Amendment to the Constitution—direct election of U.S. senators by the people rather than by their state legislatures. Following the success of reforms made at the national level, the progressives were successful in gaining reforms in government at state and local levels.

This era saw the continued growth of the U.S. role in foreign affairs. Under the administration of Theodore Roosevelt, the strength of U.S. armed forces was greatly increased. Roosevelt's foreign policy was summed up in the slogan "Speak softly and carry a big stick," backing up the efforts of diplomacy with a strong military. During the years before the outbreak of World War I, evidence of U.S. emergence as a world power could be seen in a number of actions. In the spirit of the Monroe Doctrine of the noninvolvement of Europe in the affairs of the western hemisphere, President Roosevelt forced Italy, Germany, and Great Britain to remove their blockade of Venezuela. In addition he gained the rights to construct the Panama Canal by threatening force and assumed the finances of the Dominican Republic to stabilize it and to prevent any intervention by Europeans. In 1916, President Woodrow Wilson ordered U.S. troops to the Dominican Republic.

See also Skill 1.9c

Skill 1.9b   Understand the causes of United States participation in the First World War and the consequences at home and abroad

When World War I began in 1914, President Woodrow Wilson declared that the United States was neutral, and most Americans opposed any involvement. U.S. involvement in the war did not occur until 1917. In 1916, Wilson was elected to a second term based on his promise to keep America out of the war. For a few months after the election, he kept his promise, but by then German submarines, or U-Boats, began conducting "unrestricted submarine warfare" against U.S. merchant shipping. British propaganda efforts and the German attack on the passenger ship *Lusitania*, which killed a number of Americans, swayed public support toward the Allied cause. Other root causes for the United States' participation in World War I included the surge of nationalism, the increasing strength of military capabilities, massive colonization for raw materials needed for industrialization and manufacturing, and military and diplomatic alliances. The United States also wished to support democracy where it existed in Great Britain and France, which were threatened by the totalitarian regimes of Germany and its allies.

In Europe, Italy and Germany had each united into one nation from many smaller states. There were revolutions in Austria and Hungary, the Franco-Prussian War, the dividing of Africa among the strong European nations, interference and intervention of western nations in Asia, and the breakup of Turkish dominance in the Balkans. France, Great Britain, Italy, Portugal, Spain, Germany, and Belgium controlled the entire continent of Africa except Liberia and Ethiopia. In Asia and the Pacific Islands, only China, Japan, and Siam (present-day Thailand) kept their independence. The others were controlled by the strong European nations.

World War I saw the introduction of new types of warfare. Tanks, airplanes, machine guns, submarines, poisonous gas, and flame throwers got their first use in World War I. Fighting on the Western front was characterized by a series of trenches that were used throughout the war until 1918.

When the war ended, pre-war empires lost tremendous amounts of territory as well as the wealth of natural resources in them. Many monarchies disappeared; smaller countries gained temporary independence; Communists seized power in Russia; and, in some cases, nationalism increased.

New, independent nations were formed and some predominately ethnic areas came under control of nations of different cultural backgrounds. Some national boundary changes overlapped, creating tensions, animosity, and political and economic confusion. The wishes and desires of every national or cultural group could not be realized or satisfied, resulting in disappointments for both; those who were victorious and those who were defeated.

Socially, total populations decreased because of war casualties and low birth rates. There were millions of displaced persons, their villages and farms destroyed. However, cities grew while women made significant gains in the work force and the ballot box. There was less social distinction and classes. Attitudes completely changed and old beliefs and values were questioned. The peace settlement established the League of Nations to ensure peace, but as we will see, it failed to do so.

Some ten months before the war ended, President Wilson proposed a program called the Fourteen Points as a method of bringing the war to an end with an equitable peace settlement. Five of these points set out general ideals, eight pertained to immediately working on resolving territorial and political problems, and the fourteenth counseled establishing the League of Nations, an organization of nations to help keep world peace.

When Germany agreed to an armistice in 1918, it assumed that the peace settlement would be drawn up on the basis of these Fourteen Points. However, the peace conference in Versailles ignored these points, and Wilson had to be content with efforts at establishing the League of Nations. Italy, France, and Great Britain, having suffered and sacrificed far more in the war than America, wanted retribution. The Versailles Treaty severely punished the Central Powers, taking away arms and territories and requiring payment of reparations. Germany received a harsher punishment than the others and, according to one clause in the treaty, was forced to assume the responsibility for causing the war.

In the United States, President Wilson lost his bid in the U.S. Senate to approve the Treaty of Versailles. The approval of the treaty would have made the United States a member of the League of Nations. However, the nation had just emerged from a bloody war to ensure that democracy would exist throughout the world. Americans did not want to accept the responsibility that resulted from its new position of power and were afraid that membership in the League of Nations would drag the United States into future conflicts in Europe. The nation eventually signed a separate agreement formally ending the conflict with opposing powers.

Skill 1.9c Demonstrate knowledge of political, economic, social, and cultural life in the "Roaring Twenties"

The decade of the 1920s saw tremendous changes in the United States, signifying the beginning of its development into today's modern society. The shift from farm to city life continued apace. Social changes and problems were occurring at such a fast pace that it was extremely difficult and perplexing for many Americans to adjust to them.

The influence of the automobile and the entertainment industry and the rejection of the morals and values of pre-World War I life, resulted in the fast-paced

"**Roaring Twenties.**" There were significant effects on events leading to the Depression of the 1930s and the Second World War. Many Americans greatly desired the prewar life and supported political policies and candidates in favor of a return to what was considered normal. As a result of the war, people wanted to end government's strong role and adopt a policy of isolating the country from world affairs.

Political

The **Eighteenth Amendment** to the Constitution, the Prohibition Amendment, banned the manufacture and sale of alcoholic beverages throughout the nation. Although well intentioned, the amendment turned numerous average Americans into law-breakers and led to the rise of organized crime. Prohibition of the sale of alcohol increased bootlegging, illegal speakeasies, jazz music, and the dances it promoted. The customers of these clubs were considered "modern," reflected by extremes in their clothing, hairstyles, and attitudes towards authority and life.

Ratification of the **Nineteenth Amendment** gave women the right to vote in all elections. The decade of the 1920s also showed a marked change in roles and opportunities for women with more and more of them seeking and finding careers outside the home. They began to think of themselves as the equal of men and not as housewives and mothers.

Social

Popular entertainment helped create a national mass culture and influenced Americans to admire, emulate, and support individual accomplishments. For example, interest increased in sports figures and the accomplishments of national heroes such as Charles Lindbergh. As wild and uninhibited as modern behavior became, this decade also witnessed an increase in a religious tradition known as "revivalism" or emotional preaching. Conservatives opposed the teaching of evolution in schools, as evidenced by the 1925 trial in Tennessee of John Scopes, a high-school science teacher.

Although many Americans demanded law and order, the administration of President Warren G. Harding was marked by widespread corruption and scandal. The decade of the 1920s also saw the resurgence of such racist organizations as the Ku Klux Klan.

Economical

The U.S. economy experienced a tremendous period of boom. Restrictions on business no longer existed because of the war and because conservatives in control adopted policies that helped and encouraged big business. To keep foreign goods from competing with U.S.-made goods, tariffs were raised to the highest level.

The legislative and executive branches of the Coolidge administration tended to favor businesses and the wealthy. The Revenue Act of 1926 significantly reduced income taxes for the wealthy. Despite the rise of labor unions, even the Supreme Court ruled in ways that further widened the gap between the rich and the middle and lower classes. In the case of *Adkins v. Children's Hospital* (1923), the Court ruled that minimum wage legislation was unconstitutional.

American manufacturers developed many new products, including refrigerators, radios, washing machines, and, most important, the automobile, that became readily available to the people. The consumer culture of the day led to rising levels of personal debt as people bought goods on installment plans. The concept of buying on credit caught on very quickly. Buying on credit, however, creates artificial demand for products people cannot ordinarily afford. This form of deficit spending has two effects: first, at some point there is less need to purchase products (because they have already been bought), and second, at some point, paying for previous purchases makes it impossible to purchase new products. This second effect exacerbated the problem of a surplus of goods.

Two industries, automotive and radio, drove the economy in the 1920s. The concentration of production and economic stability in the automotive industry and the production and sale of radios was expected to last forever. When these two industries declined because of decreased demand, they caused the collapse of other industries upon which they were dependent (e.g., rubber tires, glass, fuel, construction, etc.).

During this decade, the government tended to support new industries rather than agriculture. During WWI, the government had subsidized farms and paid ridiculously high prices for grains. Farmers had been encouraged to buy and farm more land and to use new technology to increase production. The nation was feeding much of Europe during and in the aftermath of the war. But when the war ended, these farm policies were cut off. Prices plummeted, farmers fell into debt, and farm prices declined. The agriculture industry was on the brink of ruin before the stock market crash.

The economy also relied on investment and luxury spending by the rich in the 1920s. During the Twenties, while investing was very healthy, investors began to expect greater returns on their investments. This desire for more money led many to make speculative investments in risky opportunities.

These risky speculative investments in the stock market were a major factor contributing to the stock market crash of 1929. Stock market speculation was spectacular throughout the 1920s. In 1929, shares traded on the New York Stock Exchange reached 1,124,800,410. In 1928 and 1929, stock prices doubled and tripled. The opportunity to achieve such profits was irresistible. In much the same way that buying goods on credit became popular, buying stock on margin allowed people to invest a very small amount of money in the hope of receiving an exceptional profit. This hope created an investing craze that drove the market higher and higher. But brokers were also charging higher interest rates on their margin loans (nearly 20 percent). If, however, the price of the stock dropped, the investor owed the broker the amount borrowed plus interest.

Skill 1.9d **Demonstrate knowledge of political, economic, and social developments during the Great Depression and the New Deal**

Stock crash

The 1929 Stock Market Crash was the powerful event that is generally interpreted as the beginning of the Great Depression in America. Although the crash of the stock market was unexpected, it was not without identifiable causes. The 1920s had been a decade of social and economic growth and hope. But the attitudes and actions of the 1920s regarding wealth, production, and investment created several trends that quietly set the stage for the 1929 disaster.

In September 1929, stock prices began to slip somewhat, yet people remained optimistic. On Monday, October 21, prices began to fall quickly. The volume traded was so high that the tickers were unable to keep up. Investors were frightened, and they started selling very quickly, causing further collapse. For the next two days prices stabilized somewhat. On **Black Thursday**, October 24, prices plummeted again. By this time investors had lost confidence. On Friday and Saturday, some leading bankers tried to stop the crash, but on Monday the 28th, prices began to fall again, declining by 13 percent in one day. The next day, **Black Tuesday, October 29**, saw 16.4 million shares traded. Stock prices fell so far that often no one was willing to buy at any price.

Great Depression

When the stock market crashed, businesses collapsed. Without demand for products, other businesses and industries collapsed. This set in motion a domino effect, bringing down the businesses and industries that provided raw materials or components to the collapsing industries. Hundreds of thousands of people became jobless. Then the jobless often became homeless. Desperation prevailed.

Another factor contributing to the Great Depression was the economic condition of Europe. The United States was lending money to European nations to rebuild after World War I. Many of these countries used this money to purchase U.S. food and manufactured goods, but they were not able to pay off their debts. While the United States was providing money, food, and goods to Europe, Americans were not willing to buy European goods. Trade barriers were enacted to maintain a favorable trade balance.

Some scholars cite several other factors as contributing to the Great Depression. First, in 1929, the Federal Reserve increased interest rates. Second, some believe that, as interest rates rose and the stock market began to decline, people began to hoard money.

Unemployment eventually reached 25 percent nationwide. Unable to afford their rents or mortgages, homeless people created makeshift towns of cardboard, scraps of wood, and tents that they called "Hoovervilles" after the increasingly unpopular President Herbert Hoover, whose hands-off approach to the economy had failed to bolster it during the downturn. Families stood in bread lines, rural workers left the Dust Bowl of the plains to search for work in California, and banks failed. More than 100,000 businesses failed between 1929 and 1932. The despair that swept the nation left an indelible scar on all who endured the Depression.

In several parts of the country, economic disaster was exacerbated by natural disaster. The Florida Keys were hit by the "**Labor Day Hurricane**" in 1935. This was one of only three hurricanes in history to make landfall as a Category 5 storm. More than 400 died in the storm, including 200 WWI veterans who were building bridges for a public works project. In the Northeast, the **Great Hurricane of 1938** struck Long Island, New York, causing more than 600 fatalities, decimating Long Island, and resulting in millions of dollars in damage to the coast from New York City to Boston.

By far the worst natural disaster of the decade came to be known as the **Dust Bowl.** Because of severe and prolonged drought in the Great Plains and previous reliance on inappropriate farming techniques, a series of devastating dust storms occurred in the 1930s that resulted in destruction, economic ruin for many, and dramatic ecological change. Plowing the plains for agriculture removed the grass and exposed the soil. When the drought occurred, the soil dried out and became dust. Wind blew the dust away. Between 1934 and 1939 winds blew the soil to the east, all the way to the Atlantic Ocean. The dust storms, called "black blizzards," created huge clouds of dust that were visible all the way to Chicago. Topsoil was stripped from millions of acres.

Crops were ruined, the land was destroyed, and people either lost or abandoned homes and farms. Fifteen percent of Oklahoma's population left. In Texas, Arkansas, Oklahoma, New Mexico, Kansas, and Colorado, more than half a million people were homeless. Many of these people journeyed west in the hope of making a new life in California. Because so many of the migrants were from Oklahoma, the migrants came to be called "**Okies**" no matter where they came from. Estimates of the number of people displaced by this disaster range from 300,000 or 400,000 to 2.5 million.

During President Roosevelt's first 100 days in office, his administration responded to this crisis with programs designed to restore the ecological balance of the Great Plains. One such program was the **Soil Conservation Service** (now the Natural Resources Conservation Service).

Recovery

Hoover's bid for reelection in 1932 failed. The new president, Franklin D. Roosevelt, won the White House on his promise to U.S. citizens of a "new deal." Upon taking office, Roosevelt and his advisers immediately launched a massive federal spending program to try to bring the Depression to an end and get the nation back on track. Congress gave the president unprecedented power to act to save the nation. Over the next several years, the most extensive and broadly based legislation in the nation's history was enacted. The legislation was intended to accomplish three goals—relief, recovery, and reform.

The first step in the Roosevelt's **"New Deal"** was to relieve suffering. This was accomplished through a number of job-creation projects. The second step, the recovery aspect, was to stimulate the economy. The third step was to create social and economic change through innovative legislation.

The National Recovery Administration attempted to accomplish the following goals:

- restore employment;
- increase general purchasing power;
- provide character-building activity for unemployed youth;
- encourage decentralization of industry and thus divert population from crowded cities to rural or semirural communities;
- develop river resources in the interest of navigation and cheap power and light;
- complete flood control on a permanent basis;
- enlarge the national program of forest protection and develop forest resources;
- control farm production and improve farm prices;
- assist home builders and home owners;
- restore public faith in banking and trust operations; and
- recapture the value of physical assets, whether in real property, securities, or other investments.

The charter of the National Recovery Administration included a statement defending the right of labor unions to exist and to negotiate with employers. This statement was interpreted by thousands as support for unions. But the Supreme Court declared such support unconstitutional. Nevertheless, these objectives and their accomplishments implied a restoration of public confidence and courage.

Among the "alphabet organizations" set up to work out the details of the recovery plan, the most prominent were:

- the **Agricultural Adjustment Administration** (AAA), designed to readjust agricultural production and prices, thereby, boosting farm income;
- the **Civilian Conservation Corps** (CCC), designed to give wholesome, useful activity in the forestry service to unemployed young men;
- the **Civil Works Administration** (CWA) and the **Public Works Administration** (PWA), designed to provide employment in the construction and repair of public buildings, parks, and highways; and
- the **Works Progress Administration** (WPA), intended to move individuals from relief rolls to work projects or private employment.

The **Tennessee Valley Authority** (TVA) was of a more permanent nature. Designed to improve the navigability of the Tennessee River and increase productivity of the timber and farm lands in its valley, this program built sixteen dams that provided water control and hydroelectric generation.

The **Public Works Administration** employed Americans on more than 34,000 public works projects at a cost of more than $4 billion. Among these projects were the construction of a highway that linked the Florida Keys and Miami, numerous highway projects, and the Boulder (now the Hoover) Dam.

To provide economic stability and prevent another crash, Congress passed the **Glass-Steagall Act**, which separated banking and investing. The Securities and Exchange Commission was created to regulate dangerous speculative practices on Wall Street. The **Wagner Act** guaranteed a number of rights to workers and unions, including the right to collectively bargain, in an effort to improve worker-employer relations. The **Social Security Act of 1935** established pensions for the aged and the infirm as well as a system of unemployment insurance.

Lasting effects

While much of the New Deal aimed to resolve the Depression immediately, certain permanent national policies emerged. The public, through its government, wanted to supervise and, to an extent, regulate business operations, from corporate activities to labor problems. These regulations included protecting bank depositors and the credit system of the country, employing gold resources and currency adjustments to aid permanent restoration of normal living, and, if possible, establishing a line of subsistence below which no citizen would be permitted to sink.

Many of the steps taken by FDR have had far-reaching effects. They eventually alleviated some of the effects the economic disaster of the Great Depression; they enacted controls that would mitigate the risk of another stock market crash; and they provided greater economic security for workers. The nation's economy, however, suffered a second decline in the late 1930s as spending decreased and interest rates increased, and it did not fully recover until the United States entered World War II.

There were negative reactions to some of the measures taken to pull the country out of the Depression. There was a major reaction to the deaths of the WWI veterans in the Labor Day Hurricane, ultimately resulting in a Congressional investigation into possible negligence. The Central Valley Project ruffled feathers of farmers who lost tillable land and some water supply to the construction of the aqueduct and the Hoover Dam. Tennesseans were initially unhappy with the changes in river flow and navigation when the Tennessee Valley Authority began its construction of dams, redirecting water to form reservoirs and to power hydroelectric plants. Some businesses and business leaders were not happy with the introduction of minimum wage laws, restrictions and controls on working conditions, and limitations of work hours for laborers. The numerous import and export tariffs of the period were the subject of controversy. Other opponents of the New Deal, such as Louisiana populist Huey Long, argued that Roosevelt's plans did not go far enough to help people.

In the long view, however, much that was accomplished under the New Deal had positive long-term effects on economic, ecological, social, and political issues for the next several decades. The Tennessee Valley Authority and the Central Valley Project in California provided reliable sources and supplies of water to major cities and electrical power to meet the needs of an increasingly electricity-dependent society. For the middle class and the poor, the labor regulations, the establishment of the Social Security Administration, and the separation of investment and banking have served the nation admirably for more than seven decades.

COMPETENCY 1.10 THE SECOND WORLD WAR AND THE POSTWAR PERIOD (1939-1963)

Skill 1.10a **Understand the causes of United States participation in the Second World War and the consequences at home and abroad**

U.S. involvement

Still suffering from the Great Depression, the U.S. population at large opposed U.S. involvement in World War II during the late 1930s and early 1940s. Roosevelt slowly increased U.S. aid to Great Britain and its allies through lend-lease and other military and economic programs. However, the nation remained formally neutral until late 1941.

The United States had opposed Japan's invasion of Southeast Asia, an effort to gain Japanese control of that region's rich resources. Consequently, the U.S. stopped all important exports to Japan, whose industries depended heavily on petroleum, scrap metal, and other raw materials. Later, Roosevelt blocked Japan's withdrawal of its funds from U.S. banks. General Tojo became the Japanese premier in October 1941 and quickly realized that the U.S. Navy was powerful enough to block Japanese expansion into Asia. Deciding to cripple the U.S. Pacific Fleet, the Japanese air force—despite the nation's continued formal attempts at diplomacy—bombed the fleet on December 7, 1941, while it was at anchor in Pearl Harbor, Hawaii. Temporarily, the attack was a success. It destroyed many aircraft and disabled much of the U.S. Pacific Fleet. In the end, however, it was a costly mistake because it quickly motivated the Americans to wage war.

Military strategy in the war as developed by Roosevelt, Churchill, and Stalin was to concentrate on Germany's defeat first, then Japan's. The start was made in North Africa, pushing Germans and Italians off the continent beginning in the summer of 1942 and ending successfully in May 1943. In 1939, before the war began, Hitler and Stalin had signed a nonaggression pact, which Hitler violated in 1941 by invading the Soviet Union. The German defeat at Stalingrad, marking a turning point in the war, was caused by a combination of entrapment by Soviet troops and the death of German troops by starvation and freezing in horrendous winter conditions. All this occurred at the same time the Allies were driving the Germans and Italians out of North Africa.

The liberation of Italy began in July 1943 and essentially ended with the surrender of German troops on the peninsula in May 1945. The third part of the strategy was D-Day, June 6, 1944, an Allied invasion of France at Normandy. At the same time, starting in January 1943, the Soviets began pushing the German troops back into central Europe, greatly assisted by supplies from Britain and the United States. By April 1945, the Allies occupied positions beyond the Rhine and the Soviets moved on to Berlin, surrounding it by April 25. Germany surrendered May 7 and the war in Europe was finally over.

Meanwhile, in the Pacific, in the six months after the attack on Pearl Harbor, Japanese forces moved across Southeast Asia and the western Pacific Ocean. By August 1942, the Japanese Empire was at its largest and stretched northeast to Alaska's Aleutian Islands, west to Burma, and south to what is now Indonesia. Invaded and controlled areas included Hong Kong, Guam, Wake Island, Thailand, part of Malaysia, Singapore, and the Philippines; in addition, the Japanese bombed Darwin on the north coast of Australia.

The raid of General Doolittle's bombers on Japanese cities and the U.S. naval victory at Midway, along with the fighting in the Battle of the Coral Sea helped turn the tide against Japan. Island-hopping by U.S. Seabees and Marines and the grueling bloody battles they fought resulted in the Japanese being gradually pushed back towards Japan.

Aftermath

After victory was attained in Europe, concentrated efforts were made to secure Japan's surrender. Truman, who assumed the presidency after Roosevelt's death, decided to use atomic weapons on the cities of Hiroshima and Nagasaki to end the war in the Pacific. The devastation of the bombing was immense, but Japan formally surrendered on September 2, 1945, aboard the U.S. battleship Missouri, anchored in Tokyo Bay. The war had finally ended.

Before the war ended in Europe, the Allies had agreed on a military occupation of Germany. It was divided into four zones, each one occupied by one of the four Allied Powers: Great Britain, France, the Soviet Union, and the United States. All four nations would jointly administer Berlin. After the war, the Allies agreed that Germany's armed forces would be abolished, the Nazi Party outlawed, and the territory east of the Oder and Neisse Rivers taken away. Nazi leaders were accused of war crimes and brought to trial at Nuremberg.

After Japan's defeat, the Allies began a military occupation directed by U.S. General Douglas MacArthur, who introduced a number of reforms, eventually ridding Japan of its military institutions and transforming it into a democratic nation. A constitution was drawn up in 1947, transferring all political rights from the emperor to the people, granting women the right to vote, and denying Japan the right to declare war. War crimes trials of twenty-five war leaders and government officials were also conducted. The United States did not sign a peace treaty until 1951. The treaty permitted Japan to rearm but took away its overseas empire.

Once more after a major world war came efforts to prevent war from occurring again throughout the world. Preliminary work began in 1943 when the United States, Great Britain, the Soviet Union, and China sent representatives to Moscow, where they agreed to set up an international organization that would work to promote peace around the earth. In 1944, the four Allied powers met again and made the decision to name the organization the United Nations. In

1945, a charter for the U. N. was drawn up and signed, taking effect in October of that year.

Global consequences

Major consequences of the war included horrendous death and destruction, millions of displaced persons, and growing Cold War tensions as a result of the beginning of the nuclear age. The death toll and casualties of World War II were more than any other war in history. Besides the losses of millions of military personnel, the devastation and destruction directly affected civilians, reducing cities, houses, and factories to ruin and rubble and totally wrecking communication and transportation systems. Millions of civilian deaths, especially in China and the Soviet Union, were the result of famine.

By the war's end, more than 12 million people were uprooted, having no place to live. Included were freed prisoners of war, those that had survived the Nazi concentration camps and slave labor camps, orphans, and people who had escaped war-torn areas and invading armies. Changing national boundary lines also caused the mass movement of displaced persons.

Germany and Japan were completely defeated; Great Britain and France were seriously weakened; and the Soviet Union and the United States became the world's leading powers. Although they had been allied during the war, the alliance fell apart as the Soviets pushed communism and the United States strove to combat it in Europe and Asia. In spite of the tremendous destruction it had suffered, the Soviet Union was stronger than ever. During the war, it took control of Lithuania, Estonia, and Latvia and by mid-1945 parts of Poland, Czechoslovakia, Finland, and Romania. It helped communist governments gain power in Bulgaria, Romania, Hungary, Czechoslovakia, Poland, and North Korea. China fell to Mao Tse-Tsung's communist forces in 1949.

Until the fall of the Berlin Wall in 1989 and the dissolution of communist governments in Eastern Europe and the Soviet Union, the United States and the Soviet Union faced off in what was called a Cold War. The possibility of the terrifying destruction by nuclear weapons loomed over both nations.

Skill 1.10b   Understand domestic and foreign developments during the Cold War

Soviet threat in Europe

The major thrust of U.S. foreign policy from the end of World War II to 1991 revolved around the postwar struggle between noncommunist nations, led by the United States, and the Soviet Union and the communist nations that were its allies. It was referred to as a "cold war" because its conflicts were not primarily fought in major armed, or "hot" war. Both the Soviet Union and the United States embarked on an arsenal buildup of atomic and hydrogen bombs as well as other nuclear weapons. Both nations could destroy each other but, because of the continuous threat of nuclear war and accidents, extreme caution was practiced on both sides. The efforts of both sides to serve and protect their political philosophies and to support and assist their allies resulted in a number of events during this more than four-decade period.

In 1946, Josef Stalin stated publicly that the presence of capitalism and its development of the world's economy made international peace impossible. In response, a U.S. diplomat in Moscow, George F. Kennan, proposed a statement of U.S. foreign policy known as **containment**. The idea and goal of the United States was to contain, or limit, the expansion of Soviet communist policies and activities. After Soviet efforts in Iran, Greece, and Turkey, U.S. President Harry Truman stated what is known as the **Truman Doctrine,** which committed the United States to a policy of intervention in order to contain the spread of communism throughout the world.

After 1945, social and economic chaos continued in Western Europe, especially in Germany. Secretary of State George C. Marshall assisted the recovery of Western Europe by proposing and implementing a program known as the European Recovery Program, or the **Marshall Plan**. Although the Soviet Union withdrew from any participation, the United States continued helping Europe regain economic stability. In Germany, the situation was critical, with the U.S. Army shouldering the staggering burden of relieving the serious problems of the German economy. In February 1948, Britain and the United States combined their two zones of influence there, and France joined them in June.

The Soviets were opposed to German unification, and in April 1948, took action to either stop it or to force the Allies to give up control of West Berlin. The Soviets blocked all road access to West Berlin from West Germany. To avoid any armed conflict, it was decided to airlift needed food and supplies into West Berlin. From June 1948 to mid-May 1949 Allied air forces flew in all that was needed for the West Berliners, forcing the Soviets to lift the blockade and permit vehicular traffic access to the city.

Hot spots in Asia
The first "hot war" in the post-World War II era was the Korean War, which began on June 25, 1950, and ended July 27, 1953. Troops from communist North Korea invaded democratic South Korea in an effort to unite both sections under communist control. The United Nations asked its member nations to furnish troops to help restore peace. Many nations responded, and President Truman sent U.S. troops to help the South Koreans. The war dragged on for three years and ended with a truce, not a peace treaty. Like Germany then, Korea remained divided. It remains divided to this day at the 38th parallel.

In 1954, the French were forced to give up their colonial claims in Indochina, the present-day countries of Vietnam, Laos, and Cambodia. Afterwards, the communist northern part of Vietnam began battling with the democratic southern part over control of the entire country. In the late 1950s and early 1960s, U.S. Presidents Eisenhower and Kennedy sent a number of military advisers to Vietnam. They also sent military aid to assist and support South Vietnam's noncommunist government. During Lyndon Johnson's presidency, the war escalated, with thousands of U.S. troops being sent to participate in combat alongside the South Vietnamese.

The Vietnam war became extremely unpopular in the United States and caused serious divisiveness among its citizens. Johnson decided not to seek reelection in 1968. It was during President Richard Nixon's second term in office that the nation signed an agreement ending the Vietnam War and restoring peace. This was done January 27, 1973, and by March 29, the last U.S. combat troops and U.S. prisoners of war left Vietnam for home. After the last Americans left Vietnam, the North Vietnamese moved into South Vietnam, uniting both sides in communist Vietnam. It was the longest undeclared war in U.S. history and it still carries the perception that it was a "lost war."

Missile crises
In 1962, during Kennedy's presidency, Soviet Premier Nikita Khrushchev and his advisors decided, as a protective measure for Cuba against an American invasion, to install nuclear missiles on the island. In October, American U-2 spy planes photographed what were identified as missile bases under construction in Cuba. Because these missiles would be within ready striking distance of the eastern United States, Kennedy announced that the United States had set up a "quarantine"—effectively, a blockade—of Soviet ships heading to Cuba to prevent the arrival of Soviet arms. The **Cuban Missile Crisis** brought the two superpowers to the brink of war, but it was eventually resolved when the Soviets removed their existing missiles from Cuba and agreed not establish missile installations there; in return, Kennedy quietly agreed to remove U.S. missiles from Turkey.

As tensions eased in the aftermath of the crisis, several agreements were made. The U.S. missiles in Turkey were removed. A telephone "hot line" was set up between Moscow and Washington to make it possible for the two heads of government to have instant contact with each other. The United States agreed to sell its surplus wheat to the Soviets.

Presidential diplomacy
Probably the highlight of the foreign policy of President Richard Nixon was his 1972 trip to China. When the communists gained control of China in 1949, the U.S. government refused to recognize the communist government. Instead, it recognized the Republic of China (ROC) on the island of Taiwan under Chiang Kai-shek as the legitimate Chinese government. The Nixon administration changed this policy and altered the nation's relations with Soviet states from that of containment to one of discussion and diplomacy.

Middle East events

During the administration of President Jimmy Carter, Egyptian President Anwar el Sadat and Israeli Prime Minister Menachem Begin met with Carter at presidential retreat Camp David. For years before this, negotiations had been taking place between the two nations, including a historic visit to Jerusalem by Sadat. After a series of meetings, the two countries agreed to sign a formal peace treaty. In 1979, the Soviet invasion of Afghanistan was perceived by Carter and his advisers as a threat to the rich oil fields in the Persian Gulf. At the time, U.S. military capability to prevent further Soviet aggression in the Middle East was weak.

Iran's Ayatollah Khomeini's extreme hatred for the United States was the result of the 1953 CIA-sponsored overthrow of Iran's Mossadegh government. The CIA had trained the Shah's ruthless secret police force, the SAVAK. The tensions within Iran led to revolution, and the ruling Shah was overthrown and replaced with the Islamic leader, the Ayatollah Khomeini. The mood of Iran turned to traditional conservative Muslim values, and a great deal of anti-Western sentiment emerged. In November 1979, sixty-six Americans were taken hostage at the U.S. Embassy in Tehran, beginning an international incident.

President Carter later froze all Iranian assets in the United States, set up trade restrictions, and approved a risky rescue attempt that failed. He had appealed to the UN for aid in gaining the release of the hostages and to European allies to join the trade embargo on Iran. Khomeini ignored UN requests for releasing the Americans while European nations refused to support the embargo so as not to risk losing access to Iran's oil. American prestige was damaged and Carter's chances for reelection were doomed. The hostages were released on the day of Ronald Reagan's inauguration as president.

Fall of communism in Europe

Perhaps the most far-reaching event of Reagan's second term was the arms-reduction agreement reached with Soviet General Secretary Mikhail Gorbachev. Gorbachev began soothing East-West tensions by stressing the importance of cooperation with the West and easing the harsh and restrictive life of the people in the Soviet Union. In retrospect, it was clearly a prelude to the events that occurred during the administration of President George H. W. Bush.

After Bush took office, it appeared for a brief period that democracy would gain a hold and an influence in China, but the brief movement was quickly and decisively crushed. The biggest surprise was the fall of the Berlin Wall in 1989, resulting in the unification of all of Germany. The loss of the communists' power in other Eastern European countries, the fall of communism in the Soviet Union, and the breakup of its satellite republics into independent nations were no less surprising. The countries of Poland, Hungary, Romania, Czechoslovakia, Albania, and Bulgaria replaced communist rule with democratic systems. The former Yugoslavia broke apart into individual ethnic enclaves, with the republics of Serbia, Croatia, and Bosnia-Herzegovina embarking on wars of ethnic cleansing among Catholics, Eastern Orthodox adherents, and Muslims.

In Russia, as in the other former republics and satellites, democratic governments were put into operation and the difficult task of changing communist economies into ones of capitalistic free enterprise began. For all practical purposes, it appeared that the tensions and dangers of the post-World War II Cold War between the U.S. and Soviet-led communism were over.

Skill 1.10c   Demonstrate knowledge of political, economic, social, and cultural life in the 1950s

President Harry Truman's administration entered the 1950s with a daunting task. A former ally, the Soviet Union under Josef Stalin, was now a rival for geopolitical influence around the world. The Cold War had begun following World War II, with East Germany and several nations of Eastern Europe falling under the Soviet sphere of control. China had recently ended a decades-long civil war that put the Communist Party under the chairmanship of Mao Tse-Tung and exiled the Guomindang (Nationalist Party) under Chiang Kai-shek to Taiwan. In Indochina (Vietnam, Laos and Cambodia), the Viet Minh under Ho Chi-Minh and forces under Vo Nguyen Giap's command had mounted a resistance to French colonial rule beginning shortly after World War II. In the minds of right-wing American politicians, these events were evidence for the "Red Menace" and a conspiracy for international domination by the communist bloc.

Truman, a Democrat, was confronted at home by a Congress controlled by the Republican Party, which carried on a series of hearings and investigations to ferret out "Reds" and communist sympathizers, starting with government agencies. The hunt soon spread to labor organizations, the arts and entertainment industry, and eventually to the infamous "blacklist" of individuals suspected of Communist Party affiliations that prevented the listed individuals from pursuing their chosen professions.

An economic boom enlivened the 1950s. The Korean War era (1950–1953) did not see the kind of general mobilization that World War II had. Most Americans were not directly affected by the war in Korea and the expansion of the economy continued. The growing middle class was spurred by the GI Bill of Rights, which gave educational, occupational, and mortgage assistance to veterans who could thus enjoy a middle-class lifestyle on an unprecedented scale.

The population boom of the babies born to veterans led to another social and cultural phenomenon, the "Baby Boomers." The election of Dwight D. Eisenhower as president in 1952 marked a continuation of economic progress and a burgeoning suburban population, fueled by low-interest Veterans Administration mortgage loans and new wealth.

After World War II and the Korean War, efforts to relieve the problems of millions of African Americans, including ending discrimination in education, housing, and jobs, and the grinding widespread poverty increased. Although President Truman ordered the Armed Forces to integrate in 1947—the same year that Jackie Robinson broke the "color barrier" of Major League Baseball—the military services were slow to integrate until the Korean War. Then, African American soldiers were assigned to front-line Army units without regard to race. The other services followed suit but only begrudgingly and out of necessity to replace personnel as casualties reduced their ranks.

The efforts of civil rights leaders found success in a number of Supreme Court decisions. The best-known case, *Brown* v. *Board of Education of Topeka* (1954), ended compulsory segregation in public schools.

Television and rock'n'roll music greatly shaped U.S. culture during the 1950s. Millions of Americans tuned into popular television programs for the first time, which helped define a new mass national culture. Teens also became more important as cultural influences with the growing popularity of rock'n'roll.

COMPETENCY 1.11   RECENT DEVELOPMENTS (1960S–PRESENT)

Skill 1.11a   Understand political developments, including the war in Vietnam, the "imperial presidency," and the new conservatism

Kennedy

The 1960 election of President John F. Kennedy signaled a new era in U.S. politics and culture. Kennedy was the first president born in the twentieth century and the second youngest to hold that office, after Theodore Roosevelt. As president, he called for Americans to serve society and the world by engaging in voluntary service at home and abroad. The Peace Corps was one of the better-known programs that Kennedy created as part of his "New Frontier."

Kennedy's mettle as a world leader was tested early in his administration. The Bay of Pigs invasion to unseat Fidel Castro from power in Cuba ended in disaster for the United States and gave Cuba a propaganda coup. The Cuban Missile Crisis nearly brought the United States to the brink of nuclear war with the Soviet Union. Kennedy also ordered military advisors to the Republic of Vietnam to support the Republic against the communist National Liberation Front (Viet Cong) who were South Vietnamese proxies for North Vietnam, thus commencing what later turned out to be a political and military quagmire for the United States.

When Kennedy was assassinated in 1963, the country faced an internal period of grief. Vice President Lyndon B. Johnson was sworn in as president after Kennedy's death in accordance with constitutional rules of succession. As president, Johnson retained Kennedy's cabinet largely intact, with few leaving, and appointed Senator Hubert H. Humphrey of Minnesota as vice president.

Johnson

The presidential election campaign of 1964 pitted Johnson against the Republican nominee, Senator Barry Goldwater of Arizona. Goldwater represented the "New Conservative" wing of his party, which advocated scaling back government from Roosevelt's New Deal and the liberal social policies of the Kennedy and Johnson administrations. The Goldwater campaign also advocated a strong military to counter the "Red Menace" of the Soviet Union, the People's Republic of China, and the communist bloc nations of the Warsaw Pact. Johnson successfully won reelection in a landslide, based partly on depicting Goldwater as a warmonger who would plunge the United States into a mutually destructive thermonuclear war with the Soviet Union.

Johnson's vision for the nation was called the "Great Society" and was built on the plans of Kennedy's "New Frontier." He won support in Congress for the largest group of legislative programs in the history of the nation. These included programs that Kennedy had been working on at the time of his death, including a new civil rights bill and a tax cut. Johnson defined the "great society" as "a place where the meaning of man's life matches the marvels of man's labor." The legislation enacted during his administration included efforts to fight disease, urban renewal, Medicare, aid to education, conservation and beautification, development of economically depressed areas, a massive "War on Poverty," voting rights for all, and control of crime and delinquency. Johnson managed an unpopular war in Vietnam and encouraged the exploration of space. During his administration, a number of new federal agencies, including the Department of Transportation, were formed, and the first black Supreme Court justice, Thurgood Marshall, was nominated and confirmed.

Vietnam

The U.S. entry into—and the escalation of—the war in Vietnam caused social conflict between supporters and opponents of the war. With active U.S. involvement from 1957 to 1973, it was the longest war participated in by the United States. It was tremendously destructive and completely divided the American public in their opinions and feelings about the war. Many were frustrated and angered by the fact that it was the first war fought on foreign soil in which U.S. combat forces were totally unable to achieve their goals and objectives. This conflict eventually led to many antiwar demonstrations and the growth of the counterculture movement.

Returning veterans faced not only a hard readjustment to normal civilian life but also bitterness, anger, rejection, and no heroes' welcome. Many suffered severe physical and deep psychological problems. The war set a precedent, with Congress and the American people actively challenging U.S. military and foreign policy. As the first "living room war," the Vietnam War also changed how citizens viewed the warmaking process and led to increased questioning of the authority of the government.

Unfortunately for Johnson, the war in Vietnam overshadowed his domestic programs and indelibly marked his legacy. It became known as "Johnson's War." The Gulf of Tonkin Resolution, enacted in late 1964 after an incident off the coast of Vietnam that involved U.S. naval ships and North Vietnamese coastal patrol boats, effectively gave the president the power to prosecute a war without a congressional declaration, as clearly stated in the Constitution. Soon afterward, in 1965, Johnson authorized the commitment of conventional military forces to Vietnam. The war proved to be a drain on the nation's economy and a growing burden for the president. Antiwar sentiment divided the nation as it hadn't since the Civil War. Eventually, the Vietnam quagmire became such a hindrance to his administration that Johnson declared, in a nationally televised address, that he would halt the bombing of North Vietnam and not be a candidate for the Democratic Party's nominee for the 1968 presidential election.

Troubles of 1968

The Vietnam War had divided the Democratic Party, and the 1968 Democratic National Convention in Chicago turned out to be highly contentious and bitterly fought, both on the floor of the convention and outside, where thousands had gathered to protest the Vietnam War. Vice President Hubert H. Humphrey became the party's nominee, but he led a divided party.

Also in 1968, the Reverend Martin Luther King, Jr., an influential leader of the civil rights movement and its most eloquent spokesman, was assassinated in Memphis, Tennessee, sparking racial riots in many U.S. cities. Senator Robert F. Kennedy of New York, the late President John F. Kennedy's younger brother, was also assassinated in Los Angeles after winning the California Democratic Primary. Before he died, it had looked very possible that he would win the party's nomination, running on an antiwar platform.

Nixon

Former Vice President Richard M. Nixon defeated the sitting Vice President Hubert Humphrey, despite a late growth of support for Humphrey in the polls. One of Nixon's campaign promises included a "secret plan" to end U.S. involvement in Vietnam. Nevertheless, the war dragged on for the length of his first term, and he ordered a widening of the war by ordering troops to invade previously neutral Cambodia in 1970. This action led to even more dissent against the war and the killing of four students at Kent State University in Ohio during a protest over the invasion of Cambodia.

In other international dealings, with a major role played by his national security advisor and later secretary of state, Henry Kissinger, Nixon undertook a bold international policy of détente with the Soviet Union and the unexpected step of opening official relations with the People's Republic of China. Given Nixon's political reputation as a staunch anti-Communist, this undertaking was surprising, even more so because China gave both political and material support to North Vietnam.

The Nixon administration was characterized as an "**Imperial Presidency**" because of his aggrandizement of presidential power—usurping powers that had been the purview of Congress and carrying on activities without the express consent of the Congress. The **Watergate scandal** resulted in the first-ever resignation of a sitting American president.

Reagan

A staunch conservative, Ronald Reagan introduced a reform program that came to be known as the Reagan Revolution. Its goal was to reduce the reliance of the American people upon government. For many, the Reagan administration restored hope in and enthusiasm for the nation. His administration's accomplishments include economic growth stimulation, curbing inflation, increasing employment, and strengthening the national defense. Nevertheless, periods of the 1980s were marked by great financial difficulty and high unemployment for the working and middle class and came at the expense of spiraling national debt. Reagan won Congressional support for a complete overhaul of the income tax code in 1986. By the time he left office, the nation had enjoyed a sustained period of overall economic growth with no major wars. He also nominated Sandra Day O'Connor as the first female justice on the Supreme Court.

See also Skills 1.10b, 1.11c

Skill 1.11b   Understand economic developments, including changes in industrial structure, the growth of the budget deficit, the impact of deregulation, and energy and environmental issues

Economic slowdown
The boom times for the economy of the 1950s slowed down by the mid and late '60s. National economic problems emerged in the late1960s as a result of the high costs of waging war in Vietnam, the arms race with the Soviet Union, and the increasing costs of growing social programs that quickly outstripped military spending as a share of the federal budget, exacerbated by an aversion for raising federal tax rates.

In order to support the unprecedented levels of spending, President Nixon instituted deficit spending, in which government spending exceeded collected revenues. This led to a dramatic increase in the national debt, as measured by the outstanding obligations in U.S. Treasury securities (bills, notes, and bonds) that were issued to cover the costs of government. The 1970s witnessed a period of high unemployment, the result of a severe recession. This was also accompanied by high inflation and wage increases, and the Nixon Administration imposed wage and price controls in August 1971 in order to lift the economy out of recession and offset the effects of "stagflation," a stagnant economy in a period of high inflation. Stagflation remained a major economic concern throughout the decade, however, with high unemployment and spiraling inflation troubling citizens into the 1980s.

Energy crisis
The U.S. appetite for nonrenewable petroleum to power cars, utilities, and industrial production grew unchecked, making the country more reliant on imports as demand outstripped domestic reserves' capacity to keep up. Persian Gulf nations provided the bulk of the imported oil that came mainly from Saudi Arabia and Iran. The United States was, therefore, dependent on a critical resource from an increasingly unstable part of the world. It was further complicated by U.S. support for Israel in the 1967 Six-Day War against Egypt, Syria, and Jordan, who were receiving aid from a number of other Arab nations, and the 1973 Yom Kippur War against Egypt and Syria, who were receiving aid from at least nine other Arab nations.

Angered by U.S. support of Israel in the Yom Kippur War, the Arab oil-producing nations of the Organization of Petroleum Exporting Countries (OPEC) cut back on oil production and boycotted exports to the United States, thus raising the price of a barrel of oil and creating a fuel shortage. Clearly, energy and fuel conservation were necessary in the American economy, especially since fuel shortages created two energy crises during the decade of the 1970s. Americans experienced shortages of fuel oil for heating and gasoline for cars and other vehicles.

Environmentalism
A great awakening to environmental concerns was evident by the mid and late 1960s as smog, polluted waterways, effects of poisons on the environment and dwindling nonrenewable resources caught the attention of the public. Rachel Carson's *Silent Spring* played a pivotal role in generating public interest in environmental issues. Major oil spills such as the Torrey Canyon spill into the English Channel in 1967 and the gigantic 1969 oil spill off the coast of Santa Barbara, California, also signaled alarming trends to come. President Nixon signed

- a bill banning DDT;
- the Environmental Protection Act of 1969, which established the Environmental Protection Agency (EPA); and
- the Occupational Safety and Health Act of 1970 (OSHA).

He also supported enactment of Clean Air and Clean Water acts.

Economic efforts
Nixon's successors in the 1970s, Presidents Ford and Carter, dealt with many of the same issues that had faced Nixon. Oil and gas prices remained generally high, and stagflation kept the nation struggling economically. Ford, like Nixon before him, attempted several, mostly unsuccessful, measure to curb inflation and jump-start the economy. He tried to reduce the role of the federal government. He reduced business taxes and lessened controls on business.

Carter's administration made significant progress by creating jobs and decreasing the budget deficit, but inflation and interest rates were at nearly record highs. There were several notable achievements, including establishing a national energy policy to deal with the energy shortage, decontrolling petroleum prices to stimulate production, civil service reform that improved government efficiency, and deregulating the trucking and the airline industries.

The Reagan administration tackled stagflation through the use of extremely high interest rates, which curbed inflation but inaugurated a time of high unemployment. In time, however, the economy stabilized and entered a period of sustained growth. Reagan's foreign policy relied on "peace through strength." Reagan set the stage for the fall of the Berlin Wall and the end of the Cold War by spending billions of dollars on national defense—a figure that could not be matched by the Soviet Union, setting the stage for its economic collapse. Yet this strategy forced the United States to rely on intense deficit spending.

Clinton

Fiscal restraint returned during President Bill Clinton's two terms. He managed to balance the federal budget for the first time since the Nixon Administration, and he left office with a $10 trillion budget surplus and a record of high economic growth. Toward the end of Clinton's presidency, the economy started to slow again. Coupling this with the economic hardships following the terrorist attacks on September 11, 2001, the budget surplus was replaced by a budget deficit during George W. Bush's first term as president.

Globalization

At the end of the twentieth century, the world witnessed unprecedented strides in communications, a major expansion of international trade, and significant international diplomatic and military activity. The Internet connected people all over the world, opening new routes of communication and providing commercial opportunities. The expansion of cell-phone usage and Internet access led to a globalized worldwide society that is interconnected as never before. In Asia, new economies matured, such as in India and China. As the technology sector expanded, so did India's economy, where high-tech companies found a highly educated work force. The formerly tightly controlled Chinese market became more open to foreign investment, which increased China's influence as a major economic power. The European Union made a bold move to a common currency, the euro, in an effort to consolidate the region's economic strength. African nations, many struggling under international debt, appealed to the international community to assist them in building their economies. In South America, countries such as Brazil and Venezuela showed growth, despite political unrest, even as Argentina suffered a near complete collapse of its economy.

Skill 1.11c   Understand major social movements and social policy initiatives in this period

President Lyndon B. Johnson continued many of the programs that John F. Kennedy started, notably passage of the **Civil Rights Act of 1964** for African-Americans, the "War on Poverty," and sustained support for the Republic of Vietnam. President Johnson pushed for the enactment of the **Voting Rights Act of 1965** to enfranchise Black voters, particularly in states of the former Confederacy, where they were actively discouraged from voting by multiple obstacles to registering to vote and, if registered, from voting, including intimidation and lynching. The Voting Rights Act also filled in some of the holes left in the Civil Rights Act.

In the 1960s, the civil rights movement under the leadership of Dr. Martin Luther King, Jr. really gained momentum. Under President Lyndon B. Johnson the Civil Rights Acts of 1964 and 1968 prohibited discrimination in housing sales and rentals, employment, public accommodations, and voter registration. President Johnson's "Great Society" programs exceeded those of Roosevelt's New Deal.

As a former public school teacher, Johnson made education a cornerstone of his policy, creating the Head Start Program. He was also responsible for getting legislation enacted to create Medicare, Job Corps, VISTA (Volunteers in Service to America, a domestic counterpart to the Peace Corps), and other programs to help the historically disadvantaged.

See also Skill 1.11a

Skill 1.11d   Understand the social and cultural effects of changes in the American family and in the ethnic composition of the United States population in this period

The first children of the Baby Boom generation born after World War II grew to maturity in this period. The Vietnam War and the Selective Service loomed large as young men who were born in 1946 became eligible for the draft in 1964 and 1965, just as the United States started deploying conventional military forces to Vietnam. Unlike in previous wars, draft-age men could be granted deferments or exemptions for educational and family reasons. Thus the upper class, wealthier and mainly white men, could avoid military service, leaving the working class and economically disadvantaged who could not afford college to serve in combat.

Youth activism in political and social activities started as part of the civil rights movement during the voter registration drives in the South for the 1964 elections in which college students participated. These students became leaders of social reform activism in later years of the decade. Such organizations as the Students for a Democratic Society (SDS) and the Youth International Party ("Yippies") also sprang up. During this growing counterculture trend, youth resisted traditional culture and society, taking up artists, rock stars, and other cultural icons of the era as models for emulation, including the use of such hallucinogenic drugs as LSD and euphoria-inducing marijuana. In 1971, the Constitution was amended to lower the voting age to eighteen.

During this period, exhibiting a new found pride was a growing trend among the nation's ethnic minorities. The African-American community found its voice in a number of civil rights organizations. Examples include the nonviolent coalition led by Rev. Martin Luther King, Jr.; the militant Black Panther Party led by Eldridge Cleaver, Huey Newton, and others; the Black Muslims led by Elijah Muhammad and Malcolm X (who later broke away from the Nation of Islam). The Nation of Islam counted among its converts Cassius Clay, the charismatic heavyweight boxing champion later known as Muhammad Ali, who also resisted the war in Vietnam by refusing induction.

Latino activism also started to come to fruition. Cesar Chavez organized Mexican-American farm workers in California, reflecting the importance and numbers of Latino workers in the U.S. economy and society. Cultural awareness among Native Americans was heightened after a takeover of Alcatraz in 1969 and the occupation of Wounded Knee, South Dakota, in 1973 by the American Indian Movement (AIM).

Gender politics became an issue as feminism and women's liberation became prominent, advocating equality for women in society and the workplace. Challenging many long-held notions of family led to the organization of the National Organization for Women (NOW), which supported an Equal Rights Amendment (ERA) to the Constitution and applauded the Supreme Court's decision in the 1973 case *Roe v. Wade.* In this decision, the Court struck down restrictions against abortion, strengthening women's reproductive rights. The gay rights movement's defining moment came with the Stonewall incident in 1969 that led to greater prominence of gay, lesbian, and transgender issues, including the American Psychiatric Association's removal in 1974 of homosexuality from classification as a mental disorder.

Skill 1.11e   Demonstrate understanding of international relations, including United States relations with the Soviet Union and its successor states and the changing role of the United States in world political and economic affairs

Throughout the Cold War era, the United States strove to limit the influence and expansion of communism around the world. This led to tense relations between the United States and the Soviet sphere during much of the 1950s, 1960s, 1970s, and early 1980s. Cold War tensions also spurred U.S. involvement in the Vietnam War. By the end of the Cold War, however, the fall of communist governments in Eastern Europe had begun to reshape international relations.

During the administration of President Jimmy Carter, Egyptian President Anwar el-Sadat and Israeli Prime Minister Menachem Begin met at presidential retreat Camp David and agreed, after a series of meetings, to sign a formal treaty of peace between the two countries. In 1979, the Soviet invasion of Afghanistan was perceived by Carter and his advisers as a threat to the rich oil fields in the Persian Gulf, but at the time U.S. military capability to prevent further Soviet aggression in the Middle East was weak.

The last year of Carter's presidential term was taken up with the fifty-three American hostages held in Iran. The shah had been deposed and control of the government and the country was in the hands of Muslim leader, Ayatollah Ruhollah Khomeini, whose extreme hatred for the United States was fueled by the 1953 CIA-orchestrated overthrow of Iran's democratically elected Mossadegh government. Also, the CIA had trained the Savak, the ruthless secret police. When the terminally-ill, exiled shah was allowed into the United States for medical treatment, a mob, supported and encouraged by Khomeini, stormed the American embassy, taking the fifty-three Americans as hostages.

President Reagan's foreign policy was, in his first term, focused primarily on the Western Hemisphere, particularly in Central America and the West Indies. U.S.

involvement in the domestic revolutions of El Salvador and Nicaragua continued into Reagan's second term, when Congress held televised hearings on what came to be known as the Iran-Contra Affair. A cover-up was exposed, showing that profits from secretly selling military hardware to Iran had been used to give support to rebels, called Contras, who were fighting in Nicaragua.

In 1983 in Lebanon, 241 American Marines were killed when an Islamic suicide bomber drove an explosives-laden truck into U.S. Marine headquarters located at the airport in Beirut. This tragic event came as part of the unrest and violence between the Israelis and the Palestine Liberation Organization (PLO) forces in southern Lebanon. In October 1983, 1,900 U.S. Marines landed on the island of Grenada to rescue a small group of U.S. medical students at the medical school and depose the leftist government.

When the Cold War ended and the Soviet Union broke apart, President George H. W. Bush supported the rise of democracy but took a position of restraint toward the new nations. Bush ordered the invasion of Panama, codenamed Operation Just Cause, to remove drug-lord General Manuel Noriega from power. Following Iraq's August 2, 1990, invasion of Kuwait, President Bush also ordered U.S. troops to Saudi Arabia to protect its vast oil fields. This military action became known as Operation Desert Shield. After Iraqi President Saddam Hussein refused to withdraw his military forces from Kuwait, President Bush, under UN authority, launched Operation Desert Storm—the largest military campaign since the Vietnam War. Thus, on January 16, 1991, the first Gulf War began, and it ended with a relative quick allied victory on February 29, 1991. Although President Bush's international affairs record was strong, and despite an overwhelming military victory in the Middle East, he was not able to turn around increased violence in America's inner cities and a struggling economy.

After the fall of the Soviet Union, the United States stood as the world's sole superpower. The nation increasingly relied on international intervention to support foreign-policy aims and to maintain global stability. During the 1990s and 2000s, the nation engaged in conflict abroad in the former Yugoslavia, the Middle East, Afghanistan, and North Africa. This came as global economic interdependence grew through the exchange of resources, and the reliance on foreign borrowing to finance the federal government contributed to the need to balance economic stability with political pressures.

See also Skills 1.10a, 1.11b

DOMAIN II.   WORLD HISTORY

COMPETENCY 2.1   PREHISTORY TO 1400 CE

Skill 2.1.a   Demonstrate knowledge of human society before approximately 3000 BCE

"Prehistory" is defined as the period of human achievements before the development of writing. The Stone Age cultures had three different periods. The **Lower Paleolithic Period** is characterized by the use of crude tools. During the **Upper Paleolithic Period**, there was a greater variety of better-made tools and implements, and the wearing of clothing, highly organized group life, and skills in art became more evident. The **Neolithic Period** featured domesticated animals; food production; the arts of knitting, spinning, and weaving cloth; fires started through friction; house building rather than living in caves; the development of institutions including the family, religion; and a form of government or the origin of the state.

Hunting and gathering societies are the earliest and most primitive form of human social groups, dating back to the **Paleolithic Age**. These groups were small bands composed of closely related individuals who established temporary camps as they roamed the land. They subsisted on gathering naturally occurring edibles and hunting for larger game; they used simple tools and instruments. Their only possessions consisted of what they could carry with them from place to place. Generally, the women, the children, and the elderly remained in their temporary camps, tending to camp chores and foraging for edible plants, insects, eggs, small mammals, and birds. The men and older adolescent males organized themselves into hunting parties that cooperatively stalked or trapped larger game. There is evidence that dogs were tamed for use in hunting. Typically, people consumed freshly killed game immediately and preserved the remainder by smoking and drying so it could be carried easily. Some hunting and gathering societies fished if they were close to a sea or a large body of water. When competing bands encountered each other, hostility resulted unless kinship ties existed to inhibit it. These groups were competing for limited resources in a given area, and one band's usual territory may not have been able to support a competing band.

The Neolithic Age marked several major changes in how people lived. Herd animals such as goats and sheep were domesticated along with pigs. Therefore, it was no longer necessary to hunt animals for meat and hides. Just as significant was the domestication of cereal crops—wheat and barley in Mesopotamia and rice in Asia. Also, pottery made its appearance during this period. With food now available from a single location, people no longer had to move around to hunt game and forage for their sustenance, and they started to live in permanent settlements. They also had a more clearly delineated division of labor, with people specializing in occupations that were not necessarily directly tied to the acquisition of food. Rudimentary metallurgy, in the form of copper smelting, was beginning to lead the societies who had it away from the Stone Age entirely.

Skill 2.1b   Understand the development of city civilizations 3000–1500 BCE

Mesopotamia, part of the "Fertile Crescent," extended from the Persian Gulf at the estuary of the Tigris and Euphrates rivers. Following the rivers in a northwesterly direction is the "Cradle of Western Civilization."

Sumer
The **Sumerians** had established walled city-states, notably at Lagash, Uruk, and Ur. The Sumerians developed a writing system that used ideographs and phonetic symbols called cuneiform. Much of what is known about Sumer comes from the tens of thousands of clay tablets that the Sumerian scribes left. Most of the information concerned commercial, economic, and administrative activities. However, thousands of tablets containing literary texts were also uncovered, implying that the Sumerians engaged in extensive trade and centralized urban planning. They also created an irrigation system of canals and dikes to take advantage of the water from the Tigris and Euphrates rivers in order to cultivate large areas of arid desert and to control the unpredictable and devastating flooding of the rivers.

In Sumerian cities, the lives of the inhabitants were highly diversified; the division of labor that first appeared in Neolithic settlements became even more specialized and, in some cases, codified and imposed on the populace by the ruling and religious elite. The ancient civilization of the Sumerians invented the wheel; developed irrigation through use of canals, dikes, and devices for raising water; devised the system of cuneiform writing; learned to divide time; and built large boats for trade.

Babylon and Assyria
The Sumerians were conquered by Akkadian-speaking Babylonian invaders under the leadership of Sargon the Great. The Babylonians were awed by the cultural sophistication of the Sumerians and retained Sumerian as the language of government and religion. Hammurabi, another notable Babylonian king, had his code of law set in stone pillars and erected throughout the territory of the empire. The Babylonians, in turn, were conquered by the Assyrians, who also adopted the Sumerian language and culture for their court and religious rituals.

The ancient **Assyrians** were warlike and aggressive empire builders, who possessed a highly organized and disciplined army that featured units of horse-drawn chariots and cavalry, elaborate siege engines, and other specialized troops to augment well-armed foot soldiers who attacked in massed formations.

Egypt

The Nile River gave rise to another ancient valley civilization, the Egyptians. The annual summer floods of the Nile supported a rich agricultural society that enjoyed surpluses that could be stored for leaner times. Two rival kingdoms emerged on the banks of the Nile. Lower Egypt was the Nile Delta in the north where the river joins the Mediterranean Sea, and Upper Egypt occupied the land south of the delta, along the banks of the Nile River approximately 800 miles to the First Cataract. Although both kingdoms were sporadically united into one during the Old Kingdom period (3000–2200 BCE), they represented two distinct cultural and political entities during that time. The Egyptians were well known for their monumental stone structures and statuary and for a highly centralized bureaucracy. The kings, known as pharaohs, were considered gods and were worshipped by their subjects.

After more than a century of intervening disorder, the Middle Kingdom period (2100–1800 BCE) saw a united kingdom, which established its capital at Thebes in the south and later moved north to Memphis for better central control. The Middle Kingdom period ended in 1800 BCE with the invasion of the Hyksos, who introduced the chariot and the bow to Egypt. Eventually, the Egyptians drove out the conquerors in 1550 BCE, and the New Kingdom period was ushered in.

Minos

The **Minoans** had a system of writing that used symbols to represent syllables in words. They built multilevel palaces containing many rooms with bright paintings on the walls; they had hot and cold running water, bathtubs, flush toilets, and sewage systems.

India

In the **Indian subcontinent**, the Indus River Valley was first settled by a Dravidian civilization that built elaborate cities at Mohenjo Daro and Harappa (modern place names) that were centrally planned, with streets and structures arranged in uniform grids, sophisticated water and sewage systems, and numerous public buildings and facilities. Archaeological evidence shows that the Indus River cities met a sudden and violent end. Most human skeletal remains that have been found show evidence of sword cuts and severe trauma. The invaders, known as Aryans, swept into the Indian subcontinent from the Central Asian steppes to the northwest via what are now Iran and Afghanistan.

China

China is considered by some historians to be the oldest uninterrupted civilization in the world. It was in existence around the same time as the ancient civilizations founded in Egypt, Mesopotamia, and the Indus Valley. Early Chinese civilization originally developed in the Huang He (Yellow River) Valley. It is shrouded in mystery, since accounts of the first era of Sage Emperors (Di) indicate unnaturally long reigns (in excess of 500 years for one emperor).

The Chinese are credited with the invention of writing, irrigation, flood control, pottery, spinning and weaving silk, jade working, divination by scapulomancy (reading portents from patterns produced by heating livestock shoulder bones and turtle plastrons), and domestication of pigs, dogs, oxen, sheep, fowl, and goats. The Chinese studied nature, astronomy, and weather; stressed the importance of family and a strong monarch who also acted on behalf of the populace as a medium to the sky spirit; and worshipped spirits that controlled natural and man-made phenomena, including their ancestors.

The Xia Dynasty followed, but its existence has not been proven with physical evidence. It exists only in legends and in the Confucian classics "Classic of Records (History)" and some of the poems contained in the "Classic of Odes (Songs)." It is considered the first Chinese dynasty because it established the pattern of rule being passed from father to eldest son.

The Xia Dynasty was overthrown by the Shang Dynasty, which was also considered legendary and existing only in literature, until the early twentieth century, when archeological evidence was unearthed where the ancient records said it would be. This dynasty set the precedent that dynasties rule because they earned that right by the **Mandate of Heaven** and proved that the ruling family was worthy. The notable features of Shang culture are a fully developed writing system (Shang Dynasty writing can still be read by modern readers of Chinese), highly sophisticated and intricate bronze casting and engraving, polished jade pieces of a luster indicating use of microabrasives (unmatched until the late twentieth century), and a formal system of social hierarchy.

Japan
Civilization in **Japan** appeared during this time, having borrowed much of its culture from China and Korea. Japan was the last of these classical civilizations to develop. The native religion was a form of nature worship, Shintoism, which worshipped Ame ("the sky above") as its principal deity. The Japanese foundation mythology recounts that the first emperor was a child of the sun goddess and that all Japanese emperors descended from him. Japan's imperial family has the longest line of continuous rule by the same family of any monarchy still in existence today.

Skill 2.1c   Demonstrate knowledge of ancient empires and civilizations 1700 BCE – 500 CE

Africa
Egypt made numerous significant contributions, including construction of the great pyramids, development of hieroglyphic writing, preservation of bodies after death, making paper from papyrus, contributing to developments in arithmetic and geometry, the invention of the method of counting in groups of one to ten (the decimal system), completion of a solar calendar, and laying the foundation for science and astronomy.

The earliest historical record of **Kush** is in Egyptian sources. They describe a region upstream from the first cataract of the Nile as "wretched." This civilization was characterized by a settled way of life in fortified mud-brick villages. They subsisted on hunting and fishing, herding cattle, and gathering grain. Skeletal remains suggest that the people were a blend of Negroid and Mediterranean peoples. This civilization appears to be the second oldest in Africa (after Egyptian).

Either the people were originally Egyptian or they were heavily influenced by Egyptians at a very early period in the development of the society. They appear to have spoken Nilo-Saharan languages. The area in which they lived is called Nubia. The capital city was Kerma, a major trading center between the northern and southern parts of Africa. For the most part, the Kushites apparently considered themselves Egyptian and inheritors of the pharaonic tradition. Their society was organized on the Egyptian model, adopting Egyptian royal titles, etc. Even their art and architecture were based on Egyptian models. But their pyramids were smaller and steeper.

During the period of Egypt's Old Kingdom (ca. 2700-2180 BCE), Kush was essentially a diffused version of Egyptian culture and religion. When Egypt came under the domination of the Hyksos, Kush reached its greatest power and cultural energy (1700-1500 BCE). When the Hyksos were eventually expelled from Egypt, the New Kingdom brought Kush back under Egyptian colonial control. The collapse of the New Kingdom in Egypt (ca. 1000 BCE) provided the second opportunity for Kush to develop independently of Egyptian control and to conquer the entire Nubian region. The capital was then moved to Napata.

In what has been called "a magnificent irony of history," the Kushites conquered Egypt in the eighth century BCE, creating the 25th dynasty. The dynasty ended in the seventh century BCE when the Assyrians defeated Egypt. The Kushites were gradually pushed farther south by the Assyrians and later by the Persians. As a result, contact with Egypt, the Middle East, and Europe was essentially cut off. They moved their capital to Meroe in about 591 BCE, when Napata was conquered. Their attention then turned to sub-Saharan Africa. Free of Egyptian dominance, they developed innovations in government and other areas.

In government, the king ruled through a law of custom that was interpreted by priests. The king was elected from the royal family. Descent was determined through the mother's line (as in Egypt), but in an unparalleled innovation the Kushites were ruled by a series of female monarchs. The Kushite religion was polytheistic, including all of the primary Egyptian gods. There were, however, regional gods that were the principal gods in their regions. There was also a lion warrior god derived from other African cultures.

The Kushite civilization was vital through the last half of the first millennium BCE, but it suffered about 300 years of gradual decline until the Nuba people eventually conquered it.

The civilizations in **Africa** south of the Sahara were developing the refining and use of iron, especially for farm implements and, later, for weapons. Trading was conducted overland using camels and at important seaports. Arab influence was extremely important, as was later contact with Indians, Christian Nubians, and Persians. In fact, trading activities were probably the most important factor in the spread of and assimilation of different ideas and stimulation of cultural growth in these civilizations.

Middle East

The **Hebrews**, also known as the ancient Israelites, instituted monotheism, the worship of one god, Yahweh. They compiled a collection of sacred writings containing worship texts, historical accounts, prophecy, instructive writings, and law, including the Ten Commandments. This compilation comprises the Old Testament of the Christian Bible.

The **Mycenaeans** changed the Minoan writing system to aid their own language and used symbols to represent syllables.

The **Phoenicians** were sea traders well known for their manufacturing skills in glass and metals and the development of their famous purple dye. They became so proficient in the skill of navigation that they were able to sail by the stars at night. Further, they devised an alphabet using symbols to represent single sounds, which was an improved extension of the Egyptian principle and writing system.

The ancient **Persians** developed an alphabet; contributed the religions/philosophies of **Zoroastrianism**, **Mithraism**, and **Gnosticism**; and allowed conquered peoples to retain their own customs, laws, and religions.

India

In **India**, the Aryan invaders from the northwest introduced the caste system, which restricted what a person could or could not do as a profession. The principle of "zero" in mathematics was invented. **Vedic Hinduism,** as practiced by the Aryans, evolved into its now recognizable form, as Dravidian states south of the Indus River were conquered, and local deities and heroes (such as Krishna, Naga, and Hanuman) were incorporated into the Hindu belief system of multiple aspects of a single godhead. Industry and commerce developed, along with extensive trading with the Near East. Outstanding advances in the fields of science and medicine were made, along with being one of the first civilizations to be active in navigation and maritime enterprises during this time.

During his conquests, Alexander the Great reached as far east as India. One strongman who met the great Alexander was **Chandragupta Maurya**, who later founded one of India's most successful dynasties. Chandragupta conquered most of what we now call India. His grandson, **Asoka**, was a more peaceful ruler, but powerful nonetheless. Asoka was also a great believer in the practices and power of Buddhism, sending missionaries throughout Asia to preach the ways of the Buddha.

Buddhism is an offshoot of Brahmanical Hindu thought, which arose during the fifth century BCE. However, unlike traditional Hinduism, Buddhism was founded by Gautama Siddartha Shakyamuni, a crown prince who, after observing suffering in the form of illness, old age, and death, and much to the dismay of his father, the maharajah, renounced the material world to seek enlightenment. Following years of practicing asceticism and austerities, the prince achieved enlightenment after meditating under a tree for 49 days. He was called the "Buddha" (a Sanskrit word meaning "Awakened One") after his enlightenment. He told his followers that life was suffering, suffering was caused by desire, desire was caused by delusion of the mind, which leads to death and rebirth, which leads to another cycle of suffering. To avoid suffering, one must get rid of the delusions that cause desire and break the cycle of life, death, and rebirth called "samsara," a concept from Hindu theology. Other concepts adapted from Hindu theology are "karma," the balancing of present action by later effect, which will trigger samsara, and "dharma," which can mean "fate," "destiny," or "unbreakable rules that govern all phenomena," depending on its context. Escape from the cycles of samsara was called "nirvana," or "extinguishment." Buddhism later split off into two main schools: Theravada ("Older Way"), or Southern, Buddhism and Mahayana ("Great Vehicle").

China
China continued to thrive. The Chinese began building the Great Wall to prevent outsiders from invading. They increased proficiency in rice cultivation through the practice of irrigation, flood control, crop rotation and terrace farming. They also increased the importance of the silk industry; and developed caravan routes across central Asia for extensive trade.

During the waning years of the Shang Dynasty, the "Yi Jing" (Classic of Change), the divination manual based on 64 hexagrams was first compiled; it is still consulted today. Continuing the dynastic cycle, the Shang Dynasty was overthrown by the Zhou Dynasty, which in turn earned the Mandate of Heaven to rule.

The early Zhou Dynasty was, several centuries later, considered by Confucius to be the "Golden Age" of rule by enlightened men of ability and moral rectitude.During fifth century BCE, the Zhou Dynasty began to disintegrate, eventually falling.

China split up into several independent kingdoms that were in a near constant state of war, with each kingdom vying for supremacy over the others in a myriad combination of alliances, which often changed. It was in this period, known as the Warring States period, one of chaos and disarray that two of the best known figures of the period, Confucius (Kong Zi) and Lao Tzu appeared (there are questions regarding whether Lao Tzu was even a real person). Confucius edited the Confucian Classics, and a collection of his teachings, the Analects, was compiled. Daoism emerged as the teachings of Lao Tzu were written down and espoused by Daoist scholars.

Eventually, after nearly 200 years of fighting, the Qin Dynasty, under Qin Shi Huang Di ("Exalted First Emperor"), gained the advantage and conquered the other kingdoms to unite China into a single empire. The Qin emperor commissioned his ministers to standardize weights and measures, and the number of Chinese characters was reduced to 3,000 from tens of thousands, by eliminating redundant and superfluous characters. The Qin dynasty was known for its harsh authoritarian rule, with an emphasis on severe punishment for even minor infractions. Within twenty years, there was a successful revolt that overthrew the Qin in 206 BCE and replaced it with the Han Dynasty.

The **Han Dynasty** lasted four centuries, longer than any other dynasty in China's history. Paper and the writing brush, in its present form, were invented during this period, and Chinese characters took the form that is familiar to today's readers. Under the Han Emperor Wu Di ("Martial Emperor"), who reigned from 141 to 87 BCE), China expanded its boundaries to their greatest extent through military conquest, including an embarkation on a campaign to rid the northern borders of the Huns. This set off a chain of events that sent westward migrations of Huns and other nomadic pastoralists into Europe.

In the aftermath of the fall of the Qin, **Confucianism** became the official political philosophy of the Han. Scholarship and the criteria for appointment to the imperial bureaucracy were based on the Five Classics: Odes, History, Rites (Etiquette), Change (Yi Jing), and the Spring and Autumn Annals (a history of a portion of the Zhou Dynasty edited by Confucius).

Additionally, scholars were expected to have a thorough knowledge of the Analects of Confucius (a collection of his teachings) and of the teachings of Mencius (Meng Zi), a Confucian scholar who expanded on the themes espoused by Confucius and his most esteemed students. The accomplishments of the Han Dynasty were so unprecedented and profound that later Chinese refer to themselves as "People of the Han" and Chinese characters have been called "Han Words" (the literal translation of the two characters that make up the word for "Chinese characters").

Daoism was one of many schools of thought that sprang up in ancient China, and, like **Confucianism**, it has endured to modern times. Its main tenet is that all phenomena are governed by natural forces that cannot be comprehended by ordinary people's minds and that resisting these forces or trying to make them act in a contrary manner leads only to frustration and just makes things worse than they already are. The two major literary works that influenced Daoism the most were the *Dao De Jing* (Discourse on the Way and Virtue) and Zhuang Zi's eponymous work the *Zhuang Zi*. Lao Zi and Zhuang Zi said that, in order to understand how these cosmic forces work, one should not seek anything since the only way to truly know something is to not think about it and to let the Way of nature run its course without interference.

Greece

The classical civilization of **Greece** reached the highest levels in man's achievements based on the foundations already laid by such ancient groups as the Egyptians, the Phoenicians, the Minoans, and the Mycenaeans.

Among the more important contributions of Greece were the Greek alphabet derived from the Phoenician letters that formed the basis for the Roman alphabet and our present-day alphabet. Extensive trading and colonization resulted in the spread of Greek civilization. The love of sports, with an emphasis on a sound body, led to the tradition of the Olympic Games. Greece was responsible for the rise of independent, strong city-states. Note the complete contrast between independent, freedom-loving Athens with its practice of pure democracy, i.e., direct, personal, active participation in government by qualified citizens, and the rigid, totalitarian, militaristic Sparta.

Other important areas that the Greeks are credited with influencing include drama, epic and lyric poetry, fables, myths centered on the many gods and goddesses, science, astronomy, medicine, mathematics, philosophy, art, architecture, and the recording of historical events. The Macedonian ruler Alexander the Great spread Hellenistic ideas to the areas he conquered and brought to the Greek world many ideas from Asia.

Rome

The ancient civilization of **Rome** lasted approximately 1,000 years in the West, including the periods of the republic and the empire, although its influence on Europe and its history lasted much longer. A very sharp contrast existed between the curious, imaginative, inquisitive Greeks and the practical, simple, down-to-earth, no-nonsense Romans, who preserved and spread the ideas of ancient Greece and other culture groups.

The contributions and accomplishments of the Romans are numerous, but their greatest included language, engineering, building, law, government, roads, trade, and the **Pax Romana,** the long period of peace that enabled free travel and trade and the spread of people, cultures, goods, and ideas all over a vast area of the known world. An important lasting influence on the modern world was Rome's development of a republican system of government that has shaped federal systems such as those of the modern United States and France.

Skill 2.1d   Understand the decline of classical civilizations and changes 500–1400 CE

Byzantine Empire

The **western Roman Empire** fell as Germanic tribes migrated to and controlled most of central and western Europe. The five major tribes were the Visigoths, the Ostrogoths, the Vandals, the Saxons, and the Franks. Internal weaknesses resulting from problems such as extended periods of political instability and overexpansion contributed greatly to the ultimate fall of Rome in 476 CE.

Bordering Europe to the east was the Byzantine Empire, which was the eastern portion of the Roman Empire after it was split in two by Emperor Diocletian. Diocletian's successor, Emperor Constantine, changed the name of the capital, Byzantium, to Constantinople, after himself. When western Rome fell in 476 CE, the Byzantine emperors, starting with Justinian, attempted to regain the lost western territories. The **Byzantines** made important contributions in art and the preservation of Greek and Roman achievements including architecture (especially in eastern Europe and Russia), the Code of Justinian, and Roman law.

Because of ineffective rulers between the seventh and ninth centuries CE, any gains were completely lost, and territorial limits reverted back to the eastern Balkans of Ancient Greece and Asia Minor. The late ninth through eleventh centuries were considered the Golden Age of Byzantium.

Although Constantine had made Christianity the official state religion of Rome, the conflict between Christian and Classical (Greek and Roman) ideals for the Byzantines was left an unresolved. There were points of contention between the Pope in Rome and the Patriarch of Constantinople, including the celibacy of priests, the language of the liturgy (Latin in the west, Greek in the east), religious doctrine, and other unreconciled issues that led to the Great Schism, which permanently split the church into the Roman Catholic and the Eastern Orthodox churches.

In secular matters, Emperor Justinian codified Roman law, summarizing a millennium of Roman legal developments into the Justinian Code. This codification laid the basis for modern western legal systems, which are still studied and used in European and American legal circles. The Byzantines combined Greco-Roman styles of architecture with those of Asia Minor to create monumental domed structures such as the Hagia Sophia church, elaborate mosaics, and a distinctive style of painting.

In western Europe, the Franks, under the leadership of Charles Martel, successfully stopped the invasion of southern Europe by the Muslims by defeating them at the Battle of Tours in 732 CE. Thirty-six years later, in 768 CE, the grandson of Charles Martel became the king of the Franks known throughout history as Charlemagne. Charlemagne was a man of war but was unique in his respect for and encouragement of learning. He made great efforts to rule fairly and to ensure just treatment for his people.

Vikings

The **Vikings** were Scandinavian seafarers who quickly gained a reputation for ruthlessness and surprise as they raided any settlement or monastery that they could reach on their swift and seaworthy longboats. The Vikings had a lot of influence at this time, spreading their ideas and knowledge of trade routes and sailing, first through their conquests and later through trade. The two main groups of Vikings were the West Vikings, from Norway and Denmark, and the East Vikings, from Sweden.

The West Vikings raided and traded with coastal areas of Britain and Ireland, Europe's Atlantic coast and as far as Sicily in the Mediterranean Sea, establishing trading outposts and permanent settlements and, in some cases, setting themselves up as rulers. They also ventured beyond the North Sea to settle in Iceland, Greenland, and North America, although Iceland was the only North Atlantic settlement that was a lasting success. The East Vikings voyaged east and south, through the Baltic nations and via the rivers of Eastern Europe to Kiev in what is now Ukraine, where they ruled as royalty and were called the "Rus." They voyaged farther south to Constantinople, where they also served as mercenaries and functionaries to the Byzantine Roman Emperor.

Middle Ages

During this time, the system of **feudalism** became the dominant feature of domestic life in western Europe. It was a system of loyalty and protection. The strong protected the weak, who returned farm labor, military service, and loyalty. Life was lived out on a vast estate called a "manor," owned by a nobleman and his family, The manor was a complete village supporting a few hundred people, mostly peasants. Improved tools and farming methods made life more bearable although most never left the manor or traveled from their village during their lifetime.

The purpose of the **Crusades** was to rid Jerusalem of Muslim control and replace it with Christian rule. This series of violent, bloody conflicts did affect trade and stimulated later explorations seeking the new, exotic products such as silks and spices. The Crusaders came into contact with other religions and cultures and learned and spread many new ideas.

Also coming into importance at this time was the era of knighthood and its code of chivalry and the tremendous influence of the Roman Catholic Church. Until the Renaissance, the Church was the only place where people could be educated. The Bible and other books were hand copied by monks in the monasteries. Cathedrals were built and were decorated with art depicting religious subjects.

With the increase in trade and travel, cities sprang up and began to grow. Craft workers in the cities developed their skills to a high degree, eventually organizing guilds to protect the quality of the work and to regulate the buying and selling of their products. City government developed and flourished, centered on strong town councils. Active in city government and the town councils were the wealthy businessmen who made up the rising middle class.

The feudal manorial system ended with the outbreak and spread of the infamous **Black Death**. This plague killed more than one-third of the total population of Europe. Those who survived and were skilled in any job or occupation were in demand. Many serfs, or peasants, found freedom and, for that time, a decidedly improved standard of living. Strong nation-states became powerful, and people developed a renewed interest in life and learning.

The Huns

In Asia, the **Huns** were a horse-riding pastoral people who originated in Asia, north of the Great Wall of China, and had finally been displaced by the Chinese emperors after centuries of border skirmishes and all-out military campaigns to drive them from the lands bordering China. They were led as far west as the eastern edges of the Roman Empire by Attila, their leader, attacking swiftly on horseback, spreading terror and havoc among their victims. After Attila suddenly and unexpectedly died after a night of celebrating his marriage to another wife, the Huns stopped their advance on Europe and either returned to Central Asia or became assimilated into the local populations where they settled.

China

After the fall of the Han Dynasty, China was once again split into different kingdoms and entered a long period of war and chaos with ever-shifting alliances and counter-alliances and a brief period of unity. At one point, China was divided into seventeen separate kingdoms. The **Sui** (pronounced "Sway") Dynasty, although lasting less than twenty years, heralded the beginning of a long period of national and cultural unity starting in 589 CE, giving way to the Tang Dynasty in 618 CE.

The **Tang Dynasty** consolidated imperial authority and is considered by many historians to be the renaissance and flowering of Chinese culture, helped by the fact that long-term stability had returned to China. The population grew to its historic high during this period, and the arts, particularly poetry, found their most creative and aesthetically pleasing levels. The Sui and the Tang introduced wide-scale government examinations for recruiting new talent into the imperial bureaucracy from the highest court ministers all the way to local county and township officials. Also, Buddhism, which had been introduced earlier, became the official state religion under the Tang, and the emperors lavishly endowed monasteries and temples. Printing was invented during the ninth century (several centuries before Gutenberg), spurred by the need to produce and distribute Buddhist literature on a wide scale.

The **Song Dynasty** was a transitional period, lasting from the late classic era to early modern times. Buddhism was rejected, and a return to Confucianism, called Neo-Confucianism, emerged. Also, the aristocratic society, which had held sway until the Tang Dynasty, virtually disappeared as a political force, ceding its authority to the landowning class and the blossoming meritocracy that came up through the government examination system, with its emphasis on Confucian learning. Although mercantile activities had been traditionally shunned by the traditional elite of China, a commercial revolution and a great expansion of the economy coincided with an unprecedented rise in population and a similar growth in agricultural production.

By the twelfth century, the Chinese were using the magnetic compass, and they made great advances in shipbuilding, which allowed them to trade with people as far away as India and the Persian Gulf. The invention of gunpowder was also a significant development in military technology, but the use of gunpowder in pyrotechnic displays became more important as a form of celebration and entertainment. One drawback to the Song Dynasty's developments in commercial and artistic pursuits was the weakening of its military power, resulting in greater vulnerability along the northern frontier.

The **Mongols** were but one of many "barbarian" pastoral peoples who rode horses, used Bactrian camels for transport of cargo, and herded flocks of sheep and goats. They were a collection of loosely affiliated tribes and clans that competed with each other for pasturage, horses, and livestock. They were united by Chinggis (also spelled "Genghis") Khan in the thirteenth century CE. As the Mongols under Chinggis conquered other neighboring territories, they gained a reputation as formidable horsemen; their cavalry attacked in swift, disciplined formations that took advantage of maneuver, surprise, and skillful and deadly use of archery, overwhelming their foes.

The Mongol Empire was highly adaptable, incorporating absorbed people's expertise. Chinggis's leading commander, Subotai, was Tuvan, a member of a distinct central Asian ethnic group with its own language. Eventually, during Chinggis's lifetime, the empire encompassed nearly all of north-central Asia and the northwest of China. After Chinggis's death, his son Ogatei assumed the title "Great Khan." Ogatei was followed by Mongke, one of Chinngis's grandsons.

To the west and south, under the rule of Chinggis's grandsons, the Mongols conquered what is now Russia, south Asia, and southwest Asia, which includes what is now Iraq, Turkey, Iran, and Afghanistan, where they acquired a ferocious reputation for wanton destruction and aggression. The most well known of Chinngis's grandsons was Khubilai, who founded the Yuan Dynasty in China and assumed the title of Emperor. When Marco Polo was a guest of the Mongol court, he wrote about Khubilai. Khubilai adopted Chinese dress and customs, left government bureaucracy and institutions fairly intact, expanded the empire into Korea, and made incursions into what is now Vietnam. His attempt to invade Japan was thwarted by a typhoon (called the "Kamikaze" in Japanese or "Divine Wind") which demolished the Mongol fleet. After the passing of Chinggis's grandsons, the Mongol Empire quickly lost control over its far-flung domain and was forced to cede political and military power. The Yuan Dynasty in China fell in 1368 CE, succeeded by an ethnically Han-Chinese dynasty.

The **Ming Dynasty** lasted from 1368 to 1644 CE and marked one of the longest eras of order and stability in government and society in world history. It was also a period of great artistic and creative achievements. However, the stability of Chinese government and society was such that it stayed relatively unaltered until the early twentieth century CE, when Imperial China ended with the 1911 Chinese Revolution. As with the Dynastic Cycle, which started with the end of the legendary Xia Dynasty, the Ming came to power as the result of a rebellion that overthrew the Mongols and expelled them from China proper. The Ming revived the purely Chinese mode of rule over China that had existed during the Tang and Song Dynasties. Confucianism and its classics were put into the forefront as the basis of all knowledge that was important for an enlightened official to possess. Ming scholarship in Confucian studies flourished and produced a myriad of texts on all subjects from commentaries on materialist philosophy to scientific texts to creative prose and poetic literature.

Although Chinese elites were traditionally anticommercial in their worldview, the Chinese economy and commercial infrastructure expanded dynamically during the Ming Dynasty, including the migration of Chinese merchants to overseas markets. The Ming Dynasty, like all the previous ones, eventually suffered from the same internal decay and official corruption that led to rebellion and the weakening of central authority that made it susceptible to external takeover.

India
In India, succeeding the Mauryas were the Guptas, who ruled India for a longer period of time and brought prosperity and international recognition to their people.

The Guptas were great believers in science and mathematics, especially how they could be used in the production of goods. They invented the decimal system and the concept of zero, two things that put them ahead of the rest of the world on the mathematics timeline. They were the first to make cotton fabrics, for example, calico, and their medical practices were much more advanced than those in Europe and elsewhere in Asia at the time. These inventions and innovations created high demand for Indian goods throughout Asia and Europe.

The idea of a united India continued after the Gupta Dynasty ended. It was especially favorable to the invading Muslims, who took over in the eleventh century, ruling the country for hundreds of years through a series of sultanates. The most famous Muslim leader of India was Tamerlane, who founded the Mogul Dynasty and began a series of conquests that expanded the borders of India. Tamerlane's grandson **Akbar** is considered the greatest Mogul. He believed in freedom of religion and is perhaps most well known for the series of buildings that he commissioned, including mosques, palaces, forts, and tombs, some of which are still standing today. During the years of Muslim rule, Hinduism continued to be respected, although it was a minority religion; Buddhism, however, died out almost entirely from the country that begot its founder.

The imposing mountains to the north of India served as a deterrent to Chinese expansion. India was more vulnerable to invaders who came from the west or by sea from the south. The Indian people were also vulnerable to the powerful monsoons, which came driving up from the south a few times every year, bringing howling winds and devastation in their wake.

Muslim conquest
Islamic (or Saracenic) civilization grew out of religious fervor shortly after the founding of Islam (Arabic for "Surrender to God") by Muhammad in the seventh century CE. Islam is a monotheistic faith that traces its traditions to the Hebrew patriarch Abraham and considers the Jewish patriarchs and prophets (especially Moses and King Solomon) and the Christian prophet Jesus Christ as earlier "Prophets of God" and venerates them accordingly. The Arabic word "Allah" and its root "'Lh" means "the Almighty" or "God" and is not a name, as "Zeus" is. Muhammad preached jihad ("holy war") in two forms: Lesser Jihad was the call to arms to spread Islam by military force, and Greater Jihad, the more important of the two, was the inner battle that an individual undertakes for the salvation of the soul and surrender to the will of God. The Quran was dictated to Muhammad as the Word of God, composed in verse in sections called "sura," each of which begins with the invocation, "In the Name of God, the Compassionate, the Merciful."

The Islamic armies spread their faith by conquering the Arabian Peninsula, conquering Mesopotamia, Egypt, Syria, and Persia by 650 CE and expanding to North Africa and most of the Iberian Peninsula by 750 CE. During this period of expansion, the Muslim conquerors established great centers of learning, universities, at Baghdad in Mesopotamia, Damascus in Syria, Alexandria in Egypt, and Cordoba in Spain. They preserved the classical knowledge of the Greeks and Romans while Europe was in the depths of the Dark Ages after the fall of the western Roman Empire. Muslim scholars are credited with great progress in the areas of science and philosophy and were responsible for accomplishments in astronomy, mathematics, physics, chemistry, medicine, literature, art, trade and manufacturing, agriculture, and a marked influence on later European scholarship and intellectual development.

Africa

In western Africa, great trading civilizations known as **Ghana, Mali,** and **Songhai** arose. These empires relied on the salt trade to develop great riches and power. Mali was a major producer of iron, tin, and leather. **Mansa Musa** was one famous West African ruler. His pilgrimage to Mecca became famous and spread knowledge about his empire's weath throughout North Africa. Timbuktu became a major center of trade and learning during this time.

Western Hemisphere

The people who lived in the Americas before Columbus arrived had a thriving, connected society. **Native Americans** in North America had a spiritual and personal relationship with the various spirits of nature and a keen appreciation of the ways of woodworking and metalworking. Various tribes dotted the landscape of what is now the United States. They struggled against one another for control of resources such as food and water but had no concept of ownership of land, since they believed that they were living on the land with the permission of the spirits. The native North Americans mastered the art of growing many crops and were willing to share that knowledge with the various Europeans who eventually showed up. Artwork made of hides, beads, and jewels was popular at this time.

The most well known empires of South America were the **Aztec,** the **Inca,** and the **Maya**. Each of these empires had a central capital city, the home of the emperor, who controlled all aspects of the lives of his subjects. The empires traded with other peoples; and if the relations soured, the results were usually absorption of the trading partners into the empire. These empires, especially that of the Aztecs, had access to large quantities of metals and jewels, and they created weapons and artwork that continue to impress historians today.

The Aztecs dominated Mexico and Central America. They conquered neighboring tribes and demanded tribute from them; this tribute was the source of so much of the Aztec riches. They also believed in a handful of gods and that these gods demanded human sacrifice in order to continue to smile on the people. The center of Aztec society was the great city of Tenochtitlan, which was built on an island so as to be easier to defend. Tenochtitlan boasted a population of 300,000 at the time of the arrival of the conquistadors. The city was known for its canals and its pyramids, none of which survive today.

The Inca Empire stretched across a vast territory down the western coast of South America, its settlements connected by a series of roads. A series of messengers ran along these roads, carrying news and instructions from the capital, Cusco. The Incas, however, did not have the wheel. The Incas are known for inventing the *quipu*, a string-based device that provided them with a method of keeping records. The Inca Empire, like the Aztec Empire, was very much a centralized state, with all income going to the state coffers and all trade going through the emperor as well. The Incas worshipped the dead, their ancestors, and nature and often took part in religious rituals.

The most advanced Native American civilization was that of the Mayas, who lived primarily in Central America. They were the only Native American civilization to develop writing, which consisted of a series of symbols that has still not been completely deciphered. The Mayas also built huge pyramids and sculptured other stone figures, mostly of the gods they worshiped. The Mayas are most famous, however, for their calendars and for their mathematics. Mayan calendars were the most accurate on the planet until the sixteenth century. The Mayas also invented the idea of zero. Maya worship resembled the practices of the Aztecs and the Incas, although human sacrifices were rare. The Mayas traded heavily with their neighbors.

See also Skills 1.2a, 1.2b

COMPETENCY 2.2   WORLD HISTORY: 1400 TO 1914

Skill 2.2a   Understand emerging global-wide interactions 1400–1800 CE

The fifteenth century was the later period of feudal society, as the medieval society had all but collapsed. Most European economies remained based on subsistence agriculture. These were also the last days of the Holy Roman Empire, and the Hapsburg Empire was strong in Europe. The Byzantine Empire was also coming to an end in the 1400s. Russia at this time was ruled by the Golden Horde. In South America, the Inca and the Aztec empires were centralized states, with all income going to the state coffers and all trade going through the emperor as well.

Renaissance

The centralized states of Europe basically came into being as a result of actions by the feudal lords and the Church. As a result of so much fighting, the stronger of the surviving lords took on the functions of kings and other members of royalty, many due to the support of the Church. Loyalty shifted from the feudal lord to the king. As the cities grew, so did commerce; market economies became more developed and trade became more important. The growth of trade resulted in greater reliance on markets. The **Renaissance** was now taking place in Europe.

The word "renaissance" literally means "rebirth," and the period signaled the rekindling of interest in the glory of the ancient Greek and Roman civilizations. It was the period in human history marking the start of many ideas and innovations leading to our modern age. The Renaissance began in Italy, with many of its ideas starting in Florence, which was controlled by the famous Medici family. Education, especially for some of the merchants, required reading, writing, math, studying law, and the writings of classical Greek and Roman writers. The combination of a renewed fascination with the classical world and a new infusion of money into the hands of those so fascinated brought on the Renaissance.

In the areas of art, literature, music, and science, the Western world changed for the better. Artists such as Leonardo da Vinci and Michaelangelo contributed to a revolution in the style and subject matter of art. In literature, humanists such as Petrarch, Boccaccio, Erasmus, and Sir Thomas More advanced the idea of being interested in life on Earth and the opportunities it can bring, rather than being constantly focused on heaven and its rewards. The monumental literary works of Shakespeare, Dante, and Cervantes found their origins in these ideas, as well as the ones that drove the painters and sculptors. In the area of political philosophy, the writings of **Machiavelli** were considered influential. All of these works, of course, owe much to Gutenberg's development of the **printing press**, which occurred during the Renaissance. Movable type facilitated the rapid spread of Renaissance ideas and innovations, thus ensuring the enlightenment of most of Western Europe.

Science advanced considerably during the Renaissance, especially in the area of physics and astronomy. Copernicus, Kepler, and Galileo were among those thinkers who led a Scientific Revolution. The Scientific Revolution was, above all, a shift in focus from **belief to evidence**. Scientists and philosophers wanted to see the proof, instead of just believing what other people told them.

Copernicus argued that the sun, not Earth, was the center of a solar system and that the other planets revolve around the sun, not Earth. This idea flew in the face of established (Church-mandated) doctrine. Building on Danish astronomer Tycho Brahe's data, German scientist Johannes Kepler instituted his theory of planetary movement, embodied in his famous Laws of Planetary Movement, and confirmed Copernicus's observations and argument that Earth revolves around the sun. The most famous defender of this idea was **Galileo Galilei**, an Italian scientist who conducted many famous experiments in the pursuit of science. He is most well known for his defense of the heliocentric (sun-centered) idea. He wrote a book comparing the two theories, but most readers could tell easily that he favored the new one.

Picking up the baton was an English scientist named **Isaac Newton**, who became perhaps the most famous scientist of all. He is known as the discoverer of gravity and a pioneering voice in the study of optics (light), calculus, and physics. More than any other scientist, Newton argued for (and proved) the idea of a mechanistic view of the world: you can see how the world works and prove how the world works through observation; if you can see these things with your own eyes, they must be so.

Changes also swept the Church during this era. The **Reformation** period consisted of two phases: the **Protestant Revolution** and the **Catholic Reformation**. The Protestant Revolution came about for religious, political, and economic reasons. The religious reasons stemmed from abuses in the Catholic Church, including fraudulent clergy with their scandalously immoral lifestyles; the sale of religious offices, indulgences, and dispensations; different theologies within the Church; and frauds involving sacred relics. The political reasons for the Protestant Revolution involved the increase in the power of rulers who were considered absolute monarchs, who desired all power and control, especially over the Church. The growth of nationalism, or patriotic pride in one's own country, was another contributing factor. Economic reasons included the greed of ruling monarchs to possess and control all the lands and wealth of the Church, the deep animosity against the burdensome papal taxation, the rise of the affluent middle class and its clash with medieval Church ideals, and the increase of an active system of intense capitalism.

The **Protestant Revolution** began in Germany with the revolt of Martin Luther against Church abuses. It spread to Switzerland where it was led by John Calvin. It began in England with the efforts of King Henry VIII to have his marriage to Catherine of Aragon annulled so he could wed another and have a male heir.

The results were the increasing support given not only by the people but also by nobles and some rulers, and of course, the attempts of the Church to stop it.

The **Catholic Reformation** was undertaken by the Church to clean up its act and to slow or stop the Protestant Revolution. The Council of Trent and the Jesuits supplied the major efforts to this end. Six major results of the Catholic Reformation included

- greater religious freedom,
- greater religious tolerance,
- more opportunities for education,
- limitations of the power and control of rulers,
- an increase in religious wars, and
- an increase in fanaticism and persecution.

These changes naturally led to the **Enlightenment**, a period of intense self-study that focused on ethics and logic. More so than at any time before, scientists and philosophers questioned cherished truths, widely held beliefs, and their own sanity in an attempt to discover why the world worked—from within. "I think; therefore I am" is one of the famous sayings from the Enlightenment. Philosophers and writers such as Descartes, Hume, and Kant became leading voices of this era.

Prevalent during the Enlightenment was the idea of the **social contract,** the belief that government existed because people wanted it to, that the people had an agreement with the government that they would submit to it as long as it protected them and didn't encroach on their basic human rights. This idea was first made famous by the Frenchman **Jean-Jacques Rousseau**, but it was also adopted by England's John Locke and America's Thomas Jefferson. **John Locke**, one of the most influential political writers of the seventeenth century, placed great emphasis on human rights and put forth the belief that, when governments violate those rights, people should rebel. He wrote the book *Two Treatises of Government* in 1690. This book had tremendous influence on political thought in the American colonies and helped shaped the U.S. Constitution and Declaration of Independence

Global exploration
The **Age of Exploration** had its beginnings centuries before in the growth of global interaction that resulted from the Crusades and, later, the Renaissance. The survivors of the Crusades made their way home to different places in Europe, bringing with them fascinating new information about exotic lands, people, customs, and desirable foods and goods such as spices and silks. The **Vivaldo Brothers** and **Marco Polo** later wrote of their travels and experiences. New ideas, new inventions, better maps and charts, and newer, more accurate navigational instruments increased knowledge. Great wealth and new methods also went to western Europe with the returning Crusaders, and these new

influences were the intellectual stimuli that eventually led to the Renaissance. The revival of interest in classical Greek art, architecture, literature, science, astronomy, and medicine, along with increased trade between Europe and Asia and the invention of the printing press helped to push the spread of knowledge and served as the impetus for the beginnings of exploration.

Trade routes between Europe and Asia were slow, difficult, dangerous, and very expensive. Whether by sea voyages on the Indian Ocean and Mediterranean Sea or by camel caravans in central Asia and the Arabian Desert, trade was still controlled by the Italian merchants in Genoa and Venice. It took months and even years for the exotic luxuries of Asia to reach the markets of western Europe. A way had to be found that would bypass traditional routes and end the control of the Italian merchants.

Prince Henry of Portugal (also called the Navigator) encouraged the Portuguese seamen who led the search for an all-water route to Asia. New types of sailing ships were built that could carry the seamen safely through the ocean waters. Experiments were conducted, resulting in newer maps, newer navigational methods, and newer instruments. The astrolabe and the compass enabled sailors to determine direction as well as latitude and longitude for exact location. Although Prince Henry died in 1460, the Portuguese kept on sailing along and exploring Africa's west coastline. In 1488, Bartholomew Diaz and his men sailed around Africa's southern tip, eventually known as the Cape of Good Hope, and headed toward Asia before returning to Europe.

The Portuguese were finally successful ten years later, in 1498, when **Vasco da Gama** and his men, continuing the route of Diaz, rounded Africa's Cape of Good Hope and sailed across the Indian Ocean to India's port of Calicut (Calcutta). Thus da Gama proved that Asia could be reached from Europe by sea.

Columbus's first transatlantic voyage was to try to prove his theory that Asia could be reached by sailing west. To a certain extent, his idea was true. It could be done but only after figuring how to go around or across or through the landmass in between. Long after Spain dispatched conquistadors to gather the wealth for the coffers of the Spanish monarchs, the British were searching valiantly for the nonexistent "Northwest Passage," a land-sea route across North America and open sea to the wealth of Asia.

Invading foreigners, particularly the Spanish conquistadors, destroyed powerful American civilizations such as those of the Incas and Aztecs. The wealth of resources in the New World was desirable to the Europeans. Slaves were imported from African countries to work in the Americas. It is estimated that in four centuries of the slave trade, more than 9.5 million slaves were sent to the Americas. The African sellers and leaders used slaves as a form of barter. They traded them for what the Europeans and others offered.

Spain, France, and England along with some participation by the Dutch led the way with expanding western European civilization in the New World. These three nations had strong monarchical governments and were struggling for dominance and power in Europe. With the defeat of the Spanish Armada in 1588, England became undisputed master of the seas. Spain lost its power and influence in Europe, and it was left to France and England to carry on the rivalry, leading to eventual British control in Asia as well. For France, claims to various parts of North America were the result of the efforts of such men as Verrazano, Champlain, Cartier, LaSalle, Father Marquette, and Joliet. Dutch claims were based on the work of Henry Hudson. John Cabot gave England its stake in North America along with John Hawkins, Sir Francis Drake, and the half brothers Sir Walter Raleigh and Sir Humphrey Gilbert.

China at the end of the eighteenth century knew very little of the outside world, and vice versa. Ming artists created beautiful porcelain pottery, but not much of it saw its way into the outside world until much later. The Manchu were known for their focus on farming and road building, two practices that were instituted in greater numbers in order to try to keep up with expanding population. Confucianism, Taoism, and ancestor worship—the staples of Chinese society for hundreds of years—continued to flourish during all this time.

The other major power in Asia was **Japan**, which developed independently and remained isolated for hundreds of years. The Sea of Japan protected Japan from invasion. Early Japanese society focused on the emperor and the farm. Japan had borrowed many ideas from China, including Buddhism, a system of writing, a calendar, and even fashion. The power of the emperor declined as it was usurped by the era of the Daimyo and his loyal soldiers, the **Samurai**. Japan flourished economically and culturally during many of these years, although the policy of isolation the country developed kept the rest of the world from knowing such things. Buddhism and local religions were joined by Christianity in the sixteenth century, but it wasn't until the mid-nineteenth century that Japan rejoined the world community.

See also Skill 2.1d

Skill 2.2b   Demonstrate knowledge of political and industrial revolutions 1750–1914

Nationalism
The overriding theme of the life in the eighteenth, nineteenth, and twentieth centuries was progress. Technological advancements brought great and terrible things in all aspects of life. New theories in economics brought great changes in the way the world does business. New theories in government brought about numerous new nations, uprisings, and wars.

During the eighteenth and especially the nineteenth centuries, **nationalism** emerged as a powerful force in Europe and elsewhere in the world. Strictly speaking, nationalism is the belief in one's own nation or people. More so than in previous centuries, the people of the European countries began to think in terms of a nation of people who had similar beliefs, concerns, and needs. This was partly a reaction to a growing discontent with the autocratic governments of the day and partly a general realization that there was more to life than the individual. People could feel a part of something like their nation, making themselves more than just an insignificant soul struggling to survive. Loyalty to one's nation included national pride, extending and maintaining sovereign political boundaries, and unification of smaller states with common language, history, and culture into a more powerful nation.

Imperialism

Nationalism precipitated several changes in government, most notably in France. Italy and Germany were each united into one nation from many smaller states. What nationalism did not do, however, was provide sufficient outlets for the sudden rise in national fervor. Especially in the 1700s and 1800s, European powers and peoples began looking to Africa and Asia in order to establish colonies: rich sources of goods, trade, and cheap labor. Africa, especially, suffered at the hands of European imperialists bent on expanding their reach outside the borders of Europe. Asia also suffered from colonial expansion, most notably in India and Southeast Asia.

Except for Liberia and Ethiopia, France, Great Britain, Italy, Portugal, Spain, Germany, and Belgium controlled the entire continent of Africa. In Asia and the Pacific Islands, only China, Japan, and Siam (present-day Thailand) kept their independence. The others were controlled by the strong European nations. An additional reason for European imperialism was the harsh, urgent demand for the raw materials needed to fuel and feed the great Industrial Revolution. The fact that these resources were not available in Europe in the huge quantities so desperately needed necessitated (and rationalized) the partitioning of the continent of Africa and parts of Asia. It was expected that, in turn, these colonial areas would purchase the finished manufactured goods.

This colonial expansion would haunt the European imperialists in a very big way, as colonial skirmishes spilled over into alliance that dragged the European powers into World War I. Some of these colonial battles were still being fought as late as the start of World War II as well.

Industrial Revolution

The **Industrial Revolution**, which began in Great Britain in the 1700s, was the development of power-driven machinery (fueled by coal and steam), leading to the accelerated growth of industry, with large factories replacing homes and small workshops as work centers. Much later developments included power based on electricity and the internal combustion engine, replacing coal and steam. The lives of people changed drastically and a largely agricultural society changed to an industrial one.

The use of machines in industry enabled workers to produce a large quantity of goods much faster than by hand. With the increase in business, hundreds of workers were hired and assigned to perform a certain job in the production process. This method of organization is called **division of labor**. By increasing the rate of production, businesses could reduce the prices of their products, thus making the products affordable for more people. As a result, sales and businesses were increasingly successful and profitable. A great variety of new products or inventions became available such as the typewriter, the telephone, barbed wire, the electric light, the phonograph, and the gasoline automobile.

Prior to the Industrial Revolution, most urban centers were either ports or centers of government. With the sudden and rapid growth of industry, urban centers began growing based on industrial production and proximity to power resources such as coal and water power. During the 1700s, the population of England went from a majority living in rural areas to a majority living in cities. As industrialization spread to other countries, a similar pattern of urbanization followed. With the advent of the railroad, moving raw materials over land became easier and less expensive, further fueling urban growth.

Political revolution

The **American Revolution** resulted in the successful efforts of the English colonists in America to win their freedom from Great Britain. After more than one hundred years of mostly self-government, the colonists resented the increased British meddling and contro., They declared their freedom, won the Revolutionary War with aid from France, and formed a new independent nation.

The **French Revolution** was the revolt of the middle and lower classes against the gross political and economic excesses of the rulers and the supporting nobility. It ended with the establishment of the first in a series of French Republics. Conditions leading to revolt included extreme taxation, inflation, lack of food, and the total disregard for the impossible, degrading, and unacceptable condition of the people on the part of the rulers, the nobility, and the Church.

Emboldened by the success of the American and French Revolutions, the Spanish and Portuguese colonies in Central and South America grew dissatisfied with their economic and political dependence on Europe, and in the early decades of the nineteenth century, several revolutionary movements gained momentum. By 1822, Argentina, Chile, Colombia, Mexico, Paraguay, Venezuela, Peru, Ecuador, and Brazil had all succeeded in their battles for independence and looked to the rest of the world for recognition and assistance. In the United States, President James Monroe announced the Monroe Doctrine, which stated that any designs by European countries to take control of their former colonies in the Western Hemisphere would be interpreted as attacks on the United States.

In Europe, France had moved into Spain and captured the Spanish King Ferdinand VII during the Napoleonic Wars, effectively weakening Spain's hold over its colonies in the Americas. The royal family of Portugal fled to Brazil, its South American colony, before Napoleon's armies reached them. Efforts by the mother countries to suppress the independence movements were thwarted by junta forces led by such figures as Miguel Hidalgo and Simon Bolivar. They were further discouraged by other countries, such as the United States and Great Britain, that were eager to gain access to South America's natural resources and lucrative markets.

In London in 1864, Karl Marx organized the first Socialist International. This radical leftist organization died off after limping along for twelve years, by which time its headquarters had moved to New York. The **Second Socialist International** met twelve years later in Paris to celebrate the anniversary of the fall of the Bastille in the French Revolution. By this time, serious factions were developing. There were the **anarchists**, who wanted to tear down everything, **communists** who wanted to tear down the established order and build another in its place, and the **democratic-socialist** majority who favored peaceful political action.

In the United States, territorial expansion occurred in the expansion westward under the banner of "Manifest Destiny." In addition, during the 1800s the United States was involved in the War with Mexico, the Spanish-American War, and support of the Latin American colonies of Spain in their quest for independence.

COMPETENCY 2.3   1914 TO THE PRESENT

Skill 2.3a   Evaluate conflicts, ideologies, and changes in the twentieth century

World War I—1914 to 1918
The causes of World War I include the surge of nationalism, the increasing strength of military capabilities, massive colonization for raw materials needed for industrialization and manufacturing, and military and diplomatic alliances. The spark that started the war was the assassination of Austrian Archduke Franz Ferdinand and his wife in Sarajevo.

There were twenty-eight nations involved in the war, not including colonies and territories. It began July 28, 1914, and ended November 11, 1918, with the signing of the Treaty of Versailles. During the course of the war, trench warfare and deadly new weapons contributed to deaths of soldiers even as a deadly influenza epidemic killed millions more.

The **Russian Revolution** began in early 1917 with the abdication of Tsar Nicholas II and the establishment of a democratic government. The extreme Marxists (Bolsheviks), who had a majority in Russia's Socialist Party, overcame the opposition and later that year did away with the provisional democratic government, setting up the world's first Marxist state.

Despite the tremendous efforts of Peter the Great during the late seventeenth and early eighteenth centuries to bring his country up to the social, cultural, and economic standards of the rest of Europe, Russia always remained a hundred years or more behind. Autocratic rule, the existence of the system of serfdom or slavery of the peasants, lack of money, defeats in wars, lack of enough food and food production, little if any industrialization—all of these contributed to conditions ripe for revolt. The Orthodox Church was steeped in political activities, and the Tsars had absolute rule. By the time the nation entered World War I, conditions were just right for revolution. Marxist socialism seemed to be the solution to all the problems. Russia had to stop its participation in the war, although it was winning a big battle. Its industry could not meet the military's needs.

Between world wars—1918 to 1939
Fascism arose following WWI. In general, fascism is the effort to create, by dictatorial means, a viable national society in which competing interests were to be adjusted to each other by being entirely subordinated to the service of the state. Fascist movements often had socialist origins. For example, in Italy, where fascism first arose in place of socialism, **Benito Mussolini** sought to impose what he called "*corporativism*." A fascist "*corporate*" state would, in theory, run the economy like a corporation for the benefit of the whole country. It would be

centrally controlled and managed by an elite who would see that its benefits would go to everyone.

The following features have been characteristic of fascism in its various manifestations:

- an origin at a time of serious economic disruption and of rapid and bewildering social change;
- a philosophy that rejects democratic and humanitarian ideals and glorifies the absolute sovereignty of the state, the unity and destiny of the people, and their unquestioning loyalty and obedience to the dictator;
- aggressive nationalism that calls for the mobilization and regimentation of every aspect of national life and makes open use of violence and intimidation;
- the simulation of mass popular support, accomplished by outlawing all but a single political party and by using suppression, censorship, and propaganda; and
- a program of vigorous action, including economic reconstruction, industrialization, and pursuit of economic self-sufficiency, territorial expansion, and war that is dramatized as bold, adventurous, and promising a glorious future.

In addition, fascist or similar regimes are at times anticommunist, as evidenced by the Soviet-German Treaty of 1939. During the period of alliance created by the treaty, Italy, Germany, and their satellite countries ceased their anticommunist propaganda. They emphasized their own revolutionary and proletarian origins and attacked the so-called plutocratic western democracies.

In theory at least, the chief distinction between fascism and communism is that fascism is *nationalist*, exalting the interests of the state and glorifying war between nations, whereas communism is *internationalist,* exalting the interests of a specific economic class (the proletariat) and glorifying worldwide class warfare. In practice, however, this fundamental distinction loses some of its validity. For in its heyday, fascism was also an internationalist movement, dedicated to world conquest, (like communism), as evidenced by the events prior to and during the Second World War. At the same time, many elements in communism, as it evolved, came to be very nationalistic as well.

World War II 1939 to 1945
Ironically, the Treaty of Versailles, which ended World War I, ultimately led to the World War II. Countries that fought in the first war were either dissatisfed over the spoils of war or were punished so harshly that resentment continued building to an eruption twenty years later.

The economic problems of both winners and losers of the first war were never resolved, and the worldwide Great Depression of the 1930s dealt the final blow to any immediate rapid recovery. Democratic governments in Europe were severely strained and weakened, which in turn gave strength and encouragement to those political movements that were extreme and made promises to end the economic chaos in their countries.

Nationalism, which was a major cause of World War I, grew even stronger and seemed to feed the feelings of discontent which became increasingly rampant. Because of unstable economic conditions and political unrest, harsh dictatorships arose in several of the countries, especially where there was no history of experience in democratic government. Germany, Japan, and Italy began to aggressively expand their borders and acquire additional territory.

In all, fifty-nine nations became embroiled in World War II, which began September 1, 1939, and ended September 2, 1945. These dates include both the European and Pacific fronts of the war. The results of this second global conflagration were more deaths and more destruction than in any other armed conflict. It completely uprooted and displaced millions of people. The end of the war brought renewed power struggles, especially in Europe and China, with many Eastern European nations, as well as China, coming under the control of communists supported and backed by the Soviet Union. With the development of atomic bombs, and their use against two Japanese cities, the world found itself in the nuclear age. The peace settlement established the United Nations, still existing and operating today.

Post-World War II—1946 to present

The post-WWII years have seen many changes in society. Nations have been involved in a global community since then, partly due to the existence of the United Nations. Governments have been more concerned with the rights of various groups, such as women and minorities. The role of women changed in the industrialized world as women joined the workforce and became political leaders. Gains have been made in human rights and the treatment of minorities. Much of this is due to the United Nations, which provides a forum for discussion and enforcement by its member nations. International treaties have also come into being to protect the rights of people.

The Cold War grew out of tensions between the United States and the Soviet Union after WWII. The Cold War was, more than anything else, an ideological struggle between proponents of democracy and those of communism. The two major players were the United States and the Soviet Union, but other countries were involved as well. The Cold War continued in varying degrees from 1947 to 1991, when the Soviet Union collapsed. Other Eastern European countries had also seen their communist governments overthrown by this time, marking the dismantling of the Iron Curtain.

One problem the world has been dealing with since WWII is population growth, especially in the less-developed countries. Economies and the food supply have to expand to accommodate a growing population. This has not been the case in many of the less-developed countries and as a result they suffer extreme poverty and have a poor quality of life.

See also Skills 1.9b, 1.10a, 1.10b, and 3.2a

Skill 2.3b   Understand contemporary trends—1991 to the present

Tremendous progress in communication and transportation has tied all parts of Earth and drawn them closer. New technologies, such as computers and cell phones, have changed the way of life for many. Technology makes the world seem a much smaller place. In many places technology has resulted in a mobile population. Popular culture has been shaped by mass production and the mass media. Mass production and technology have made electronic goods affordable to most people in wealthy nations. This is the day of the cell phone. The **Internet** and e-mail allow people anywhere in the world to be in touch with others and to learn about world events.

Globalization has tied much of the world together economically. Outsourcing is now popular because of technological advances. Call centers for businesses in Europe and America are now located in India and Pakistan, while manufacturing jobs have shifted to areas of the world with low labor costs.

Terrorism became a major security threat around the world from the 1990s on. Major terrorist attacks, often executed by small groups of extremists, have taken place on nearly every continent. A series of 2001 attacks in the United States led to lengthy wars in Iraq and Afghanistan that, at times, involved NATO allies. In 2011, democracy movements that spread through Middle Eastern nations such as Egypt created what became known as the **Arab Spring.**

COMPETENCY 3.0   BASIC POLITICAL CONCEPTS

Skill 3.0a   Demonstrate understanding of why government is needed

Historically the functions of government, or people's concepts of government and its purpose and function, have varied considerably. In the theory of political science, the function of government is to secure the common welfare of the members of the given society over which it exercises control. In different historical eras, governments have attempted to achieve the common welfare by various means in accordance with the traditions and ideology of the given society.

At its heart, the primary purpose of modern democratic government is to organize people together into a society that agrees upon basic rules and aims. Government makes and enforces laws that reflect both fundamental human rules, such as the wrongness of murder, and broad social aims, such as the protection of individual liberties or the provision of social services. Government also serves as a way for people to work together to provide public goods and services, such as roads and schools, that would otherwise be too expensive and far-reaching for a small group to provide.

Skill 3.0b   Demonstrate knowledge of political theory

Political science is the study of political life and different forms of government, including elections, political parties, and public administration. In addition, political science studies the values of justice, freedom, power, and equality. U.S. political scientists may organize political study into six main fields:

1. Political theory and philosophy,
2. Comparative governments,
3. International relations,
4. Political behavior,
5. Public administration, and
6. U.S. government and politics.

Some contributors to political theory include the following:

Aristotle and Plato were Greek philosophers who believed that political order was to be the result of political science and that this political order would ensure maximum justice while at the same time remaining totally stable.

Saint Thomas Aquinas elaborated further on Aristotle's theories and adapted them to Christianity, emphasizing certain duties and rights of individuals in the governmental process. He also laid emphasis on government rule according to those rights and duties. Aquinas helped lay the foundation of the idea of modern constitutionalism by stating that government was limited by law.

Niccolo Machiavelli, author of *The Prince,* was the famous politician from Florence who disregarded the ideals of Christianity in favor of realistic power politics.

Thomas Hobbes, whose most famous work was *Leviathan,* believed that a person's life is a constant, unceasing search for power, and he believed in the state's supremacy to combat this.

John Locke was one of the most influential political writers of the seventeenth century. He put great emphasis on human rights and put forth the belief that, when governments violate those rights, people should rebel. He wrote the *Two Treatises of Government* in 1690. This work had tremendous influence on political thought in the American colonies and helped shaped the U.S. Constitution and the Declaration of Independence.

Montesquieu and Rousseau were proponents of "liberalism," the willingness to change ideas, policies, and proposals to solve current problems. They also believed that individual freedom was just as important as any community's welfare. Rousseau's *Social Contract* argued for the idea that people entered into a free agreement with their government to achieve shared goals. This idea greatly influenced the Framers of the Constitution.

David Hume and Jeremy Bentham believed that "the greatest happiness of the greatest number was the goal of politics."

John Stuart Mill wrote extensively of the liberal ideas of his time.

Johann Gottlieb Fichte and Friedrich Hegel were well-known German philosophers who contributed significantly in the eighteenth century. Johann Gottlieb Fichte and Friedrich Hegel supported a liberalism which included ideas about nationalism and socialism. Immanuel Kant's liberalism included the idea of universal peace through world organization.

Some basic tenets of political theory have influenced the practice of government in the United States. **Law** is the set of established rules or accepted norms of human conduct in their relationship with other individuals, organizations, and institutions. The rule of law recognizes that the authority of the government is to be exercised only within the context and boundaries established by laws that are enacted according to established procedure and publicly disclosed.

In order to structure and maintain a society and the various safeties of the people, the rule of adherence to the law is considered universal for all who live within the jurisdiction to which laws apply. Failure to adhere to the laws of the state or the nation is punishable under the legal code.

Civil disobedience, however, is the refusal to obey certain laws, regulations, or requirements of a government because those laws are believed to be detrimental to the freedom or right of the people to exercise government-guaranteed personal and civil liberties. Civil disobedience, in principle, can be nonviolent in the steps taken to resist or refuse to obey these laws. Notable examples of the exercise of civil disobedience have included Henry David Thoreau's refusal to pay taxes in protest against slavery and against the Mexican-American War. Dr Martin Luther King, Jr., led the Civil Rights Movement of the 1960s on the principle and within the established techniques of nonviolent civil disobedience. Internationally, Gandhi was a major nonviolent leader who used this theory to help secure India's independence from Great Britain.

Skill 3.0c   Demonstrate understanding of political concepts such as legitimacy, power, authority, and responsibility

The political concepts of **legitimacy, power, authority, and responsibility** are all interrelated. Legitimacy refers to the moral correctness of a political system. If the political system is deemed to be morally correct, it will be accepted by its citizens. The citizens will agree to obey the laws and rules of that system because they accept its legitimacy. When the citizens no longer accept the legitimacy of a regime, the political system is overthrown—which is different from being changed via an election. An election is a part of the political system. A political system's legitimacy is enhanced when it is recognized or acknowledged by another government. Democracy is a political system with legitimacy.

Political authority refers to the people in the various offices within the political system. Their political authority lies in their ability to coerce people to comply with the wishes of the political system. Their political authority stems from the acceptance of the legitimacy of the political system or the citizens would not accept their ability to coerce.

Political power refers to the ability of those with political authority to do or to influence. If the orders of a legitimate representative of the political system are not obeyed, the military can enforce those orders.

Political responsibility is the moral obligation of citizens and government to do the morally correct thing. For example in the case of genocide and other atrocities, the political responsibility is to speak out and fight the atrocities.

Skill 3.0d   Demonstrate understanding of various political orientations

At its most basic, a **political orientation** is simply the lens through which individuals or groups view government and politics. In the United States, for example, common political orientations include **liberal** and **conservative.** Each of these orientations relies on a different ideology to organize the proper role of government; liberals believe in wide-scale government programs and social support, and conservatives support small government through limited spending and social involvement.

Political orientation may also refer to views on the proper form of national government. A person living in a monarchy, for example, may follow a political orientation that supports that form of government; in comparison, a citizen of a republic may view political activity through the context of representative democracy.

COMPETENCY 3.1   UNITED STATES POLITICAL SYSTEM

Skill 3.1a   **Demonstrate understanding of the constitutional foundation of the United States government, including knowledge of the basic content and structure of the United States Constitution, and of the processes of constitutional interpretation and amendment**

The Constitution is the basis for government in the United States. Shortly after ratification, the founding fathers received and passed the first ten amendments, collectively known as the **Bill of Rights**. These amendments were established to protect an individual's rights, such as the freedom of speech and the right to a trial by jury with representation. This document establishes a federal system that divides power between the central government and the states. It also splits power among three federal branches and provides a system of checks and balances to prevent the taking of too much power by one particular branch. These ideas are laid out through a series of Articles giving details about the specifics of the federal government system and through a group of twenty-seven amendments that reshape or clarify various points.

As a constitutional government and political system, the basis of all laws and all decisions and enforcement of laws is the Constitution. The Constitution establishes the process by which laws can be written and enacted, the basis for their legitimacy within the context of the principles documented in the Constitution, and the means of interpretation and enforcement of those laws by the police and the courts.

Laws are introduced, debated, and passed by Congress, with both houses of Congress passing the same version of the law. Then the president must sign the law. Once signed, the law is considered enacted and is enforced. Challenges to the constitutionality of the law and questions of interpretation of the law are handled by the federal court system. Each state has the authority to make laws covering anything not reserved to the federal government. State laws cannot negate federal laws.

An amendment is a change or addition to the Constitution. Amending the United States Constitution is extremely difficult to do. Two-thirds of both houses of Congress must propose and then pass an amendment. Alternatively, two-thirds of the state legislatures can call a convention to propose an amendment. Then the proposed amendment must be ratified by three-fourths of the state legislatures. To date, only twenty-seven amendments to the Constitution have passed. An amendment may be used to cancel out a previous one; for example, the Eighteenth Amendment, known as Prohibition, was nullified by the Twenty-first Amendment.

A key element in the failure of some amendments has been the time limit that Congress may impose when proposing an amendment. A famous example of an amendment that came close but did not reach the threshold for ratification before the deadline expired was the Equal Rights Amendment. This amendment was proposed in 1972 but could not muster enough support for passage, even though its deadline was extended to ten years from the original seven.

The Constitution has been interpreted in different ways at different times by different people. The Supreme Court has the role of offering a final judicial interpretation of the Constitution through its power to rule that certain laws are constitutional or unconstitutional. Lower courts may also interpret the Constitution.

See also Skill 3.1b

Skill 3.1b   Demonstrate knowledge of the functions and powers of the legislative, executive, and judicial branches of government, and of the relationships among them

In the United States, the three branches of the federal government, the **executive**, the **legislative**, and the **judicial**, divide up their powers thus:

Legislative—Article I of the Constitution established the legislative or law-making branch of the government called the Congress. It is made up of two houses, the House of Representatives and the Senate. Voters in all states elect the members who serve in each respective House of Congress. The legislative branch is responsible for making laws, raising and printing money, regulating trade, establishing the postal service and the federal courts, approving the president's appointments, declaring war, and supporting the armed forces. Congress also has the power to change the Constitution itself and to impeach (bring charges against) the president. Impeachment charges are brought by the House of Representatives and tried in the Senate.

Executive—Article II of the Constitution created the executive branch of the government, headed by the president, who leads the country, recommends new laws, and can veto bills passed by the legislative branch. As the chief of state, the president is responsible for carrying out the laws of the country and the treaties and declarations of war passed by the legislative branch. The president also appoints federal judges and is commander-in-chief of the military when it is called into service.

Other members of the executive branch include the vice president (also elected), various appointees (such as ambassadors and presidential advisors), members of the armed forces, and other employees of government agencies, departments, and bureaus. The president's appointments of government officials must be approved by the legislative branch.

Judicial—Article III of the Constitution established the judicial branch of government, headed by the Supreme Court. The Supreme Court has the power to rule that a law passed by the legislature or an act of the executive branch is illegal and unconstitutional. Citizens, businesses, and government officials can, in an appeal capacity, ask the Supreme Court to review a decision made in a lower court if someone believes that the ruling by a judge is unconstitutional. The judicial branch also includes the lower federal courts, known as federal district courts, that have been established by Congress. These courts try lawbreakers and review cases referred from other courts. Supreme Court justices, after being nominated by the president, must be approved by the Senate.

In the United States, the term "checks and balances" refers to the ability of each branch of government (executive, legislative, and judicial) to "check" or limit the actions of the others. Examples of checks and balances are the executive branch limiting the legislature by power of veto over bills and appointments in the court system. The judicial branch limits the power of the legislature by judicial review and the ability to rule laws unconstitutional. The judicial branch may also determine that executive orders are unconstitutional. The legislature checks the executive by the power of impeachment.

Skill 3.1c   Demonstrate knowledge of the formation and operation of political institutions not established by the Constitution, such as political parties and interest groups, and of the role of the media and public opinion in American political life

Although not part of the U.S. Constitution, and even opposed by early government leaders, political parties have been a part of U.S. political life since the 1790s. The first two parties that developed were led by Thomas Jefferson as the Secretary of State and Alexander Hamilton as the Secretary of the Treasury. Hamilton wanted the federal government to be stronger than the state governments. Jefferson believed that the state governments should be stronger. Jefferson interpreted the Constitution strictly and argued that the Constitution does not grant the federal government the power to create a national bank. Hamilton interpreted the Constitution much more loosely.

In time, factions developed behind these varying ideas. Hamilton and his supporters were known as Federalists, because they favored a strong federal government. The Federalists had the support of the merchants and the ship owners in the Northeast and of some planters in the South. Small farmers, craft workers, and some of the wealthier landowners supported Jefferson and the Democratic-Republicans.

By 1816, after losing a string of important elections (Jefferson was reelected in 1804, and James Madison, a Democratic-Republican, was elected in 1808), the Federalist Party ceased to be an effective political force and soon passed off the national stage. By the late 1820s, new political parties had grown up. The **Democratic**-Republican Party, or simply the **Republican Party**, had been the major party for many years, but differences within it about the direction the country was headed in caused a split after 1824. Those who favored strong national growth took the name **Whigs,** after a similar party in Great Britain, and united around then President John Quincy Adams. Many business people in the Northeast as well as some wealthy planters in the South supported it.

By the time of the Civil War, the present major political parties had been formed. The Democratic-Republicans had slowly evolved into the modern Democratic Party, and the newer Republican Party emerged to oppose the spread of slavery. Despite the influence of third parties, ranging from the anti-immigrant Know-Nothings in the mid-1850s to the agricultural Populist Party in the late 1800s to the modern Libertarian Party, the two major parties have largely controlled the political discussion in the United States.

Another powerful political influence is **special interest groups** of a political nature. These groups contain people who want to effect political change or maintain the status quo. Special interest groups may exist to support a particular idea or cause, such as environmental protection, or to help a certain industry, location, or candidate.

A **free press** is essential to maintaining responsibility and civic-mindedness in government and in the rest of society. The U.S. broadcast, print, and electronic media serve as societal and governmental watchdogs. The press allows government leaders to share information about their plans, political analysts to offer commentary and debate, and investigative journalists to pursue and expose governmental wrongdoing.

Because the United States is a representative democracy, its leaders are subject to the influence of **public opinion,** or the ideas about certain topics that U.S. citizens have. Widespread public support or opposition to certain practices or laws may lead to their passage or repeal, and many elected leaders closely follow public opinion regarding their performance. Public opinion is usually gauged by professional pollers.

Skill 3.1d   Demonstrate understanding of the relationship among federal, state, and local governments

The U.S. Constitution divides certain powers between the national and the state governments.

Powers delegated to the federal government	Powers reserved to the states
• to tax	• to regulate intrastate trade
• to borrow and coin money	• to establish local governments
• to establish postal service	• to protect general welfare
• to grant patents and copyrights	• to protect life and property
• to regulate interstate & foreign commerce	• to ratify amendments
• to establish courts	• to conduct elections
• to declare war	• to make state and local laws
• to raise and support the armed forces	
• to govern territories	
• to define and punish felonies and piracy on the high seas	
• to fix standards of weights and measures	
• to conduct foreign affairs	

The concurrent powers of the federal government and states are

- both may levy taxes;
- both may borrow money;
- both may charter banks and corporations;
- both may establish courts;
- both may make and enforce laws;
- both may take property for public purposes; and
- both may spend money to provide for the public welfare.

The implied powers of the federal government are

- to establish banks or other corporations, implied from delegated powers to tax, borrow, and to regulate commerce;
- to spend money for roads, schools, health, insurance, etc., implied from powers to establish post roads, to tax to provide for general welfare and defense, and to regulate commerce;
- to create military academies, implied from powers to raise and support an armed force;
- to locate and generate sources of power and sell surplus, implied from powers to dispose of government property, commerce, and war powers; and

- to assist and regulate agriculture, implied from power to tax and spend for general welfare and regulate commerce;

Thus, the federal and state governments operate in a federal system. Over time, the federal government has gradually assumed more influence over the states through legislation and, in modern times, the allocation of federal funds. Nevertheless, states retain their Constitutional powers. Local governments, such as city or county governments, operate under the auspices of state constitutions. These smaller bodies typically have responsibility for the day-to-day functioning of a place. For example, local governments may oversee police and fire departments, public water systems, schools and libraries, and city services.

Skill 3.1e   Demonstrate understanding of political behavior at both the individual and group levels, including elections and other forms of political participation

The most basic way for citizens to participate in the political process is to vote. Since the passing of the Twenty-third Amendment in 1965, U.S. citizens who are at least eighteen years old are eligible to vote. Elections are held at regular intervals at all levels of government, allowing citizens to weigh in on local matters as well as those of national scope.

Citizens wishing to engage in the political process to a greater degree have several paths open to them, such as participating in local government. Counties, states, and sometimes neighborhoods are governed by locally elected boards or councils that meet publicly. Citizens can usually address these boards, bringing their concerns and expressing their opinions on matters being considered. Citizens may even wish to stand for local election and join a governing board or seek support for higher office.

Supporting a political party is another means by which citizens can participate in the political process. Political parties support member candidates in election campaigns and endorse certain platforms that express general social and political goals. Political parties make much use of volunteer labor, with supporters making telephone calls, distributing printed material, and campaigning for the party's causes and candidates. Political parties solicit donations to support their efforts as well. Contributing money to a political party is another form of participation citizens can undertake.

Yet another form of political activity is to support an issue-related political group. Several political groups work actively to sway public opinion on various issues or on behalf of a segment of American society. These groups may have representatives who meet with state and federal legislators to "lobby" them—to provide them with information on an issue and persuade them to take favorable action.

COMPETENCY 3.2   OTHER FORMS OF GOVERNMENT

Skill 3.2a   Demonstrate understanding of the structures of various forms of government

Governments may be divided into a few broad categories. **Limited governments** exercise political authority that is limited in some way, often by a constitution or other founding document. Under a limited government, all people and the government must follow established laws. **Unlimited governments**, however, exercise total, unfettered political authority. These types of governments are more likely to experience abuse of power.

Types of governments may also be characterized by the number of people who have political authority. A government with just one leader uses the rule-of-one form. Under the rule of few, a select, elite group oversees the government. Democratic forms of government rely on the rule of many. Governments that are based on the will of many are more likely to serve the needs of both the majority and the minority groups within that society.

Some major forms of government are:

Communism: This political and economic system is characterized by the ideology of class conflict and revolution and of government ownership of the means of production and distribution of goods and services. Historically, communism was practiced in the Soviet Union; the largest communist country today is China. The centralized control exercised by communist governments has typically resulted in economic and political hardships for its citizens.

Dictatorship: The rule by an individual or small group of individuals (oligarchy) that centralizes all political control in itself and enforces its will with a strong police force. Dictatorships may exist with varying degrees of success, but they often become repressive.

Fascism: A belief, as well as a political system, opposed ideologically to communism, though similar in basic structure, with a one-party state, centralized political control, and a repressive police system. However, fascism tolerates private ownership of the means of production though, overall, it maintains tight control. Central to its belief is the idolization of the leader, a "cult of the personality," and, most often, an expansionist ideology. Examples have been German Nazism and Italian fascism.

Monarchy: The rule of a nation by a monarch, a nonelected and usually hereditary leader, most often a king or a queen. Most monarchies today are constitutional monarchies, under which an elected legislative body such as a parliament shares authority with the monarch.

Parliamentary System: A system of government with a legislature, usually involving a multiplicity of political parties and often coalition politics. There is a division between the head of state and the head of government. The head of government is usually known as a prime minister. This person is typically the leader of the largest political party. The head of government and the cabinet members usually both sit and vote in the parliament. The head of state is most often an elected president (though, in the case of a constitutional monarchy such as Great Britain, the sovereign may take the place of a president as head of state). A government may fall when a majority in parliament votes "no confidence" in the government.

Presidential System: A system of government with a legislature; it can involve few or many political parties and no division between the head of state and the head of government. The president serves in both capacities. The president is elected either by direct or indirect vote. A president and the members of the cabinet usually do not sit or vote in the legislature, and the president may or may not be the head of the largest political party. A president can thus rule even without a majority in the legislature. He can be removed from office before an election only for major infractions of the law.

Socialism—Political belief and economic system in which the state takes a guiding role in the national economy and provides extensive social services to its population. It may or may not own the means of production outright, but even where it does not, it exercises tight control. It usually promotes democracy, (democratic socialism), though the heavy state involvement produces excessive bureaucracy and usually inefficiency. Taken to an extreme, socialism may lead to communism as government control increases and democratic practices decrease.

COMPETENCY 3.3 INTERNATIONAL RELATIONS

Skill 3.3a Demonstrate knowledge of the functions and powers of international organizations, such as the United Nations

Alliances are developed among nations on the basis of political philosophy, economic concerns, cultural similarities, religious interests, or for military defense. Some of the most notable alliances today are

- the United Nations,
- the North Atlantic Treaty Organization,
- the Caribbean Community,
- the Common Market,
- the Council of Arab Economic Unity, and
- the European Union.

The United Nations began in the waning days of World War II. It brought the nations of the world together to discuss their problems rather than fight about them. UNICEF, a worldwide children's fund, has been able to achieve great things in just a few decades of existence. Other peace-based organizations like the International Red Cross and Medicines sans Frontiers (Doctors Without Borders) have seen their membership and their efficacy rise during this time as well.

<u>DOMAIN IV.</u>   **GEOGRAPHY**

COMPETENCY 4.0   THEMES

Skill 4.0a   Identify relative and absolute location and the physical and human characteristics of "place"

Location and place are two core ideas in the study of geography. Every point on Earth has a specific location that is determined by an imaginary grid of lines denoting latitude and longitude. Parallels of latitude measure distances north and south of the origin line called the equator. Meridians of longitude measure distances east and west of the origin line called the prime meridian. Geographers use latitude and longitude to pinpoint a place's absolute, or exact, location.

To know the absolute location of a place is only part of the equation. It is also important to know how that place is related to other places—in other words, to know that place's relative location. Words such as north, south, east, and west typically describe physical relative location. Relative location may also deal with the interaction that occurs between and among places. It refers to the many ways—by land, by water, even by technology—that places are connected.

The theme of place refers to both the physical and the human characteristics of a given place and how those characteristics shape that place to give it a unique character. Physical characteristics include factors such as topography, climate, and location. Human characteristics describe the people who live in a place and may include language, dress, religion, government, or other human-made factors.

Skill 4.0b   Demonstrate understanding of human-environment interactions

Just as the physical characteristics of a place shape the lives of the people who live there, humans shape their natural environment. Physical factors such as climate and available natural resources can determine what kinds of housing humans construct or what economic activities take place in a certain region. For example, people who live near a coastline are likely to rely on fishing or other water-based industries as part of their economy, but people living inland probably do not.

Humans can change their environments to suit their particular needs and interests, such as through the construction of cities, transportation routes, or factories. These adaptations can result in the extinction of species or changes to the habitat itself. For example, deforestation damages the stability of mountain surfaces. One particularly devastating example is the removal of the grasses of the Great Plains for agriculture. Tilling the ground and planting crops left the soil unprotected. Sustained drought dried out the soil into dust. When windstorms occurred, the topsoil was stripped away and blown all the way to the Atlantic Ocean.

See also Skill 4.2a

Skill 4.0c   **Identify significant types of movement such as migration, trade, and the spread of ideas**

Migration is the movement of people from one place to another. Often, migration is used to describe long-distance movement of groups, but it can also refer to shorter moves or to the actions of just a few.

Trade is the movement and exchange of goods between differing groups. The movement of goods often results in the exchange of cultural ideas and practices through cultural diffusion. **Cultural diffusion** is the movement of cultural ideas or materials among populations independent of the movement of those populations. Cultural diffusion can take place when two or more populations are close to one another, through direct interaction, or across great distances through mass media and other routes. Historically, the spread of Buddhism from India to other parts of Asia is an example of cultural diffusion. A contemporary example of cultural diffusion is the spread of the popularity of American movies to other nations.

COMPETENCY 4.1   MAP SKILLS

Skill 4.1a   Read and interpret various types of maps

Among the more common illustrations used in geography are various types of **maps** and **globes.** These depictions of Earth's surface show land and information in either a flat, two-dimensional form (maps) or a spherical three-dimensional form (globes).

The four main properties of maps are

- the size of the areas shown on the map,
- the shapes of the areas,
- consistent scales, and
- straight-line directions.

A map can be drawn so that it is correct in one or more of these properties. No map can be correct in all of them.

Maps thus have advantages and disadvantages. The major problem of all maps is that it is impossible to reproduce exactly on a flat surface an object shaped like a sphere. In order to put Earth's features onto a map they must be stretched in some way. This stretching is called **distortion.** Distortion does not mean that maps are wrong; it simply means that they are not perfect representations of Earth or its parts.

Cartographers understand the problems of distortion. They try to design their maps so that there is as little distortion as possible. The process of putting the features of Earth onto a flat surface is called **projection**. All map projections have differing types of distortion. One common map projection used today is the **Mercator projection**.

Maps showing physical features often try to show information about the elevation, or **relief,** of the land. **Relief maps** usually give more detail than simply showing the overall elevation (distance above or below sea level) of the land's surface. They also show the shape of the land surface: flat, rugged, or steep. Relief is usually indicated by colors; for instance, all areas on a map that are at a certain elevation will be shown in the same color. Another way to show relief is by using **contour lines**. These lines connect all points of a land surface in a particular area that are the same height.

To properly analyze a given map, one must be familiar with the various parts and symbols that most modern maps use. For the most part, these parts and symbols are standardized, with different maps using similar parts and symbols, which can include the following:

Title—All maps should have a title that tells you what information is to be found on the map.

Legend—Most maps have a legend which tells the reader about the various symbols that are used on that particular map and what the symbols represent (also called a **map key**).

Grid—A grid is a series of lines that are used to find exact places and locations on the map. Several different kinds of grid systems are in use; however, most maps do use the longitude and latitude system, known as the **geographic grid system**.

Compass rose—Most maps have some directional system to show which way the map is being presented. Often, a small compass rose will be present, with arrows showing the four basic directions: north, south, east, and west.

Scale—The scale is used to show the relationship between a unit of measurement on the map and the actual measurement on Earth. Maps are drawn to many different scales. Some maps show a lot of detail for a small area. Others show a greater span of distance. In any event, one should always be aware of just what scale is being used. For instance, for a small area, the scale might be 1 inch = 10 miles. For a map showing the whole world, the scale might be 1 inch = 1,000 miles. One must look at the map key in order to see what units of measurements the map is using.

See also Skill 4.1d

Skill 4.1b   Determine distance, direction, latitude, longitude, and the location of physical features

Distance is the measurement between two points on a map. Measurement can be in terms of a number of units such as feet, yards, miles, meters, or kilometers. Distance is often correct on equidistant maps only in the direction of latitude.

On a map that has a large scale, 1:125,000 or larger, distance distortion is usually insignificant. An example of a large-scale map is a standard topographic map. On these maps, measuring straight-line distance is simple. Distance is first measured on the map using a ruler. This measurement is then converted into a real-world distance using the map's scale. For example, if we measured a distance of 10 centimeters on a map that had a scale of 1:10,000, we would multiply 10 (distance) by 10,000 (scale). Thus, the actual distance in the real world would be 100,000 centimeters.

Direction may be characterized as either cardinal direction or intermediate direction. The cardinal directions are north, south, east, and west. The intermediate directions include northeast, southeast, southwest, and northwest. Direction is usually shown on a map using a compass rose.

Geographers may use **latitude** or **longitude** to determine location. Parallels of latitude are imaginary lines that encircle Earth from east to west. They are parallel to the Equator, which serves to divide north and south latitude. A line of latitude, or parallel, of 30 degrees north has an angle that is 30 degrees north of the plane represented by the equator. The maximum value that latitude can attain, either north or south, is 90 degrees.

Lines of **longitude** circle Earth from north to south and measure position on Earth's surface relative to a point found at the center of Earth. This central point is also located on Earth's rotational or **polar** axis. There are 180 degrees of longitude on either side of a starting meridian, which is known as the **prime meridian**. The prime meridian has a designated value of 0 degrees. Measurements of longitude are defined as being either west or east of the prime meridian.

Physical maps are usually the best way to find and show the physical features of a certain place. Physical features such as bodies of water, mountains, and plains are shown in various ways on maps and globes. Often, a map key or various labels indicate how to locate these features.

Skill 4.1c   Recognize and describe spatial patterns

Maps come in a variety of formats. While general reference maps show where something is in relation to other points, thematic maps describe attribute(s) about that place. These types of maps are sometimes referred to as graphic essays. A thematic map, also known as a statistical or special purpose map, emphasizes the spatial variation of one or a small number of geographic distributions. These distributions may be physical phenomena such as climate or human characteristics such as population density and health issues. Location is important to provide a reference base of where selected phenomena are occurring.

Skill 4.1d   Using a legend or key

Most maps have a legend, or **map key**, that tells the reader about the various symbols that are used on that particular map and what the symbols represent. Map keys may rely on shading, line patterns, dots, or symbols to show various types of information. For example, a resource map may show small images of the various natural resources depicted on the map, such as oil, wheat, or coal. A population density map would likely use different shades of the same color, with light colors indicating sparsely populated area and darker colors showing densely populated areas.

COMPETENCY 4.2   PHYSICAL GEOGRAPHY

Skill 4.2a   **Demonstrate knowledge of landforms and water, climate, and vegetation and natural resources**

A **landform** is any large physical feature on Earth's surface. Examples of landforms include continents, mountains, valleys, and islands. **Bodies of water** include the five oceans—Atlantic, Pacific, Indian, Arctic, and Southern—along with smaller features such as seas, lakes, rivers, and even ponds and streams.

Weather is the day-to-day condition of the air in a locality; it includes atmospheric conditions such as temperature, air pressure, wind, and moisture or precipitation (rain, snow, hail, or sleet). **Climate** is average weather, or daily weather conditions for a specific region or location over a long or extended period of time. A study of the climate of an area will include information gathered on the area's monthly and yearly temperatures and its monthly and yearly amounts of precipitation.

Natural resources are naturally occurring substances that are considered valuable in their natural form. Natural resources may be renewable, meaning that they regenerate themselves, or nonrenewable, meaning that they cannot be replaced. Renewable resources include solar power, trees, wind, and plant and animal life. Plant life may be known as **vegetation.** Nonrenewable resources include oil, coal, natural gas, and other mineral resources.

See also Skill 1.1b

Skill 4.2b   **Demonstrate understanding of human impact on the environment**

Humans can influence their environments in positive or negative ways. Conservation and restoration efforts help keep natural environment strong even as people rely on them to provide resources. People may build dams, level terrain, or make other changes to the physical terrain of an area.

People generally live in communities or settlements. Settlements begin in areas that offer the natural resources to support life, i.e., food and water. When people gain the ability to manage the environment, populations become more concentrated. Cities are major hubs of human settlement. The concentrations of populations and the divisions of these areas among the various groups that constitute cities can differ significantly. North American cities are different from European cities in terms of shape, size, population density, and modes of transportation. Hubs of human population have a great impact on the environment. People build structures and transportation systems and use up natural resources. Pollution may damage air and water systems.

See also Skill 4.0b

COMPETENCY 4.3 HUMAN GEOGRAPHY

Skill 4.3a   Demonstrate knowledge of human geography, including cultural geography; economic geography; political geography; and population geography

Human geography is the study of how people interact with their physical landscape. Geographers often divide human geography include several basic categories. These include:

Cultural geography is the study of cultural traits and characteristics, such as cultural norms, language, religion, ethnicity, and gender; it also includes the study of cultural patterns and diffusion

Economic geography is the study of how economic systems and activities shape groups; it includes such concerts as economic globalization; primary, secondary, and tertiary activities; and varying levels of economic development around the world.

Political geography is the study of how politics and government shape groups; it includes the study of various forms of government, the relationship between resources and government, and the nature and formation of political boundaries.

Population geography is the study of the composition, spatial patterns, and movement of groups; it includes such concepts as population density, population policies, and immigration.

COMPETENCY 4.4 REGIONAL GEOGRAPHY

Skill 4.4a   Demonstrate knowledge of the geography of the major regions of the world

The **region** is the basic unit of the study of geography. Earth's surface is 70 percent water and 30 percent land. Physical features of the land surface include mountains, hills, plateaus, valleys, and plains. Other minor landforms include deserts, deltas, canyons, mesas, basins, foothills, marshes, and swamps. Earth's water features include oceans, seas, lakes, rivers, and canals.

Mountains are landforms with rather steep slopes that rise 2,000 feet or more above sea level. Mountains are found in groups called mountain chains or mountain ranges. At least one range can be found on six of Earth's seven continents. North America has the Appalachian and the Rocky Mountains; South America, the Andes; Asia, the Himalayas and the Urals; Australia, the Great Dividing Range; Europe, the Alps; and Africa, the Atlas, Ahaggar, and Drakensburg Mountains.

Hills are elevated landforms rising to an elevation of about 500 to 2000 feet. They are found everywhere on earth including Antarctica, where they are covered by ice.

Plateaus are elevated landforms that are usually level on top. Depending on location, they range from being an area that is very cold to one that is cool and healthful. Some plateaus are dry because mountains that keep out any moisture surround them. Some examples include the Kenya Plateau in East Africa, which is very cool. The plateau extending north from the Himalayas is extremely dry while those in Antarctica and Greenland are covered with ice and snow.

Plains are described as areas of flat or slightly rolling land, usually lower than the landforms next to them. Sometimes called lowlands (and sometimes located along **seacoasts**), they support the majority of the world's people. Some are found inland, and many have been formed by large rivers, resulting in extremely fertile soil for the successful cultivation of crops and numerous large settlements of people. In North America, the vast plains areas extend from the Gulf of Mexico north to the Arctic Ocean and between the Appalachian and the Rocky Mountains. In Europe, rich plains extend east from Great Britain into central Europe and on into the Siberian region of Russia. Plains in river valleys are found in China (the Yangtze River valley), India (the Ganges River valley), and Southeast Asia (the Mekong River valley).

Valleys are land areas found between hills and mountains. Some have gentle slopes containing trees and plants; others have steep walls and are referred to as canyons. One example is Arizona's Grand Canyon of the Colorado River.

Deserts are large dry areas of land receiving ten inches or less of rainfall each year. Among the better known deserts are Africa's large Sahara Desert, the Arabian Desert on the Arabian Peninsula, and the desert outback covering roughly one third of Australia.

Deltas are areas of lowlands formed by soil and sediment deposited at the mouths of rivers. The soil is generally very fertile, and most fertile river deltas are important crop-growing areas. One well-known example is the delta of Egypt's Nile River, known for its production of cotton.

Mesas are hills or mountains with steep sides and flat tops. Sometimes plateaus are also called mesas. Basins are considered to be low areas drained by rivers or low spots in mountain areas. Foothills are a low series of hills found between a plain and a mountain range. Marshes and swamps are wet lowlands where plants such as rushes and reeds grow.

Seas are smaller than oceans and are mostly surrounded by land. Some examples include the Mediterranean Sea, found between Europe, Asia, and Africa, and the Caribbean Sea, touching the West Indies, and South and Central America. A lake is a body of (usually) fresh water surrounded completely by land. The Great Lakes in North America are a good example.

Rivers, considered a nation's lifeblood, usually begin as very small streams formed by melting snow and rainfall, flowing from higher to lower land, emptying into a larger body of water, usually a sea or an ocean. Examples of important rivers for the people and countries affected by and/or dependent on them include the Nile, the Niger, and the Congo rivers of Africa; the Rhine, the Danube, and the Thames rivers of Europe; the Yangtze, the Ganges, the Mekong, the Hwang He, and the Irrawaddy rivers of Asia; the Murray-Darling River in Australia; the Rio Grande in Mexico; and the Orinoco River in South America. River systems are made up of large rivers and the numerous smaller rivers, or tributaries, flowing into them. Examples include the vast Amazon River system in South America and the Mississippi River system in the United States.

Canals are man-made water passages constructed to connect two larger bodies of water. Famous examples include the **Panama Canal** across Panama's isthmus, connecting the Atlantic and the Pacific Oceans and the **Suez Canal** in the Middle East between Africa and the Arabian Peninsula, connecting the Red and the Mediterranean seas.

DOMAIN V.   ECONOMICS

COMPETENCY 5.0   MICROECONOMICS I

Skill 5.0a   Understand the definition of economics and identify the factors of production and explain how they are used

Economics is a study of how a society allocates its scarce **resources** to satisfy what are basically unlimited and competing **wants**. Economics can also be defined as the study of the production, distribution, and consumption of goods and resources subject to the constraint of scarce resources. Each of these definitions may look as if they are referring to different things, but both of them are the same. A resource is an input into the production process. Resources are limited in supply. There are not enough of them to produce all of the goods and services that society wants. Resources are called factors of production, and there are four factors of production: **labor, capital, land, and entrepreneurs**.

Labor refers to all kinds of labor used in the production process. It doesn't matter if the labor is skilled or unskilled, part-time or full-time. All laborers are selling their ability to produce goods and services. Capital refers to anything that is made or manufactured to be used in the production process. Included in this definition are plant, equipment, machines, tools, etc. Land is not only land itself but also all natural resources such as lumber, minerals, and oil. The entrepreneur is the individual who has the ability to combine the land, the labor, and the capital to produce a good or a service. Entrepreneurs bear the risks of failure and loss, and they are the ones who will gain from the profits if the product or service is successful.

Every good and service that is produced uses some combination of each of the four inputs. The combination used is called the production process. The production process is classified according to the way the four factors are combined to produce the output. If the production technique uses a lot of machinery and very few laborers, it is called capital intensive. If the production process requires many workers and very little machinery, it is said to be labor intensive.

Skill 5.0b   Demonstrate understanding of scarcity, choice and opportunity cost

Scarcity means that choices have to be made. If society decides to produce more of one good, this means that there are fewer resources available for the production of other goods. Assume a society can produce two goods; let's call them "good X" and "good Y." The society uses resources in the production of each good. If, for example, producing one unit of good X uses three units of resources needed to make good Y, then producing one more unit of good X results in a decrease of three units of good Y. In effect, one unit of good X "costs" three units of good Y. This cost is referred to as opportunity cost.

Opportunity cost is the value of the sacrificed alternative, what had to be given up in order to have the output of good X. Opportunity cost does not refer just to production. Your opportunity cost of studying with this guide is the value of what you are not doing because you are studying, whether it is watching TV, spending time with family, working, or whatever. Every **choice** has an opportunity cost.

Skill 5.0c   Demonstrate knowledge and application of the production possibilities curve to illustrate efficiency, unemployment, and tradeoffs

The scarcity of resources places a constraint on the kinds and amounts of goods and services that a society can produce, distribute, and consume. Because resources are limited in supply, society wants to use them efficiently. People do not want to waste resources. They want to obtain the greatest amount of output possible for their available supply of resources. In order to achieve efficiency, two conditions must be fulfilled: full employment and full production.

Full employment refers to having all resources employed. Idle resources result in lower levels of output. **Full production** means that resources are employed in their most productive capacity. A resource should be doing what it does best in order to make the greatest contribution to output. Full production cannot be achieved without allocative and productive efficiency. A society has achieved allocative efficiency when its resources are being used to produce the goods wanted by that society. Productive efficiency means those goods are being produced without waste, that the lowest-cost method of production is being used.

Production Possibilities Curve

All of these concepts come together in the Production Possibilities Curve (PPC). If we assume a two-good economy, capital goods and consumer goods, with fixed resources and fixed technology, the PCC represents the maximum amount of output that the society can achieve given efficient production. For example, if the economy uses all of its resources to produce capital goods, it can have 500 units of capital goods and no consumer goods. Its choices are as follows: If it produces 100 consumer goods, then it can have only 450 capital goods; 200 consumer goods and 375 capital goods, 300 consumer goods and 275 capital goods, 400 consumer goods and 150 capital goods, and 500 consumer goods and no capital goods. The opportunity cost is the amount of capital goods given up to produce consumer goods.

The first 100 consumer goods have an opportunity cost of 50 capital goods, the second 100 have an opportunity cost of 75 capital goods, and so on. Plotting the above capital-good/consumer-good combinations results in a downward sloping curve that is bowed outward. This is the PPC.

Every point on the curve represents efficient production. Every point represents a trade-off between capital goods and consumer goods. If society wants more consumer goods, it must give up some capital goods.

Points to the left of the curve represent inefficient production. If society is at a point inside the curve, then there is underemployment or unemployment. If society has unemployed resources, it is producing a lower level of output. Employing those unemployed resources means a higher quantity of output, and society will move from the point inside the curve to the curve itself. Society may have full employment of its resources, but not all the resources are employed in their most productive capacity. If this is the case, society is not obtaining the most output it can with its available supply of resources and is still at a point to the left of the PPC. Employing these resources in the most productive capacity will move them to a point on the curve where they are efficient. Points to the right of or outside the PPC are unattainable. The society must experience economic growth by an increase in the supply of factors and/or technological progress.

Skill 5.0d   Demonstrate knowledge of economic systems

Economic systems refer to the arrangements a society has devised to answer what are known as the Three Questions: *What goods to produce? How to produce the goods?* and *For whom are the goods being produced?* Different economic systems answer these questions in different ways.

In a **market economy,** consumers vote for the products they want with their spending. Goods acquiring enough dollar votes are profitable, signaling to the producers that society wants their scarce resources used in this way. This is how the "What" question is answered under the free enterprise system. The producer then works in accordance with the goods consumers want, looking for the most efficient, or lowest–cost, method of production. The lower the firm's costs for any given level of revenue, the higher the firm's profits. This is the way in which the "How" question is answered. The "For whom" question is answered in the marketplace by the determination of the equilibrium price. Price serves to ration the goods to those who can and will transact at the market price or better. Those who can't or won't are excluded from the market. This mechanism results in market efficiency, or obtaining the most output from the available inputs that are consistent with the preferences of consumers. Society's scarce resources are being used the way society wants them to be used.

The opposite of the free enterprise system is the **command economy**. In a command economy, the government makes all of the economic decisions about what goods and services are produced produced, how they are produced, and for whom they are produced. The Soviet Union and other communist countries primarily used a command economy; today, communist nations such as China now have some free enterprise combined with the command system.

In between the two extremes is the **mixed economy.** This system uses both markets and government-controlled planning. Planning is usually used to direct resources at the upper levels of the economy, with markets being used to determine prices of consumer goods and wages. Under a mixed economy, the government may control utility companies or other major industries. Nearly all contemporary nations, including the United States, have some elements of a mixed economy.

Skill 5.0e   **Demonstrate understanding of the concepts of absolute and comparative advantage, free trade, and the impacts of trade barriers such as tariffs and quotas**

Trade theory is based on prices and costs. A nation has an **absolute advantage** in the production of a good when it can produce that good more efficiently than the other nations can. It is comparative advantage that is the basis for international trade. Trade that takes place on the basis of comparative advantage results in lower output prices and higher resource prices. According to trade theory, nations or regions should specialize in the production of the good that they can produce at a relatively lower cost than the other country can. In other words, if in country A one unit of X costs one unit of Y and in country B one unit of X costs three units of Y, good X is cheaper in country A and good Y is cheaper in country B. It takes only one third of a unit of X to produce one unit of Y in country B, whereas it takes one unit of Y in country A. Therefore, country B has the comparative advantage in the production of Y and country A has the comparative advantage in the production of good X. Economic theory states that each country should specialize in the production of the good in which it has the comparative advantage and trade for the other good. This means country B should use all of its resources to produce good Y and trade for good X. Country A should do the opposite and specialize in the production of good X and trade for good Y. Specialization and trade on this basis result in lower prices in both countries/regions and greater efficiency in the use of resources.

Each country will also experience increased consumption, since it is getting the maximum amount of output from its given inputs by specializing according to comparative advantage. Each country or region can consume its own goods and the goods it has traded for.

The introduction of national or international competition into a market can result in greater efficiency if the trade is without restrictions such as tariffs or quotas. Trade barriers cause inefficiencies by resulting in higher prices and lower quantities. A **tariff** is a tax that is added to the price of the import or export. The purpose is to raise the price of the import so people will buy the domestic good. This leads to higher employment levels in the domestic industry and unemployment in the foreign industry. Resources have shifted in the wrong direction because of the tariff. Tariffs are a way of exporting unemployment to the foreign country.

Quotas are limits set on the physical number of units imported or exported. An import quota limits the number of units entering a country; an export quota limits the number of units leaving the country. The result of limiting the quantity is to cause a higher price. Whether the trade barrier is a tariff or a quota, the result is to reduce the volume of international trade. All of the benefits that were achieved with free trade are being lost. The results of trade barriers are lower levels of production, consumption, employment, and income.

Trade theory says that **free trade** is best. It results in the highest level of efficiency for the world. It results in the greatest levels of output, production, consumption, income, and employment. Any form of interference with free trade, such as tariffs and quotas, deters from the highest level of efficiency. The world has less output from its available inputs. There are lower levels of income and employment. This is why there is a movement on for trade liberalization.

Skill 5.0f   Demonstrate understanding of property rights, incentives, and the role of markets

Property rights perform an important function in our economy. Owners of physical or intellectual property own their property under U.S. law. Money shifts through the economy as those property rights are transferred.

Incentives are economic reasons to pursue a particular course of action, such as the drive for profit. Entrepreneurs, for example, are willing to undertake the risk of new business ventures for the incentive of monetary gain. Resources move into higher than normal rate of return industries because they are attracted by the profit potential. Inventors are willing to take the risk of spending time and money trying to come up with new products in the hope of monetary gain. These examples represent the ways financial incentives operate in a market economy.

Without a profit incentive, there would be no reason for firms to spend millions and billions on research and development and technological progress would be almost nonexistent. This was a problem in the planned economies during the Soviet era. Since the means of production were owned by the state, there was no incentive to improve technology or to develop new production processes. The individual had no reason to take the risks involved in entrepreneurial activities because there was nothing in it for him but a letter of commendation. The results were slow, inefficient production processes. In a market economy, the entrepreneur is willing to take the risks and knows there is a good probability that his or her business will fail, but there is also a chance that it will succeed.

The existence of economic profits in an industry functions as a market signal to firms to enter the industry. Economic profits means there is an above normal rate of return in that industry. As the number of firms increases, the market supply curve shifts to the right. Assuming that cost curves stay the same, the expansion continues until the economic profits are eliminated and the industry is earning a normal rate of return. Depending on the level of capital intensity, this process might take a few or many years. The easier it is to shift resources from one industry to another, the faster the process will be. Resources will go where they earn the highest rate of return, especially if they are in a situation where they are earning a lower than normal rate of return.

Profits are the market signal that indicates the proper allocation of resources in accordance with consumer preferences.

Skill 5.0g **Demonstrate understanding of the supply and demand model and its application in the determination of equilibrium price in competitive markets**

In a market economy, the markets function on the basis of supply and demand and if markets are free, the result is an efficient allocation of resources. The seller's supply curve represents the different quantities of a good or service the seller is willing and able to bring to the market at different prices during a given period of time. The seller has to have the good and has to be willing to sell it. The supply curve represents the selling and production decisions the seller makes based on the costs of production. The costs of production of a product are based on the costs of the resources used in its production. The costs of resources are based on the scarcity of the resource. The scarcer a resource is, relatively speaking, the higher its price. A diamond costs more than paper because diamonds are scarcer than paper is. All of these concepts are embodied in the seller's supply curve.

The same thing is true on the buying side of the market. The buyer's preferences, tastes, income, etc.—all of the buying decisions—are embodied in the demand curve. The demand curve represents the various quantities of a good or a service the buyer is willing and able to buy at different prices during a given period of time. The buyer has to want the good and be willing and able to purchase it. He may want a Ferrari but can't afford one; therefore, he is not a part of the relevant market demand.

The demand side of the market is showing us what buyers are willing and able to purchase, and the supply side of the market is showing us what sellers are willing and able to supply. But we don't know anything about what buyers and sellers actually do buy and sell without putting the two sides together. If we compare the buying decisions of buyers with the selling decisions of sellers, the place where they coincide represents the market equilibrium. This is where the demand and supply curves intersect. At this one point, the quantity demanded is equal to the quantity supplied. This price-quantity combination represents an efficient allocation of resources.

Consumers are basically voting for the goods and services that they want with their dollar spending. When a good accumulates enough dollar votes, the producer earns a profit. The existence of profits is the way the market signals the seller that he is using society's resources in a way that society wants them used. Consumers are obtaining the most satisfaction that they can from the way their society's scarce resources are being used. When consumers do not want a good or service, they don't purchase it and the producers don't accumulate enough dollar votes to have profits. **Losses** are the markets' way of signaling that consumers don't want their scarce resources used in the production of that particular good or service and that they want their resources used in some other manner. Firms that incur losses eventually go out of business. They either have a product that consumers don't want or they have an inefficient production process that results in higher costs and, therefore, higher prices. Higher costs than the competitors' means that there is inefficiency in production. All of this occurs naturally in a market economy.

Skill 5.0h   Demonstrate understanding of market surpluses and shortages

Market surpluses and shortages exist when the market is not in equilibrium. This occurs when there is an inequality between quantity supplied and quantity demanded. In other words, the market price does not equate quantity demanded with quantity supplied. Let's look at a situation with a price above the market equilibrium price. The higher price results in a larger quantity supplied, as sellers are willing to supply larger quantities at higher prices than they are at lower prices. The higher price also means that buyers don't want as many units of output. Buyers are willing and able to buy larger quantities at lower prices, not at higher prices. So the higher price results in a situation in which the quantity supplied is greater than the quantity demanded, and there is a **surplus** of the good. The seller begins to offer the surplus goods at a lower price.

As the price comes down, more buyers are willing to buy the good. A lower price results in a larger quantity demanded. So the price continues to fall until the surplus is eliminated and the market is back at equilibrium, where quantity demanded is equal to quantity supplied.

Let's consider the effects of a price below the market equilibrium. At the lower price, sellers do not want to sell as much. The lower price results in a smaller quantity supplied by sellers. The lower price means an increase in quantity demanded by buyers, who want to buy larger quantities at lower prices than at higher prices. The result is a situation in which the quantity demanded exceeds the quantity supplied. There is a **shortage** in the market. Because of the shortage of the good, buyers who want the good begin to bid up the price.

The higher price results in more producers being willing to sell the good. As the price rises, there is a decrease in the quantity demanded of consumers, who will buy fewer units of a good at higher prices than at lower prices. This process of bidding up prices continues until the shortage has been eliminated and that market is back in equilibrium, where the quantity demanded equals the quantity supplied.

Whenever there is a situation of disequilibrium in a market, the market will function to eliminate the inequality. A surplus of goods will cause the price to fall; a shortage of goods will cause the price to rise. A disequilibrium situation will never last for long in a market because the market functions in such a way that it will eliminate the disequilibrium. This is called the rationing function of prices.

Skill 5.0i   Demonstrate understanding of the role of government and the impact of price ceilings, price floors, and taxes on market outcomes

Government may play a role in determining the price of certain goods and services. In a command economy, governments play a large role in this way. In other economic systems, its role is lessened.

A **price floor** is the minimum price that may be charged for a good. For example, the federally mandated minimum wage is a price floor for the cost of labor. A **price ceiling** is the maximum price that may be charged for a good. A rent-controlled apartment is subject to a price ceiling. Price floors and price ceilings can exert different levels of influence. If a price floor or ceiling is within the price range determined by market forces, it has no effect. If a price floor is above the market equilibrium price, it can create a surplus of goods as consumers decline to pay inflated prices. Equally, if a price ceiling is below the market equilibrium price, it can create a shortage as consumers rush to take advantage of low prices.

Taxes have a complex influence on market outcomes. One common government tax, the **tariff,** can directly shape the market. A tariff typically places a tax on imported or exported goods. Tariffs can thus raise the price of imported goods in comparison to domestic goods, making domestic goods more attractive to consumers. However, low tariffs—or the absence of tariffs altogether—encourage increased cross-border trade, which can in turn raise overall demand for a product or result in increased supply and so lower consumer prices.

Skill 5.0j   Demonstrate understanding of the concept of market failure and public policy

A **market failure** takes place when supply and demand are not equal within a market. This results in a lack of equilibrium, inefficient use of resources, and, consequently, problems for the economy. Market failures may be caused by inequalities in market power—the ability to influence prices—the need to allow people to use certain goods despite their inability to pay, and the boom and bust cycle, among others.

Public policy is the regulation and goals outlined by the government in a particular area. In economics, government policy may shape how the government spends its money within the economy, how businesses are regulated, and what laws and regulations control factors such as prices and taxes. Different political parties and leaders tend to have different economic goals, and thus public policy may be inconsistent over time. For example, during the 1920s, public policy supported unfettered business growth and profit-taking. A few years earlier, during World War I, public policy tightly controlled the supply of certain war goods and established price controls and rationing.

COMPETENCY 5.1 MICROECONOMICS II

Skill 5.1a Demonstrate knowledge of types of market structure and the characteristics and behavior of firms in perfect competition, monopoly, oligopoly, and monopolistic competition

There are four kinds of market structures in the output market: **perfect competition, monopoly, monopolistic competition, and oligopoly**. Each of these market structures differs in terms of competition.

Perfect competition is the most competitive of all market structures. For the most part, perfect competition is a theoretical extreme. Products are homogeneous in this market structure. The numerous firms sell a product identical to that sold by all other firms in the industry. There are a large number of buyers and a large number of sellers, and no one buyer or seller is large enough to affect market price. The price is thus determined entirely by supply and demand. This means the individual firm faces a horizontal or perfectly elastic demand curve. Buyers and sellers have full market information, and there are no barriers to entry. A barrier to entry is anything that makes it difficult for firms to enter or leave the industry.

The opposite of perfect competition is a monopoly, a market structure in which only one seller sells a unique product for which there are no substitutes. The firm is the only supplier of the good, so the firm can control the price. High barriers to entry allow monopolies to exist and remain the only producer of a certain product. These barriers to entry, such as a very high fixed cost structure, function to keep new firms from entering the industry. Pure monopolies are rare and are illegal in the U.S. economy.

In between the two extremes are the two market structures that typical U.S. firms fall into. An **oligopoly** is a market structure in which there are a few sellers of products that may be either homogeneous, such as steel, or heterogeneous, such as automobiles. There are high barriers to entry, which is why there are only a few firms in each industry. Each firm has some degree of monopoly power but not as much as a monopolist. The firms of an oligopoly are dependent on one another. Each firm must consider the actions of its rivals when making any decisions. This is referred to as a mutual interdependence in decision making. If Ford offers rebates, Chrysler will also offer rebates to keep its customers.

Monopolistic competition is the market structure you see in shopping centers. There are numerous firms, each selling similar products, but not identical, such as brand name shoes or clothing. Products are close substitutes for one another. Each firm has a small market share, since no one firm is large enough to dominate the industry. Barriers to entry are not as high as in oligopoly, which is why there are more firms. It is relatively easy for most firms to enter or leave the industry.

Skill 5.1b   Demonstrate understanding of factor markets and the determination of income distributions and the returns to factors of production

There are input and output markets in the economy. **Output markets** refer to the market in which goods and services are sold. The **input market** is the market in which factors of production, or resources, are bought and sold. Inputs, or factors of production, fall into four broad categories: land, labor, capital, and entrepreneurs. Each of these four inputs is used in the production of every good and service.

When the consumer goes to the local shoe store to buy a pair of shoes, the shoes are the output and the consumer is taking part in the output market. However, the shoe store is a participant in both the input and the output markets. The sales clerk and the store's workers are hiring out their resource of labor in return for a wage rate. They are participating in the input market. In a market-oriented economy, all of these markets function on the basis of supply and demand, whether they are input or output markets. The equilibrium price is determined where the buying decisions of buyers coincide with the selling decisions of sellers. This is true whether the market is an input market with a market rate of wage or an output market with a market price of the output. This results in the most efficient allocation of resources.

A firm's production decisions are based on its costs. Every product is produced using inputs, or factors of production. The firm utilizes these factors in the input, or resource, market. The production process refers to the method in which resources are combined to produce a good or service. Each factor of production earns its factor income in the resource market.

Labor earns income, also called wages, capital earns interest, land earns rent, and the entrepreneur earns profit. The labor market illustrates the variation in market structure. There can be a competitive market structure, such as the market for unskilled labor. The laborer is the wage-taker with the wage rate more or less given. Labor markets can also be unionized. When there is a union, the wage rate and benefits are negotiated by the employer and the union representatives.

The factor income for capital is **interest,** the rate, or percent, being determined by the intersection of the demand for loanable funds curve and the supply of loanable funds curve. The supply of loanable funds comes from savings. When people save their money, they are delaying consumption. They must receive a payment to induce them to save. This payment is called interest. Lenders pay a price for borrowed funds, which is also interest. The interest rate equates the quantity of loanable funds demanded with the quantity of loanable funds supplied and represents the payment to owners of capital.

Land is a factor that is fixed in supply, so it has a perfectly inelastic supply curve. No matter what the price is, it can't result in an increased supply of land. Rent, the factor payment to land, is thus determined solely by demand.

Profit is the factor income for the entrepreneur. Profit is equal to total revenue minus total cost. It is the entrepreneur's reward for the risk incurred.

See also Skill 5.0a

COMPETENCY 5.2 MACROECONOMICS I

Skill 5.2a   Demonstrate understanding of gross domestic product (GDP) and its components

Macroeconomics refers to the functioning of the economy on the national level and the functioning of the aggregate units that comprise the national economy.

A nation's overall economic performance may be measured by its Gross Domestic Product (GDP). GDP is a monetary measure of the economy's output during a specified time period. The economy's output can be measured in two ways, both of which give the same result: the expenditures approach and the incomes approach. Basically, what is spent on the national output by each category of the economy is equal to what is earned producing the national output by each of the factors of production. The two methods have to be equal.

The macro economy consists of four broad sectors: **consumers, businesses, government,** and the **foreign sector**. In the expenditures approach, GDP is determined by the amount of spending in each sector. GDP is equal to the consumption expenditures of consumers plus the investment expenditures of businesses plus spending of all three levels of government plus the net export spending in the foreign sector.

To complete the tabulation of GDP from the incomes approach, we have to adjust for two nonincome charges. First are indirect business taxes, such as property taxes and sales taxes. Second is depreciation, or the amount of capital that is worn out producing the current term's output. Both indirect business taxes and depreciation are subtracted from the gross amount, and the figure remaining is GDP. This figure is identical to the figure computed in the expenditures approach.

Skill 5.2b   Demonstrate understanding of how unemployment is measured and its causes and consequences

Economists may also measure a society's economic level with other economic indicators. The **unemployment rate** measures the proportion of a society's labor force that cannot find work, despite efforts to do so. The labor force consists of people aged sixteen or older who are working or who want to work and are actively seeking employment. It does not include people who cannot work because they are too young or are institutionalized or those who do not want to work, such as the retired population or the parent that stays home with the children.

There are certain situations that cause these figures to be inaccurate. First, the figures do not account for underemployment or for people who are working part-time while looking for full-time employment. They just ask if the person is employed; it doesn't matter if it is full-time employment or part-time employment. This practice tends to understate the unemployment rate. The figures also do not account for the discouraged worker. This is the worker who has given up trying to find employment. The figures treat him as being out of the labor force because he is not actively looking for employment. This practice also understates the published unemployment figures.

Unemployment tends to rise during times of economic recession. Companies need fewer goods or take in lower profits, resulting in cost-cutting measures through the reduction of labor forces. As companies shrink, fewer new jobs are created, and more people compete for the same openings. This may result in long-term unemployment for some workers. High unemployment rates tend to drag down the economy at large as consumers have less money to spend or experience lowered consumer confidence. This creates a cycle in which companies need fewer products or workers, keeping employment and spending down—thus lowering overall demand for a company's products and the workers that make or service them,

Skill 5.2c   Demonstrate understanding of inflation and its causes and consequences

An economy that is growing too rapidly and has too high a level of spending has **inflation**, a period of rises in the price level as buyers bid up prices to obtain the given supply of goods and services. Inflation results in a dollar with less purchasing power. When there is, say, five percent inflation, this means that the $100 that bought $100 worth of goods last year buys just $95 worth of goods this year. Goods and services are more expensive.

Inflation affects different people in different ways. Some people are affected more than others are. How inflation affects people depends on the individual position. People on fixed incomes feel the effects of inflation more than people who have flexible incomes. Social security benefits are an example of a fixed income. The recipients cannot request a raise like working people can. They lose purchasing power during periods of inflation. The value of tangible assets increases during inflation. If you own assets, such as a house, you experience an increase in your net worth because of inflation. On the other hand, the amount of your savings account is fixed and has less purchasing power because of inflation.

Inflation is a situation in which the appropriate governmental action is to slow down the economy. The government can implement policies that result in less spending in the economy to end the inflation.

See also Skill 5.3b

COMPETENCY 5.3   MACROECONOMICS II

Skill 5.3a   Demonstrate understanding of national income determination using aggregate demand and supply analysis

Aggregate supply and demand analysis considers the interaction of supply and demand at the national level. Aggregate supply comprises all of the broad factors influencing national economic supply, such as labor and resource costs, interest rates, and availability of investment capital. Aggregate demand describes the sum of all national spending and consumption by government, businesses, and individuals, as well as the value of exports.

National income falls into equilibrium when aggregate supply and aggregate demand are in balance. Economic theory suggests that employment is a key factor is determining whether this balance is achieved. When underemployment takes place, the overall equilibrium point of the national economy tends to decline.

Skill 5.3 b   Demonstrate understanding of fiscal policy and its instruments

Fiscal policy consists of changing the level of taxes and government spending to influence the level of economic activity. These are known as **contractionary** monetary and fiscal policy. Contractionary monetary policy will result in the banking system having less money available for loans. Aspects of contractionary monetary policy consist of raising the reserve ratio, raising the discount rate and selling bonds. Contractionary fiscal policy consists of raising taxes and/or decreasing government spending. If there is less money to spend in the economy, it takes the pressure off prices because there is a decrease in aggregate demand, which slows down the economy and stops the rising price level. Expansionary fiscal policy consists of lowering taxes and raising government spending to stimulate a sluggish economy and generate higher levels of employment. Changes take place in government revenues and expenditures when fiscal policy is used.

The **federal budget** is government expenditures and revenues for a fiscal year. The government's budget does not have to balance. Whenever there is a budget deficit the budget deficit has to be financed. The government can finance its deficit by borrowing or by the process of money creation. When government borrows, it sells bonds and uses the funds acquired by the bond sales to finance its deficit. Money creation refers to increasing the reserves in the banking system.

Expansionary fiscal policy—lowering taxes and increasing government spending—puts the budget in a deficit position where government is spending more than it is taking in. Every year that the federal government has a budget deficit that is financed by borrowing, the size of the national debt increases and so do the interest payments on the debt.

See also Skill 5.3c

Skill 5.3c   Demonstrate understanding of the Federal Reserve System and monetary policy

Nations need a smoothly functioning banking system in order to experience economic growth. The **Federal Reserve System** (Fed) provides the framework for the monetary system in the United States. The Fed implements monetary policy through the banking system, and it is a tool used to promote economic stability at the macro level of the economy. There are three components of monetary policy: the **reserve ratio**, the **discount rate**, and **open market operations**. Changes in any of these three components affect the amount of money in the banking system and, thus, the level of spending in the economy.

The reserve ratio refers to the portion of deposits that banks are required to hold as vault cash or on deposit with the Fed. The purpose of this reserve ratio is to give the Fed a way to control the money supply. These funds can't be used for any other purpose. When the Fed changes the reserve ratio, it changes the money creation and lending ability of the banking system. When the Fed wants to expand the money supply, it lowers the reserve ratio, leaving banks with more money to lend. This is one aspect of expansionary monetary policy. When the reserve ratio is increased, banks have less money to make loans with; this is a form of contractionary monetary policy, which leads to a lower level of spending in the economy.

Another way in which monetary policy is implemented is by changing the discount rate. When banks have temporary cash shortages, they can borrow from the Fed. The interest rate on the funds they borrow is called the **discount rate**. Raising and lowering the discount rate is a way of controlling the money supply. Lowering the discount rate encourages banks to borrow from the Fed, instead of restricting their lending to deal with the temporary cash shortage. Encouraging banks to borrow increases their lending ability, which results in a higher level of spending in the economy. Lowering the discount rate is a form of expansionary monetary policy. Discouraging bank lending by raising the discount rate is a form of contractionary monetary policy.

The final tool of monetary policy is called open market operations. This consists of the Fed buying or selling government securities with the public or with the banking system. When the Fed sells bonds, it is taking money out of the banking system. The public and the banks pay for the bonds, thus resulting in fewer dollars in the economy and a lower level of spending. The sale of bonds is a form of contractionary monetary policy that leads to a lower level of spending in the economy. The Fed is expanding the money supply when it buys bonds from the public or the banking system because it is paying for those bonds with dollars that enter the income-expenditures stream. The result of the Fed buying bonds is an increase in the level of spending in the economy.

Skill 5.3d   Demonstrate understanding of the major concepts in international finance and investment

All nations have records of their international transactions. A nation's international transactions are recorded in the balance of payments. The balance of payment consists of two major accounts: the current account, which gives the figures for the exchange of goods, services, and unilateral transfers; and the capital account, which provides the figures for capital flows resulting from the exchange of real and financial assets. The current account contains the balance of trade, which equals a nation's merchandise imports minus its merchandise exports. If the nation's exports are greater than its imports, it has a trade surplus. If its imports are greater than its exports, it has a trade deficit. Adding in the category of exports and imports of services gives the balance on goods and services. Adding unilateral transfers, military expenditures, and other miscellaneous items yields the balance on current account. The capital account consists of strictly financial items in various categories. The last category is statistical discrepancies, which is a balancing entry so that the overall balance of payments always balances. This has to do with floating exchange rate regimes. It is the trade account that is watched closely today.

The exchange rates of most currencies today are determined in a floating exchange rate regime. In a clean float, supply and demand factors for each currency in terms of another are what determine the equilibrium price or the exchange rate. A clean float is a market functioning without any government interference, purely on the basis of demand and supply. Sometimes nations will intervene in the market to affect the value of their currency vis-à-vis the other currency. This situation is referred to as a managed, or dirty, float. A government is not required to intervene to maintain a currency value, as they were under a regime of fixed exchange rates.

A government that intervenes in the currency market now does so because it wants to, not because it is required to intervene to maintain a certain exchange rate value. For example, if the U.S. government thinks the dollar is depreciating too much against the Canadian dollar, the U.S. government will buy U.S. dollars in the open market and pay for them with Canadian dollars. This increases the demand for U.S. dollars and increases the supply of Canadian dollars. The U.S. dollar appreciates, or increases in value, and the Canadian dollar depreciates, or decreases in value, in response to the government intervention. A stronger U.S. dollar means Canadian goods are cheaper for Americans and American goods are more expensive for Canadians.

In the international economy, capital flows where it earns the highest rate of return, regardless of national borders. If the interest rate is higher in London than it is in New York, dollars will be converted into pounds, which results in dollar depreciation and pound appreciation, as capital flows into London in response to the higher interest rate.

The weaker dollar means that U.S. exports are more attractive to foreigners. It also means that U.S. citizens pay a higher price for imports. Markets today are truly international when it comes to capital flows.

Skill 5.3e   Demonstrate understanding of the determinants of long run economic growth

Economic growth can be defined as increases in real output over time. The growth rate is computed as the difference between the growth rates in two periods divided by the growth rate in the first period. Obviously, nations want to see their growth rates increase. Nations experience economic growth when there is an increase in the supply of resources or when they use their existing resources more efficiently. Total output will increase whenever there is an increase in labor and a corresponding increase in productivity. There are many factors that enter into this.

Supply factors are factors that affect the physical capabilities of the economy. They involve the quantity and quality of resources. The first factor is natural resources, and this involves the quantity and quality of natural resources that a country has. Human resources are the second factor, and this involves the quantity and quality of the labor force. The quality of the labor force has to do with productivity or how much output it is producing. Factors affecting productivity have to do with education and training; health; nutrition; government policies in health, safety, and the environment; and the amount and quality of capital such as equipment and machinery available for the worker to use.

This last factor is determined by the level of investment and is called the stock of capital, which is the third factor. Here the capital-to-labor ratio is important because it shows the amount of capital a worker has to work with. If a nation has a growing labor force, it needs growth in its capital stock in order to experience growth. Higher levels of investment lead to higher growth rates. At the same time, the economy needs public investment in order to improve and expand the infrastructure. The last factor is technological progress. Technological progress results in new and more productive production processes. These supply factors determine the economy's ability to grow.

The other side of the growth rate has to do with the demand side of the economy. There must be sufficient demand in the economy to generate economic growth. Aggregate demand has to grow steadily to absorb the increased output that comes with growth. The economy must have full employment and full production in order to experience the highest levels of growth. Not only must all factors be employed; they must be employed in their most productive capacity.

Skill 5.3f   Demonstrate understanding of current national and international issues and controversies

Some current national and international issues and controversies involve employment and trade issues. In today's world, markets are international, and nations are all part of a global economy. No one nation has all of the resources needed to be totally self-sufficient in everything it produces and consumes. Membership in a global economy means that what one nation does affects other nations because economies are linked through international trade, commerce, and finance. They all have open economies. International transactions affect the levels of income, employment, and prices in each of the trading economies. The relative importance of trade is based on what percentage of Gross Domestic Product trade constitutes. In a country like the United States, trade represents only a small percent of the GDP. In other nations, trade may represent more than 50 percent of the GDP. For those countries, changes in international transactions can cause economic fluctuations and many problems.

Trade barriers are one way that economic problems are caused in other countries. Suppose the domestic government is confronted with rising unemployment in the domestic industry due to cheaper foreign imports. Consumers are buying the cheaper foreign import instead of the higher priced domestic good. In order to protect domestic labor, government imposes a tariff, thus raising the price of the more efficiently produced foreign good. The result of the tariff is that consumers buy more of the domestic good and less of the foreign good.

The problem is that the foreign good is the product of the foreign nation's labor. A decrease in the demand for the foreign good means foreign producers don't need as much labor, so they lay off workers in the foreign country. The result of the trade barrier is that unemployment has been exported from the domestic country to the foreign country.

Treaties such as the North American Free Trade Agreement (NAFTA) are a way of lowering or eliminating trade barriers on a regional basis. As trade barriers are lowered or eliminated, labor and output markets change. Some grow, some shrink. These adjustments are taking place now for Canada, the United States, and Mexico. Membership in a global economy adds another dimension to economics, in terms of aiding developing countries and in terms of national policies that are implemented.

COMPETENCY 6.0 SOCIALIZATION

Skill 6.0a **Demonstrate understanding of the role of socialization in society and of positive and negative sanctions in the socialization process**

Socialization is the process by which humans learn the expectations their society has for their behavior so that they might successfully function within that society.

Socialization takes place primarily in children as they are taught and learn the rules and norms of their culture. Children grow up eating the common foods of a culture and develop a taste for these foods, for example. By observing adults and older children, they learn about gender roles and appropriate ways to interact.

Socialization also takes place among adults who change their environment and are expected to adopt new behaviors. Joining the military, for example, requires a different type of dress and behavior than civilian culture. Taking a new job or going to a new school are other examples of situations where adults must re-socialize.

Two primary ways that socialization occurs are through positive and negative sanctions. Positive sanctions are rewards for appropriate or desirable behavior, and negative sanctions are punishments for inappropriate behavior. Recognition from peers and praise from a parent are examples of positive sanctions that reinforce expected social behaviors. Negative sanctions might include teasing by peers for unusual behavior or punishment by a parent.

Sanctions can be either formal or informal. Public awards and prizes are ways a society formally reinforces positive behaviors. Laws that provide for punishment of specific infractions are formal negative sanctions.

COMPETENCY 6.1 PATTERNS OF SOCIAL ORGANIZATION

Skill 6.1a   Demonstrate knowledge of folkways, mores, laws, beliefs, and values

Sociologists have identified three main types of norms that cultures use to define behavioral expectations. Each are associated with different consequences if they are violated. These norms are called folkways, mores, and laws.

Folkways are the informal rules of etiquette and behaviors that a society follows in day-to-day practice. Forming a line at a shop counter or holding a door open for an elderly person are examples of folkways in many societies. Someone who violates a folkway— by pushing to the front of a line, for instance—might be seen as rude but is not thought to have done anything immoral or illegal.

Mores are stronger than folkways in the consequences they carry for not observing them. Examples of mores might include honesty and integrity. Cheating on a test or lying might violate a social more, and a person who does so may be considered immoral.

Laws are formal adoptions of norms by a society with formal punishment for their violation. Laws are usually based on the mores of a society. The more that it is wrong to kill is codified in a law against murder, for example. Laws are the most formal types of social norm, as their enforcement is specifically provided for. Folkways and mores, on the other hand, are primarily enforced informally by the fellow members of a society.

The folkways, mores, and laws of a society are based on the prevailing beliefs and values of that society. Beliefs and values are similar and interrelated systems.

Beliefs are those things that are thought to be true. Beliefs are often associated with religion, but beliefs can also be based on political or ideological philosophies. "All men are created equal" is an example of an ideological belief.

Values are what a society thinks is right and wrong and are often based on and shaped by beliefs. The value that every member of the society has a right to participate in government might be considered to be based on the belief that "all men are created equal," for instance.

Skill 6.1b   Demonstrate understanding of social stratification

Social stratification is the division of a society into different levels based on factors such as race, religion, economic standing, or family heritage. Various types of social stratification may be closely related. For instance, stratification by race may result in people of one race being relegated to a certain economic class as well.

The pioneering sociologist Max Weber theorized that there are three components of social stratification: class, status, and political power.

Social class, as Weber defined it, is based on economics and a person's relationship to the economic market. For example, a factory worker is of a different social class than a factory owner. Social status is based on noneconomic factors such as honor or religion. Political status is based on the relationships and influence one has in the political domain.

The economic revolutionary Karl Marx identified social stratification as the source of exploitation of one level of society by another and based his theory of revolution and economic reform on this belief.

Mobility between social strata may differ between societies. In some societies, a person may move up or down in social class because of changes in one's personal economic fortunes. Political status can change when prevailing political thought shifts. Some systems of stratification are quite formal, however, as in the former caste system in India. In these systems, lines between strata are more rigid, with employment, marriage, and other social activities tightly defined by one's position.

COMPETENCY 6.2   SOCIAL INSTITUTIONS

Skill 6.2a   **Demonstrate understanding of the roles of the following social institutions and of their interactions: the family, education, government, religion, and the economy**

Sociologists have identified five different types of institutions around which societies are structured: family, education, government, religion, and economy. These institutions provide a framework for members of a society to learn about and participate in a society and also allow for a society to perpetuate its beliefs and values to succeeding generations.

The **family** is the primary social unit in most societies. It is through the family that children learn the most essential skills for functioning in their society such as language and appropriate forms of interaction. The size of the family unit varies among cultures, with some including grandparents, aunts, uncles, and cousins as part of the basic family, who may all live together. The family is also related to a society's economic institutions, as families often purchase and consume goods as a unit. A family that works to produce its own food and clothing, as was the case historically in many societies, is also a unit of economic production.

Education is an important institution in a society because it allows for the formal passing on of a culture's collected knowledge. The institution of education is connected to the family because that is where a child's earliest education takes place. Educational traditions within a society are also closely associated with economic institutions because some levels of employment require specific academic achievement.

A society's **governmental** institutions often embody its beliefs and values. Laws, for instance, reflect a society's values by enforcing its ideas of right and wrong. The structure of a society's government can reflect that society's ideals about the role of an individual in his society. A democracy may emphasize that an individual's rights are more important than the needs of the larger society, while a socialist governmental institution may place the needs of the whole group first in importance.

Religion is frequently the institution from which spring a society's primary beliefs and values; religion can be closely related to other social institutions. Many religions have definite teachings on the structure and importance of the family, for instance. In some societies, the head of the government is also the head of the predominant religion, or the government may be operated on religious principles. Historically, formal educational institutions in many societies were primarily religious, and all religions include an educational aspect to teach their beliefs.

A society's **economic** institutions define how an individual can contribute and receive economic reward from his society. In highly developed systems, economic institutions may be closely tied to governmental institutions, each informing and regulating the other. Economic institutions are also linked to family institutions, as workers are often supporting more than one person with their wages. A society's economic institutions might affect its educational goals by creating a demand for certain skills and knowledge.

COMPETENCY 6.3   THE STUDY OF POPULATIONS

Skill 6.3a   Demonstrate knowledge of populations, including the impact on society of changes in population growth and distribution, migration, and immigration

A **population** is a group of people living within a certain geographic area. Populations are usually measured on a regular basis by census, which also measures age, economic, ethnic, and other data. Populations change over time because of many factors, and these changes can have significant impact on cultures.

When a population grows in size, it becomes necessary for it to either expand its geographic boundaries to make room for new people or to increase its density. Population density is simply the number of people in a population divided by the geographic area in which they live. Cultures with a high population density are likely to have different ways of interacting with one another than those with low density, as people live in closer proximity to one another.

As a population grows, its economics need to change. If a population's production or purchasing power does not keep pace with its growth, its economy can be adversely affected. The age distribution of a population can impact the economy as well, if the number of young and old people who are not working is disproportionate to the number of those who are.

Growth in some areas may spur both inward or outward migration. People may wish to move to a geographic region that is less densely populated, or they may flock to densely populated zones seeking jobs. This redistribution of population also places demands on the economy, since infrastructure is needed to connect these new areas to older population centers and land is put to new use.

Populations can grow naturally, as when the rate of birth is higher than the death rate, or by adding new people from other populations through immigration. Immigration is often a source of societal change as people from other cultures bring their institutions and language to a new area. Immigration also impacts a population's educational and economic institutions as immigrants enter the workforce and place their children in schools.

Populations can also decline in number. Two factors of population decline are when the death rate exceeds the birth rate and the migration of people to another area. War, famine, disease, and natural disasters can also dramatically reduce a population. The economic problems from population decline can be similar to those from overpopulation because economic demands may be higher than can be met. In extreme cases, a population may decline to the point where it can no longer perpetuate itself and its members and their culture either disappear or are absorbed into another population.

COMPETENCY 6.4 MULTICULTURAL DIVERSITY

Skill 6.4a Define the concepts of ethnocentrism and cultural relativity

Ethnocentrism and **cultural relativity** are terms used by sociologists to describe two ways of thinking about other cultures in relation to one's own culture. These terms have been expanded to describe two general ways that cultures view themselves and other cultures.

Ethnocentrism is the belief that one's own culture is the central, and usually superior, culture, and it views all other cultures in terms of how they are different. An ethnocentric view usually considers the different practices of other cultures as inferior or even "savage."

Psychologists have suggested that ethnocentrism is a naturally occurring attitude. For the large part, people are most comfortable among other people who share their same upbringing, language, and cultural background, and they are likely to judge other cultural behaviors as alien or foreign.

In the objective study of other cultures, however, ethnocentrism can skew the way the behaviors of other cultures are interpreted. Current thinking is that the study of another culture should not be made in terms of the observer's own culture but only in relation to the other culture's attributes. This is called cultural relativity. Cultural relativity aims to remove the biases and prejudices inherent in ethnocentrism to produce a clearer and more complete picture of other cultures.

Skill 6.4b Demonstrate knowledge of variation in race, ethnicity, and religion

Race is a term most generally used to describe a population of people that share certain common physical traits. Skin color and facial features have traditionally been used to categorize individuals by race. The term has generated some controversy among sociologists, anthropologists, and biologists as to what race and racial variation mean. Biologically speaking, a race of people shares a common genetic lineage. Socially, race can be more complicated to define, with many people identifying themselves as part of a racial group even as others might not, despite shared genetic lineage. This self-perception of race, and the perception of race by others, is perhaps more crucial than any genetic variation when trying to understand the social implications of variations in race.

An **ethnic group** is a group of people who identify themselves as having a common social background and set of behaviors and who perpetuate their culture by traditions of marriage within their own group. Ethnic groups often share a common language and ancestral background and frequently exist within larger populations with which they interact. Ethnicity and race are sometimes interlinked but differ in that many ethnic groups can exist within a population of people thought to be of the same race. Ethnicity is based more on common cultural behaviors and institutions than it is on common physical traits.

Religion can be closely tied to ethnicity, as it is frequently one of the common social institutions shared by an ethnic group. Like ethnicity, religion varies in practices and beliefs even within the large major religions. Some religions and religious sects link their beliefs closely to their ancestry and so are closely linked to the concept of race.

Variations in race, ethnicity, and religion—both real and perceived—are primary ways in which cultures and cultural groups are defined. They are useful in understanding cultures but can also be the source of cultural biases and prejudices.

Eight major religions are commonly practiced today around the world. All of these religions have divisions or smaller sects within them; not one of them is completely unified.

Judaism is the oldest of the eight major religions and was the first to teach and practice the belief in monotheism. Judaism puts an emphasis on learning and law. The Jewish sacred text, known as the Torah, consists of what Christians call the Old Testament, including the ten commandments.

Christianity grew out of Judaism and spread in the first century CE throughout the Roman Empire, despite persecution. A later schism resulted in the western (Roman Catholic) and eastern (Orthodox) parts. Protestant sects developed as part of the Protestant Revolution.

The name "Christian" means one who is a follower of Jesus Christ. Christians follow his teachings and examples, living by the laws and principles of the Bible.

Islam was founded in Arabia by Mohammed, who preached about one God known as Allah. Islam spread through trade, travel, and conquest. Followers of Islam, called Muslims, live by the teachings of their sacred text, the Quran, and of their prophets.

Hinduism was begun by people called Aryans around 1500 BCE and spread into India. The Aryans blended their culture with the culture of the Dravidians, the natives that they conquered. Although this origin theory has long been adhered to by historians, some modern scholars have contested its validity. Today, Hinduism has many sects and promotes worship of hundreds of gods and goddesses and belief in reincarnation. Though forbidden today by law, a prominent feature of Hinduism in the past was a rigid adherence to and practice of the caste system.

Buddhism developed in India from the teachings of Prince Gautama, known as the Buddha, and spread to most of Asia. Its beliefs opposed the worship of numerous deities, the Hindu caste system, and the supernatural. Worshippers must be free of attachment to all things worldly and devote themselves to finding release from life's suffering.

Confucianism is a Chinese philosophy based on the teachings of the Chinese philosopher Confucius. There is no clergy and no belief in a deity or in life after death. It emphasizes political and moral ideas with respect for authority and ancestors. Rulers were expected to govern according to high moral standards.

Daoism is a native Chinese belief system with veneration for many deities and natural phenomena. It teaches all followers to make the effort to achieve the two goals of happiness and immortality. Practices and rituals include meditation, prayer, magic, reciting scriptures, special diets, breath control, beliefs in geomancy, fortune telling, astrology, and communicating with the spirits of the dead.

Shinto is the native religion of Japan; it developed from folk beliefs and the worship of spirits and demons in animals, trees, and mountains. According to its mythology, deities created Japan and its people, which resulted in worshipping the emperor as a god. Shinto never had strong doctrines on salvation or life after death.

Skill 6.4c   Demonstrate understanding of the prevalence and consequences of discrimination and prejudice

Prejudice is the prejudging of something or someone without firsthand experience. It often involves making judgments based on stereotypes or the automatic rejection of a behavior or practice that seems unusual or foreign.

Discrimination takes place when a person or group acts out of prejudice to harm or deny privileges to another person or group. Discrimination takes place between all races and ethnic groups and between men and women at all levels of society. It can occur between individuals or groups.

In some cases, discrimination based on prejudice is official government policy and is reflected in the laws of a society. The United States has a history of official racial discrimination, for example. The enslavement of black people was legal and common until the end of the Civil War in the mid nineteenth century. However, once blacks were freed, dominant prejudicial thinking at the time was that they did not possess the intelligence or moral ability to participate equally in society. As a result, various laws were passed that discriminated against blacks' voting rights, property ownership, and education. These "Jim Crow" laws also regulated how and where blacks could participate in commerce. Jim Crow laws remained in effect in many areas of the United States until the mid 1960s.

These racial prejudices also led to a two-tiered educational system in many parts of the country, with black children segregated into black schools. While these schools were supposed to receive the same support as other schools, in practice they were often poorly maintained and understaffed, and they did not always have current teaching materials.

While official discrimination toward anyone on the basis of race is no longer legal in the United States, it is still common and widespread. Unofficial and *de jure* discrimination can be equally damaging. In competitive situations such as applying for a job, racial or gender prejudices of the person making the hiring decision may result in one or more candidates being discriminated against. A similar scenario may play out when a landlord is deciding to whom an apartment will be rented. This kind of discrimination, when it occurs systematically, has the consequence of relegating groups of people to a lower economic level.

Skill 6.4d   Demonstrate understanding of the concept of pluralism

Cultural pluralism is the simultaneous existence of several cultures and ethnic groups, with each afforded the protection and ability to observe their cultural institutions. It is also sometimes called **multiculturalism**.

The concept of cultural pluralism calls for mutual respect among ethnic groups and cultures, allowing them to exist together and perpetuate their cultures. As an ideal, multiculturalism aims to provide equal access and status to all cultures and so is often described in terms of civil rights, especially in reference to minority ethnic groups. Multiculturalism calls for official support of these ideals in the form of legislation and encourages this approach in school curricula.

Proponents of multiculturalism believe it also leads to the interchange of ideas, art, music, and other cultural features among groups. This interchange, it is thought, furthers the understanding and acceptance of a culturally pluralistic society, reducing prejudice and discrimination.

Multiculturalism can be controversial in some societies, especially those experiencing high rates of immigration. In some of these societies, there are a significant number of people who feel that newcomers should aim to assimilate into the dominant culture as much as possible and that multiculturalism should not receive official support or endorsement. As a result of this countermovement, some groups have passed official language laws and other regulations intended to encourage or require a certain amount of assimilation by immigrants.

COMPETENCY 6.5   SOCIAL PROBLEMS

Skill 6.5a   Demonstrate understanding of major contemporary social problems, including causes, consequences, and proposed solutions

The list of major social problems facing the world is long, with each culture approaching them based on its own values and beliefs. Four broad areas in which social problems are affecting the world today are the global economy, the environment, education, and health.

Economic—Increasing globalization has forced societies to adapt their production and economic strategies to suit these changing conditions. As some countries are able to capitalize on the emergence of new markets, the gap between these rich nations and those poor countries that cannot participate is widening. Economic forces are also attracting immigrants from poorer countries to those with job opportunities, creating social stresses. Rising food costs have raised levels of hunger in many impoverished nations, even causing political disturbances and riots in places such as Mexico and Thailand.

International organizations such as the United Nations and the World Bank have programs to assist developing nations with loans and education so they might join the international economy. Many countries are taking steps to regulate immigration.

Environmental—The effect that the growing world population is having on the global environment is a subject of great concern and some controversy. Increased demand for food and fuel are creating environmental stresses that may have worldwide consequences.

The use of fossil fuels such as coal and natural gas, for instance, are widely thought to be contributing to the gradual warming of the planet by creating "greenhouse gases." The effects of this warming may include the rising of world sea levels and adverse changes in climate. Because oil and gas are non-renewable resources, continual exploration must take place to identify new sources. This drilling itself impacts the environment and presents potential pollution danger from pipelines and oil spills.

The international community has attempted to place limits on the production of greenhouse gases, but not all developed countries have agreed to these protocols. Many countries have placed limits on emissions from factories and automobiles in an effort to reduce the amount of pollution that enters the atmosphere. Alternative clean energy resources are being researched.

Education—As the world's economy changes, educational needs change to provide a skilled workforce, and a society's ability to educate its people is crucial to participating in this economy. Likewise, educational institutions contribute to the artistic, cultural, and academic advancement of a nation.

Disparity in educational opportunities within and between nations can contribute to social and economic disparities. Failure to keep pace with international demands for certain fields of education can leave a country at a disadvantage. In many developing regions, women also face particular challenges in receiving adequate education in comparison to men.

Health—In most developed countries, the population is living longer and placing a higher demand on health-care systems. This in turn places a burden on the larger society as taxes used to support the health-care system rise, in the case of socialized medicine, or health insurance costs increase, as in private systems. In the United States, people who are unemployed or otherwise unable to obtain health insurance are often unable to meet the high costs of health care.

Diseases such as AIDS and other viruses are rampant in some parts of the world. Treatments can be difficult to come by either because of their high costs, or because of a lack of organization to distribute them. International aid organizations exist to provide treatment to disease victims and to assist local governments in developing plans to reduce disease transmission.

COMPETENCY 6.6   HOW CULTURES CHANGE

Skill 6.6a   Demonstrate understanding of how cultures change

Innovation is the introduction of new ways of performing work or organizing societies. It can spur drastic changes in a culture. Prior to the innovation of agriculture, for instance, human cultures were largely nomadic and survived by hunting and gathering their food. Agriculture led directly to the development of permanent settlements and a radical change in social organization. Likewise, technological innovations in the Industrial Revolution of the nineteenth century changed the way work was performed and transformed the economic institutions of western cultures. Recent innovations in communications are changing the way cultures interact today.

Cultural diffusion is the movement of cultural ideas or materials between populations independent of the movement of those populations. Cultural diffusion can take place when two populations are close to one another, through direct interaction, or across great distances, through mass media and other routes. American movies are popular all over the world, for instance. Hockey, a traditional Canadian pastime, has become a popular sport in the United States. These are both examples of cultural diffusion.

Adaptation is the process that individuals and societies go through in changing their behavior and organization to cope with social, economic and environmental pressures.

Acculturation is an exchange or adoption of cultural features when two cultures come into regular direct contact. An example of acculturation is the adoption of Christianity and western dress by many Native Americans in the United States.

Assimilation is the process by which a minority ethnic group largely adopts the culture of the larger group it exists within. These groups are typically immigrants moving to a new country, as with the European immigrants who traveled to the United States at the beginning of the twentieth century. These groups assimilated into a shared U.S. culture.

Extinction is the complete disappearance of a culture. Extinction can occur suddenly, such as from disease, famine, or war, when the people of a culture are completely destroyed. It may occur slowly as a culture adapts, acculturates, or assimilates to the point at which its original features are lost.

Bibliography

Adams, James Truslow. *The March of Democracy*. Vol 1, *The Rise of the Union*. New York: Charles Scribner's Sons, 2006.

Barbini, John & Warshaw, Steven. *The World Past and Present*. New York: Harcourt, Brace, Jovanovich, 2006.

Berthon, Simon & Robinson, Andrew. *The Shape of the World*. Chicago: Rand McNally, 2006.

Bice, David A. *A Panorama of Florida II*, 2nd. ed. (Marceline, Missouri: Walsworth Publishing Co., Inc., 2006).

Bram, Leon, ed. *Funk and Wagnalls New Encyclopedia*. United States of America, 2006.

Burns, Edward McNall & Ralph, Philip Lee. *World Civilizations Their History and Culture*, 5th ed. (New York: W.W. Norton & Company, Inc., 2006).

Dauben, Joseph W. *The World Book Encyclopedia*. Chicago: World Book, Inc. A Scott Fetzer Company, 2006.

De Blij, H.J. & Muller, Peter O. *Geography Regions and Concepts*, 6th ed. (New York: John Wiley & Sons, Inc., 2006).

Encyclopedia Americana. Danbury, Connecticut: Grolier Incorporated, 2006.

Encyclopedia Britannica. Chicago, IL: Britannica, 2012.

Heigh, Christopher, ed. *The Cambridge Historical Encyclopedia of Great Britain and Ireland*. Cambridge: Cambridge University Press, 2006.

Hunkins, Francis P. & Armstrong, David G. *World Geography People and Places*. Columbus, Ohio: Charles E. Merrill Publishing Co. A Bell & Howell Company, 2006.

Jarolimek, John; Anderson, J. Hubert & Durand, Loyal, Jr. *World Neighbors*. New York: Macmillan Publishing Company. London: Collier Macmillan, 2006.

McConnell, Campbell R. *Economics—Principles, Problems, and Policies*, 10th ed. (New York: McGraw-Hill Book Company, 2006).

Millard, Dr. Anne & Vanags, Patricia. *The Usborne Book of World History*. London: Usborne Publishing Ltd., 2006.

Novosad, Charles, ed. *The Nystrom Desk Atlas*. Chicago: Nystrom Division of Herff Jones, Inc., 2006.

Patton, Clyde P.; Rengert, Arlene C.; Saveland, Robert N.; Cooper, Kenneth S. & Cam, Patricia T. *A World View*. Morristown, New Jersey: Silver Burdette Companion, 2006.

Schwartz, Melvin & O'Connor, John R. *Exploring A Changing World*. New York: Globe Book Company, 2006.

The Annals of America: Selected Readings on Great Issues in American History 1620-1968. United States of America: William Benton, 2006.

Tindall, George Brown & Shi, David E. *America—A Narrative History*, 4th ed. (New York: W.W. Norton & Company, 2006).

Todd, Lewis Paul & Curti, Merle. *Rise of the American Nation*, 3rd ed. (New York: Harcourt, Brace, Jovanovich, Inc., 2006).

Tyler, Jenny; Watts, Lisa; Bowyer, Carol; Trundle, Roma & Warrender, Annabelle *The Usbome Book of World Geography*. London: Usbome Publishing Ltd., 2006.

Willson, David H. *A History of England*. Hinsdale, Illinois: The Dryder Press, Inc. 2006.

Sample Test

1. The continent of North America includes all but which of the following countries: *(Rigorous) (Skill 1.1a)*

   A. Canada

   B. Mexico

   C. Cuba

   D. Ecuador

2. Which river is the longest in the United States? *(Easy) (Skill 1.1a)*

   A. Rio Grande

   B. St. Lawrence

   C. Mississippi

   D. Colorado

3. The Mediterranean-type climate is characterized by: *(Average) (Skill 1.1b)*

   A. Hot, dry summers and mild, relatively wet winters

   B. Cool, relatively wet summers and cold winters

   C. Mild summers and winters, with moisture throughout the year

   D. Hot, wet summers and cool, dry winters

4. Which location may be found in Canada? *(Rigorous) (Skill 1.1b)*

   A. 27 N 93 W

   B. 41 N 93 E

   C. 50 N 111 W

   D. 18 N 120 W

5. The climate of southern Florida is the _____ type. *(Average) (Skill 1.1b)*

   A. humid subtropical

   B. marine west coast

   C. humid continental

   D. tropical wet-dry

6. Apartments built out of cliff faces; shared government by adult citizens; absence of aggression toward other groups and perhaps the oldest representative government in the world. These factors characterize the Native American group known as: *(Average) (Skill 1.2b)*

   A. Pueblos

   B. Comanches

   C. Seminoles

   D. Sioux

7. The Native Americans of the eastern woodlands lived on: *(Average) (Skill 1.2b)*

   A. Buffalo and crops such as corn, beans, and sunflowers

   B. Chiefly farming of squash, beans, and corn

   C. A variety of game (deer, bear, moose) and crops (squash, pumpkins, corn)

   D. Wolves, foxes, polar bears, walruses, and fish

8. One tribe of Indians formed a representative government referred to as the _____ Confederacy. *(Easy) (Skill 1.2b)*

   A. Cherokee

   B. Seminole

   C. Wampanoag

   D. Iroquois

9. Columbus first reached western hemisphere lands in what is now: *(Easy) (Skill 1.3a)*

   A. Florida

   B. Bermuda

   C. Puerto Rico

   D. Bahamas

10. Which one of the following is *not* a reason why Europeans came to the New World? *(Rigorous) (Skill 1.3b)*

    A. To find resources in order to increase wealth

    B. To establish trade

    C. To increase a ruler's power and importance

    D. To spread Christianity

11. How many oceans cover Earth? *(Easy) (Skill 1.1b)*

    A. 3

    B. 4

    C. 5

    D. 6

12. During the early years of colonization in New France, what commodity was the livelihood for many people, both in New France and in France? *(Easy) (Skill 1.3c)*

    A. Wampum

    B. Fish

    C. Gold

    D. Fur

13. The middle colonies of the Americas were: *(Average) (Skill 1.3d)*

   A. Maryland, Virginia, North Carolina

   B. New York, New Jersey, Pennsylvania, Delaware

   C. Rhode Island, Connecticut, New York, New Jersey

   D. Vermont and New Hampshire

14. Slavery arose in the southern colonies partly as a perceived economical way to: *(Average) (Skill 1.3d)*

   A. Increase the owner's wealth through human beings used as a source of exchange

   B. Cultivate large plantations of cotton, tobacco, rice, indigo, and other crops

   C. Provide Africans with humanitarian aid, such as health care, Christianity, and literacy

   D. Keep ships' holds full of cargo on two out of three legs of the "triangular trade" voyage

15. Which of the following was *not* a leading a factor leading to the American Revolution? *(Rigorous) (Skill 1.4a)*

   A. The desire for an imperial state

   B. Belief in equality

   C. Belief in no taxation without representation

   D. The desire for freedom

16. France decided in 1777 to help the American colonies in their war against Britain. This decision was mostly based on: *(Rigorous) (Skill 1.4a)*

   A. The naval victory of John Paul Jones over the British ship *Serapis*

   B. The survival of the terrible winter at Valley Forge

   C. The success of colonial guerilla fighters in the South

   D. The defeat of the British at Saratoga

17. **The Bill of Rights was mostly written by:** *(Average) (Skill 1.4b)*

   A.   Thomas Jefferson

   B.   James Madison

   C.   George Washington

   D.   Alexander Hamilton

18. **Which issue most divided the members of the nation's first two political parties?** *(Rigorous) (Skill 1.5a)*

   A. The exact duties of each branch of government

   B. The outcome of the election of 1800

   C. The relative qualities of Hamilton and Jefferson

   D. The proper application of the Constitution

19. **The Second Great Awakening refers to:** *(Easy)(Skill 1.5b)*

   A.   Religious movements

   B.   Political movements

   C.   Military movements

   D.   Industrialization

20. **The area of the United States was effectively doubled through purchase of the Louisiana Territory under which President?** *(Easy) (Skill 1.5b)*

   A.   John Adams

   B.   Thomas Jefferson

   C.   James Madison

   D.   James Monroe

21. **Which one of the following was *not* a reason why the United States went to war with Great Britain in 1812?** *(Rigorous) (Skill 1.5b)*

   A. Resentment over the sale, exploration, and settlement of the Louisiana Territory

   B. The westward movement of farmers because of the need for more land

   C. Canadian fur traders were agitating the northwestern Indians to fight American expansion

   D. Britain continued to seize American ships on the high seas and force American seamen to serve aboard British ships

22. Under the new Constitution, the most urgent of the many problems facing the new federal government was that of: *(Average) (Skill 1.5c)*

    A. Maintaining a strong army and navy

    B. Establishing a strong foreign policy

    C. Raising money to pay salaries and war debts

    D. Setting up courts, passing federal laws, and providing for law enforcement officers

23. What was a major source of contention between American settlers in Texas and the Mexican government in the 1830s and 1840s? *(Rigorous) (Skill 1.6a)*

    A. The Americans wished to retain slavery, which had been outlawed in Mexico

    B. The Americans had agreed to learn Spanish and become Roman Catholic, but failed to do so

    C. The Americans retained ties to the United States, and Santa Ana feared the power of the U.S.

    D. All of the above were contentious issues between American settlers and the Mexican government

24. The right of the states to declare invalid any act of Congress that they felt was unjust was known as the: *(Average) (Skill 1.6a)*

    A. Declaration of Independence

    B. Missouri Compromise

    C. Monroe Doctrine

    D. Doctrine of Nullification

25. The belief that the United States should control all of North America was called: *(Easy) (Skill 1.6b)*

    A. Westward Expansion

    B. Pan Americanism

    C. Manifest Destiny

    D. Nationalism

26. The "Trail of Tears" relates to: *(Average) (Skill 1.6b)*

    A. The removal of the Cherokees from their native lands to Oklahoma Territory

    B. The revolt and subsequent migration of the Massachusetts Pilgrims under pressure from the Iroquois

    C. The journey of the Nez Perce under Chief Joseph before their capture by the U.S. Army

    D. The 1973 standoff between federal marshals and Native Americans at Wounded Knee, S.D.

27. The tensions between the North and the South before the Civil War mostly stemmed from: *(Rigorous) (Skill 1.7a)*

    A. Political differences

    B. Cultural differences

    C. Economic differences

    D. Historical differences

28. Of the following groups of states, which were slave states? *(Average) (Skill 1.7a)*

    A. Delaware, Maryland, Missouri

    B. California, Texas, Florida

    C. Kansas, Missouri, Kentucky

    D. Virginia, West Virginia, Indiana

29. What was one social effect of the expansion of the railroad during the nineteenth century? *(Rigorous) (Skill 1.8a)*

    A. Increased immigration from Europe

    B. Expanded trade between the eastern and western United States

    C. The decline of labor unions

    D. The establishment of standardized time zones

30. What event sparked a great migration of people from all over the world to California in the 1840s? *(Easy) (Skill 1.8a)*

    A. The birth of labor unions

    B. California statehood

    C. The invention of the automobile

    D. The gold rush

31. **What technological development most influenced the growth of the American West?** *(Rigorous) (Skill 1.8a)*

    A. The steamboat

    B. The cotton gin

    C. The telegraph

    D. The railroad

32. **The Industrial Revolution contributed directly to all of the following except:** *(Rigorous) (Skill 1.8b)*

    A. Decline of the agricultural economy

    B. Urbanization

    C. Economic growth

    D. The Civil War

33. **Increased immigration in the late 1800s led to all of the following except** *(Rigorous) (Skill 1.8c)*

    A. The rise of political machines

    B. The growth of factories

    C. The construction of the Transcontinental Railroad

    D. The increase of the overall urban population

34. **The American labor union movement started gaining new momentum:** *(Rigorous) (Skill 1.8d)*

    A. During the building of the railroads

    B. After 1865 with the growth of cities

    C. With the rise of industrial giants such as Carnegie and Vanderbilt

    D. During the war years of 1861–1865

35. **Which of the following was *not* a factor in the United States' entry into World War I?** *(Rigorous) (Skill 1.9b)*

    A. The closeness of the presidential election of 1916

    B. The German threat to sink all allied ships, including merchant ships

    C. The desire to preserve democracy as practiced in Britain and France as compared to the totalitarianism of Germany

    D. The sinking of the *Lusitania* and the *Sussex*

36. The stock market crash of 1929 directly contributed to the beginning of: *(Average) (Skill 1.9d)*
   A. World War I

   B. The Marshall Plan

   C. The Great Depression

   D. The Second Industrial Revolution

37. The international organization established to work for world peace at the end of the First World War was the: *(Easy) (Skill 1.10a)*

   A. League of Nations

   B. United Federation of Nations

   C. United Nations

   D. United World League

38. What Supreme Court ruling ended school segregation? *(Average) (Skill 1.10c)*

   A. *Miranda v Arizona*

   B. *Mapp v Ohio*

   C. *Brown v Board of Education*

   D. *Marbury v Madison*

39. In issuing an ultimatum for Soviet ships not to enter Cuban waters in October 1962, President John F. Kennedy, as part of his decision, used the provisions of the: *(Rigorous) (Skill 1.10b, 1.11a)*

   A. Monroe Doctrine

   B. Declaration of the Rights of Man

   C. Geneva Convention

   D. Truman Doctrine

40. Which of the following developments is most closely associated with the Neolithic Age? *(Average) (Skill 2.1a)*

   A. Human use of fire

   B. First use of stone chipping instruments

   C. Domestication of plants

   D. Development of metallurgical alloys

41. China first became important during the same era as the rise the *(Average) (Skill 2.1b)*

   A. Egyptians

   B. Japanese

   C. Greeks

   D. Maya

42. Which ancient civilization is credited with being the first to develop irrigation techniques through the use of canals, dikes, and devices for raising water? *(Average) (Skill 2.1b)*

    A. The Sumerians

    B. The Egyptians

    C. The Babylonians

    D. The Akkadians

43. The politics of classical Athens is best described by which of the following? *(Average) (Skill 2.1c)*

    A. Limited democracy, including both slaves and free men

    B. One-man dictatorial rule

    C. Universal democracy among free owners of property

    D. Oligarchy with a few families controlling all decisions

44. The first ancient civilization to introduce and practice monotheism was the: *(Easy) (Skill 2.1c)*

    A. Sumerians

    B. Hebrews

    C. Phoenicians

    D. Minoans

45. The principle of zero in mathematics is the discovery of the ancient civilization found in: *(Average) (Skill 2.1c)*

    A. Egypt

    B. Persia

    C. India

    D. Babylon

46. An early cultural group was so skillful in navigating on the seas that they were able to sail at night guided by stars. They were the: *(Average) (Skill 2.1c)*

    A. Greeks

    B. Persians

    C. Minoans

    D. Phoenicians

47. A historian might compare the governmental systems of the Roman Empire and the twentieth century United States with regard to which of the following commonalities? *(Average) (Skill 2.1c)*

    A. Totalitarianism

    B. Technological development

    C. Constitutional similarities

    D. Republican federalism

48. Development of a solar calendar, invention of the decimal system, and contributions to the development of geometry and astronomy are all the legacy of: *(Average) (Skill 2.1c)*

A. The Babylonians

B. The Persians

C. The Sumerians

D. The Egyptians

49. Chinese civilization is generally credited with the original development of which of the following sets of technologies: *(Average) (Skill 2.1d)*

A. Movable type and mass production of goods

B. Wool processing and domestication of the horse

C. Paper and gunpowder manufacture

D. Leather processing and modern timekeeping

50. Which of these empires did *not* control Western Africa through powerful trading connections? *(Rigorous) (Skill 2.1d)*

A. Ghana

B. Mali

C. Berber

D. Songhai

51. During the Age of Exploration, who first desired to find a completely nautical route to Asia?: *(Average) (Skill 2.2a)*

A. The Portuguese

B. The Spanish

C. The English

D. The Dutch

52. The period of intellectual and artistic rebirth in Europe was called: *(Easy) (Skill 2.2a)*

A. Age of Exploration

B. Colonialism

C. Renaissance

D. Imperialism

53. The ideas and innovations of the period of the Renaissance were spread throughout Europe mainly because of: *(Rigorous) (Skill 2.2a)*

A. Extensive exploration

B. Craft workers and their guilds

C. The invention of the printing press

D. Increased travel and trade

54. **The first explorer to reach India by sailing around the southern tip of Africa was:** *(Average) (Skill 2.2a)*

   A. Amerigo Vespucci

   B. Vasco da Gama

   C. Ferdinand Magellan

   D. John Cabot

55. **Which of these was *not* a cause of the Protestant Revolution?** *(Rigorous (Skill 2.2a)*

   A. The rise of Calvinism

   B. The sale of religious offices

   C. The growth of nationalism

   D. The power of absolute monarchs

56. **Who is considered to be the most important figure in the spread of Protestantism across Switzerland?** *(Average) (Skill 2.2a)*

   A. Calvin

   B. Zwingli

   C. Munzer

   D. Leyden

57. **Bartholomeu Diaz discovered which cape near the southern tip of Africa?** *(Average) (Skill 2.2a)*

   A. Cape Horn

   B. Cabo Bojador

   C. Cape of Good Hope

   D. Cape Hatteras

58. **Which of these rulers led classical India?** *(Easy) (Skill 2.2a)*

   A. Akbar

   B. Asoka

   C. Genghis Khan

   D. Mansa Musa

59. **What conclusion is best supported by the lengthy search for a Northwest Passage?** *(Rigorous) (Skill 2.2a)*

   A. Europeans had a thirst for knowledge and exploration

   B. Europeans did not believe geographical information from native peoples

   C. Europeans wanted a water route to Asia

   D. Europeans had little interest in long-distance trade

60. In Western Europe, the achievements of the Renaissance were unsurpassed and made these countries outstanding cultural centers on the continent. All of the following were accomplishments except: *(Rigorous) (Skill 2.2a)*

A. Invention of the printing press

B. A rekindling of interest in the learning of classical Greece and Rome

C. Growth in literature, philosophy, and art

D. Better military tactics

61. Which event most influenced the rise of the French Revolution? *(Rigorous) (Skill 2.2b)*

A. Industrial Revolution

B. American Revolution

C. Protestant Revolution

D. Glorious Revolution

62. Colonial expansion by Western European powers in the 18th and 19th centuries was due primarily to: *(Average) (Skill 2.2b)*

A. Building and opening the Suez Canal

B. The Industrial Revolution

C. Marked improvements in transportation

D. Complete independence of all the Americas and loss of European domination and influence

63. Great Britain became the center of technological and industrial development during the nineteenth century chiefly on the basis of: *(Average) (Skill 2.2b)*

A. Central location relative to the population centers of Europe

B. Colonial conquests and military victories over European powers

C. Reliance on exterior sources of financing

D. Resources of coal and production of steel

64. It can be reasonably stated that the change in the United States from primarily an agricultural country into an industrial power was due to all of the following except: *(Rigorous) (Skill 2.2b)*

   A. Tariffs on foreign imports

   B. Millions of hardworking immigrants

   C. An increase in technological developments

   D. The change from steam to electricity for powering industrial machinery

65. What was an immediate effect of the Russian Revolution? *(Rigorous) (Skill 2.3a)*

   A. World War I began

   B. Russia left World War I

   C. The Cold War began

   D. Russia declared war on Germany in World War II

66. Of all the major causes of both World Wars I and II, the most significant one is considered to be: *(Rigorous) (Skill 2.3a)*

   A. Extreme nationalism

   B. Military buildup and aggression

   C. Political unrest

   D. Agreements and alliances

67. The conflict between fascism and communism mostly stemmed from disagreements over: *(Rigorous) (Skill 2.3a)*

   A. The role of government

   B. Control of the means of production

   C. The importance of the military

   D. The emphasis on national or international goals

68. Since World War II, population growth has mostly been a problem because of *(Rigorous) (Skill 2.3a)*

   A. Inadequate technological development

   B. Declining global health

   C. Limited food supply

   D. Decreasing literacy rates

69. The Cold War mostly stemmed from *(Rigorous) (Skill 2.3a)*

   A. Geographical and social issues

   B. Political and economic disagreements

   C. Ethical and intellectual divides

   D. Governmental and cultural splits

70. Increased _____ is both a cause and an effect of greater economic interdependence. *(Rigorous) (Skill 2.3b)*

A. globalization

B. consumer demand

C. scarcity

D. unemployment

71. Which of these technological developments has had the least significant impact in the 21st century? *(Rigorous) (Skill 2.3b)*

A. Automobile

B. Internet

C. Cell phone

D. E-mail

72. Which force has *not* shaped changing world events in the 21st century? *(Rigorous) (Skill 2.3b)*

A. Communist expansion

B. Global terrorism

C. Religious extremism

D. Arab democratic movements

73. What is *not* a purpose government laws? (Rigorous) (Skill 3.0a)

A. Maintain order

B. Catch criminals

C. Keep people safe

D. Establish guidelines for behavior

74. Who first suggested the idea of the "social contract"? *(Easy) (Skill 3.0b)*

A. Jean-Jacques Rousseau

B. Thomas Hobbes

C. Niccolo Machiavelli

D. William Shakespeare

75. Public administration, such as public officials in the areas of budgets, accounting, distribution of public funds, and personnel management would be a part of the field of: *(Average) (Skill 3.0b)*

A. Anthropology

B. Sociology

C. Law and taxation

D. Political science and economics

76. **A political scientist might use all of the following except:** *(Rigorous) (Skill 3.0b)*

   A. An investigation of government documents

   B. A geological timeline

   C. Voting patterns

   D. Polling data

77. **In the United States, checks and balances refers to:** *(Average) (Skill 3.1a)*

   A. The ability of each branch of government to limit the actions of others

   B. The creation of a series of guaranteed rights

   C. The balance of power between the federal government and the states

   D. The recognition of minority rights alongside majority rule

78. **In the Constitutional system of checks and balances, a primary "check" which accrues to the president is the power of:** *(Average) (Skill 3.1a)*

   A. Executive privilege

   B. Approval of judges nominated by the Senate

   C. Veto of Congressional legislation

   D. Approval of judges nominated by the House of Representatives

79. **The term that best describes how the Supreme Court can block laws that may be unconstitutional from being enacted is:** *(Average) (Skill 3.1a)*

   A. Jurisprudence

   B. Judicial Review

   C. Exclusionary Rule

   D. Right of Petition

80. **Constitutions are formally changed by:** *(Average) (Skill 3.1a)*

   A. Amendments

   B. Court decisions

   C. Laws

   D. Referendums

81. Collectively, the first ten amendments to the Constitution are known as the: *(Easy) (Skill 3.1a)*

A. Articles of Confederation

B. Mayflower Compact

C. Bill of Rights

D. Declaration of the Rights of Man

82. Why is the system of government in the United States referred to as a federal system? *(Average) (Skill 3.1d)*

A. There are different levels of government

B. There is one central authority in which all governmental power is vested

C. The national government cannot operate except with the consent of the governed

D. Elections are held at stated periodic times, rather than as called by the head of the government

83. Which branch is responsible for carrying out the laws of the country? *(Easy) (Skill 3.1b)*

A. Judicial

B. Executive

C. Legislative

D. Supreme Court

84. Which of the following is *not* a branch of government? *(Rigorous) (Skill 3.1b)*

A. Executive branch

B. Federal branch

C. Legislative branch

D. Judicial branch

85. The _____ branch of government is made up of House of Representatives and the Senate. *(Easy) (Skill 3.1b)*

A. judicial

B. executive

C. legislative

D. supreme Court

86. Which one of the following is *not* a function or responsibility of the U.S. political parties? *(Rigorous) (Skill 3.1e)*

A. Conducting elections or the voting process

B. Obtaining funds needed for election campaigns

C. Choosing candidates to run for public office

D. Making voters aware of issues and other public affairs information

87. Which of the following are *not* local governments in the United States? *(Rigorous) (Skill 3.1e)*

A. Cities

B. Townships

C. School boards

D. All of these are forms of local government

88. The head of state of a monarchy might be called a: *(Easy) (Skill 3.2a)*

A. President

B. King

C. Prime minister

D. Dictator

89. _____ is the effort to create, by dictatorial means, a viable national society in which competing interests are to be adjusted to each other by being entirely subordinated to the service of the state although it will tolerate some private ownership of the means of production. *(Easy) (Skill 3.2a)*

A. Dictatorship

B. Parliamentary system

C. Anarchism

D. Fascism

90. The movement of cultural ideas or materials between populations is known as: *(Rigorous)(Skill 4.0c)*

A. Adaptation

B. Innovation

C. Acculturalization

D. Cultural diffusion

91. Absolute location is identified by: *(Average) (Skill 4.0a)*

A. Direction

B. Latitude and longitude

C. City and state

D. Regional characteristics

92. All of these are examples of human-environment interaction except: *(Rigorous) (Skill 4.0b)*

A. Agriculture

B. Map-making

C. Mining

D. Building suburbs

93. The influence of physical characteristics on how people live is part of which theme of geography? *(Rigorous) (Skill 4.0b)*

    A. Regions

    B. Location

    C. Movement

    D. Human-environment interaction

94. Relief maps can be depicted in different ways. One way is the use of: *(Easy) (Skill 4.1a)*

    A. Great Circle Route

    B. Opisometer

    C. Meridians

    D. Contour Lines

95. Meridians, or lines of longitude, not only help in pinpointing locations, but are also used for: *(Average) (Skill 4.1b)*

    A. Measuring distance form the poles

    B. Determining direction of ocean currents

    C. Determining the time around the world

    D. Measuring distance to the equator

96. The study of spatial patterns would be used by people in the field of: *(Easy) (Skill 4.1c)*

    A. Political science

    B. Anthropology

    C. Geography

    D. Sociology

97. Which of these is the best example of a thematic map? *(Average) (Skill 4.1c)*

    A. A map showing election results

    B. A map showing rivers

    C. A map showing state capitals

    D. A map showing landforms

98. What information might a map key best show? *(Average) (Skill 4.1d)*

    A. Population density

    B. Map distortion

    C. Boundary location

    D. Cardinal direction

99. A physical geographer would be concerned with which of the following groups of terms? *(Average) (Skill 4.2a)*

A. Landform, biome, precipitation

B. Scarcity, goods, services

C. Nation, state, administrative subdivision

D. Cause and effect, innovation, exploration

100. Which of these is *not* a division of human geography? *(Rigorous) (Skill 4.3a)*

A. Cultural geography

B. Economic geography

C. Physical geography

D. Population geography

101. Which question might a cultural geographer ask? *(Rigorous) (Skill 4.3a)*

A. What is the highest point in this nation?

B. How does religion shape this region?

C. Which political system is used in this country?

D. What level of economic development has this region reached?

102. How do deltas most shape human activity? *(Rigorous) (Skill 4.4a)*

A. By providing adequate farmland

B. By discouraging settlement

C. By offering drinking water supplies

D. By serving as natural borders between countries

103. Which of the following is not a river? *(Rigorous) (Skill 4.4a)*

A. Yangtze

B. Rio Grande

C. Arctic

D. Ganges

104. The basic unit of study in geography is: *(Easy) (Skill 4.4a)*

A. The region

B. A country

C. One mile

D. A culture

105. **An economist might engage in which of the following activities?** *(Rigorous) (Skill 5.0a)*

A. An observation of the historical effects of a nation's banking practices

B. The application of a statistical test to a series of data

C. Introduction of an experimental factor into a specified population to measure the effect of the factor

D. An economist might engage in all of these

106. **Economics is best described as:** *(Average) (Skill 5.0b)*

A. The study of how money is used in different societies

B. The study of how different political systems produce goods and services

C. The study of how human beings use limited resources to supply their necessities and wants

D. The study of how human beings have developed trading practices through the years

107. **In order to achieve efficiency, two conditions must be fulfilled:** *(Average) (Skill 5.0c)*

A. Low unemployment and low inflation

B. Full employment and full production

C. Full employment and stable monetary supply

D. Access to resources and full production

108. **Capitalism and communism are alike in that they are both:** *(Average) (Skill 5.0d)*

A. Organic systems

B. Political systems

C. Centrally planned systems

D. Economic systems

109. **Which of the following is *not* a significant influence within the free enterprise system?** *(Rigorous) (Skill 5.0d)*

A. Government planning

B. Markets

C. Entrepreneurs

D. Innovation

110. In a command economy: *(Average) (Skill 5.0d)*

    A. The open market determines how much of a good is produced and distributed

    B. The government determines how much of a good is produced and distributed

    C. Individuals produce and consume a specified good as commanded by their needs

    D. The open market determines the demand for a good, and then the government produces and distributes the good

111. One method of trade restriction used by some nations is: *(Easy) (Skill 5.0e)*

    A. Limited treaties

    B. Floating exchange rate

    C. Bill of exchange

    D. Import quotas

112. The interaction of supply and demand most affect: *(Rigorous) (Skill 5.0g)*

    A. Scarcity

    B. Prices

    C. Production

    D. Entrepreneurship

113. What is a major difference between monopolistic competition and perfect competition? *(Rigorous) (Skill 5.1a)*

    A. Perfect competition has many consumers and suppliers, while monopolistic competition does not

    B. Perfect competition provides identical products, while monopolistic competition provides similar, but not identical, products

    C. Entry to perfect competition is difficult, while entry to monopolistic competition is relatively easy

    D. Monopolistic competition has many consumers and suppliers, while perfect competition does not

114. Of the following, the best example of an oligopoly in the United States is: *(Average) (Skill 5.1a)*

    A. Automobile industry

    B. Food services

    C. Cleaning services

    D. Clothing manufacturing

115. Savings most contributes to the growth of the economy by *(Rigorous) (Skill 5.1b)*

   A. Decreasing consumer spending

   B. Increasing the overall money supply

   C. Providing funds for investment

   D. Encouraging inflation

116. The _____ is a monetary measure of the economy's output during a spedivied time period and is used by all nations to measure and compare national production. *(Easy) (Skill 5.2a)*

   A. float rate

   B. gross domestic product (GDP)

   C. unemployment rate

   D. national output

117. Inflation is the result of the economy _____? *(Average) (Skill 5.2c)*

   A. expanding too slowly

   B. remaining stable

   C. expanding too quickly

   D. expanding in conjunction with the unemployment rate

118. As a sociologist, you would be most likely to observe: *(Average) (Skill 6.0a)*

   A. The effects of an earthquake on farmland

   B. The behavior of rats in sensory-deprivation experiments

   C. The change over time in Babylonian obelisk styles

   D. The behavior of human beings in television focus groups

119. All of the following are basic institutions around which societies are organized except: *(Rigorous) (Skill 6.2a)*

   A. Education

   B. Religion

   C. Corporation

   D. Family

120. In sociology, populations are usually measured by all of the following EXCEPT: *(Rigorous) (Skill 6.3a)*

A. People's jobs

B. People's education levels

C. People's interaction with the natural environment

D. People's relative health levels

121. Which term best relates to the naturally occurring attitude that people, for the most part, are most comfortable with others like themselves? *(Average) (Skill 6.4a)*

A. Pluralism

B. Discrimination

C. Ethnocentrism

D. Racial Bias

122. The native metaphysical outlook of Japan, usually characterized as a religion, is: *(Rigorous) (Skill 6.4b)*

A. Daoism

B. Shinto

C. Nichiren Shoju

D. Shaolin

123. The world religion which includes a caste system is: *(Easy) (Skill 6.4b)*

A. Buddhism

B. Hinduism

C. Sikhism

D. Jainism

124. What concept calls for mutual respect between ethnic groups and cultures, allowing them to exist together and perpetuate their cultures? *(Average) (Skill 6.4d)*

A. Syllogism

B. Conformance

C. Discrimination

D. Cultural pluralism

125. Which of the following is *not* one of the four broad areas affecting modern social problems? *(Rigorous) (Skill 6.5a)*

A. Assimilation

B. Environment

C. Education

D. Health

Answer Key

1.	D	34.	B	67.	D	100.	C
2.	C	35.	A	68.	C	101.	B
3	A	36.	C	69.	B	102.	A
4.	C	37.	A	70.	A	103.	C
5.	A	38.	C	71.	A	104.	A
6.	A	39.	A	72.	A	105.	D
7.	C	40.	C	73.	B	106.	C
8.	D	41.	A	74.	A	107.	B
9.	D	42.	A	75.	D	108.	D
10.	B	43.	C	76.	B	109.	A
11.	C	44.	B	77.	A	110.	B
12.	D	45.	C	78.	C	111.	D
13.	B	46.	D	79.	B	112.	B
14.	B	47.	D	80.	A	113.	B
15.	A	48.	D	81.	C	114.	A
16.	D	49.	C	82.	A	115.	C
17.	B	50.	C	83.	B	116.	B
18.	D	51.	A	84.	B	117.	C
19.	A	52.	C	85.	C	118.	D
20.	B	53.	C	86.	A	119.	C
21.	A	54.	B	87.	D	120.	C
22.	C	55.	A	88.	B	121.	C
23.	D	56.	A	89.	D	122.	B
24.	D	57.	C	90.	D	123.	B
25.	C	58.	B	91.	B	124.	D
26.	A	59.	C	92.	B	125.	A
27.	C	60.	D	93.	D		
28.	A	61.	B	94.	D		
29.	D	62.	B	95.	C		
30.	D	63.	D	96.	C		
31.	D	64.	A	97.	A		
32.	D	65.	B	98.	A		
33.	C	66.	A	99.	A		

Rigor Table

	Easy %20	Average Rigor %40	Rigorous %40
Question #	2, 8, 9, 11, 12, 19, 20, 25, 30, 37, 44, 52, 58, 74, 81, 83, 85, 88, 89, 94, 96, 104, 111, 116, 123	3, 5, 6, 7, 13, 14, 17, 22, 24, 26, 28, 36, 38, 40, 41, 42, 43, 45, 46, 47, 48, 49, 51, 54, 56, 57, 62, 63, 75, 77, 78, 79, 80, 82, 91, 95, 97, 98, 99, 106, 107, 108, 110, 114, 117, 118, 121, 124	1, 4, 10, 15, 16, 18, 21, 23, 27, 29, 31, 32, 33, 34, 35, 39, 50, 53, 55, 59, 60, 61, 64, 65, 66, 67, 68, 69, 70, 71, 72, 73, 76, 84, 86, 87, 90, 92, 93, 100, 101, 102, 103, 105, 109, 112, 113, 115, 119, 120, 122, 125

Rationales with Sample Questions

1. The continent of North America includes all but which of the following countries: *(Rigorous) (Skill 1.1a)*

A) Canada

B) Mexico

C) Cuba

D) Ecuador

Answer: D. Ecuador

North America consists of (A) Canada; the United States of America; (B) Mexico; the Caribbean island nations of the West Indies including (C) Cuba, Jamaica, Haiti, and the Dominican Republic; and the "land bridge" of Middle America, including Panama, Honduras, El Salvador, Nicaragua, Guatemala, and others. (D) Ecuador is a part of South America.

2. Which river is the longest in the United States: *(Easy) (Skill 1.1a)*

A . Rio Grande

B. St. Lawrence

C. Mississippi

D. Colorado

Answer: C. Mississippi

The (C) Mississippi River is the longest river in the United States, extending from the U.S.-Canada border to the Gulf of Mexico, draining the Ohio River from the east and the Missouri River to the west. It is 2,320 miles long. Other significant rivers are the (B) St. Lawrence at 744 miles, which connects Lake Erie to the Atlantic Ocean, and the (A) Rio Grande, (1885 miles) forming most of the border between Mexico and the United States. The (D) Colorado River is in the southwestern United States and northwestern Mexico approximately 1,450 miles long.

3. The Mediterranean-type climate is characterized by *(Average) (Skill 1.1b)*:

    A. Hot, dry summers and mild, relatively wet winters

    B. Cool, relatively wet summers and cold winters

    C. Mild summers and winters, with moisture throughout the year

    D. Hot, wet summers and cool, dry winters

Answer: A. Hot, dry summers and mild, relatively wet winters

Westerly winds and nearby bodies of water create stable weather patterns along the west coasts of several continents and along the coast of the Mediterranean Sea, after which this type of climate is named. Temperatures rarely fall below the freezing point and have a mean between 70 and 80 degrees F in the summer. Stable conditions make for little rain during the summer months.

4. Which location may be found in Canada? *(Rigorous) (1.1b)*

    A. 27 N 93 W

    B. 41 N 93 E

    C. 50 N 111 W

    D. 18 N 120 W

Answer: C. 50 N 111 W

(A) 27 North latitude, 93 West longitude is located in the Gulf of Mexico. (B) 41 N 93 E is located in northwest China. (D) 18 N 120 W is in the Pacific Ocean, off the coast of Mexico. (C) 50 N 111 W is located near the town of Medicine Hat in the province of Alberta, in Canada.

5. The climate of Southern Florida is the _____ type. *(Average) (Skill 1.1b)*

   A. humid subtropical

   B. marine west coast

   C. humid continental

   D. tropical wet-dry

Answer: A. humid subtropical

The (B) marine west coast climate is found on the western coasts of continents. Florida is on the eastern side of North America. The (C) humid continental climate is found over large land masses, such as Europe and the American Midwest, not along coasts such as where Florida is situated. The (D) tropical wet-dry climate occurs within about 15 degrees of the equator, in the tropics. Florida is subtropical. Florida is in a (A) humid subtropical climate, which extends along the East Coast of the United States to about Maryland and along the Gulf coast to northeastern Texas.

6. Apartments built out of cliff faces; shared government by adult citizens; absence of aggression toward other groups; and perhaps the oldest representative government in the world. These factors characterize the Native American group known as: *(Average) (Skill 1.2b)*

   A. Pueblos

   B. Comanches

   C. Seminoles

   D. Sioux

Answer: A. Pueblos

The famous (A) Pueblos, a culture comprising a number of tribes, are called after the communal dwellings where they live. They wear clothes made of wool and woven cotton, farm crops in the middle of desert land, create exquisite pottery and Kachina dolls, and have one of the most complex religions of all the tribes. They are perhaps best known for the challenging vista-based villages that they once constructed in openings in the sheer faces of cliffs and for their adobes, mud-brick buildings that house their living and meeting quarters. The ancient Pueblos chose their own chiefs. This is perhaps one of the oldest representative governments in the world. The present-day Pueblo culture is represented by the Hopi in Arizona and by the Zuni and the Taos, among others, in New Mexico.

7. **The Native Americans of the eastern woodlands lived on:** *(Average)* *(Skill 1.2b)*

   A. Buffalo and crops such as corn, beans, and sunflowers

   B. Chiefly farming of squash, beans, and corn

   C. A variety of game (deer, bear, moose) and crops (squash, pumpkins, corn)

   D. Wolves, foxes, polar bears, walruses, and fish

Answer: C. A variety of game (deer, bear, moose) and crops (squash, pumpkins, corn)

(A) Buffalo live in the plains habitat found in western and midwestern North America. (B) & (C) While the Native Americans did farm the "three sisters" of corn, squash and beans, the woods of the east also meant that a variety of game (deer, bear, moose) was widely available for them to hunt. However, (D) wolves, foxes, walruses, polar bears, and fish are found together only within the Arctic Circle, not in eastern woodlands.

8. **One tribe of Indians formed a representative government referred to as the _____ Confederacy.** *(Easy) (Skill 1.2b)*

   A. Cherokee

   B. Seminole

   C. Wampanoag

   D. Iroquois

Answer: D. Iroquois

Five of the (D) Iroquois tribes formed a Confederacy, a shared form of government. Living in the Southeast were the (B) Seminoles and Creeks, a huge collection of people who are best known, however, for their struggle, especially led by the great Osceola, against Spanish and English settlers. The (A) Cherokee also lived in the Southeast. They were one of the most advanced tribes, living in domed houses and wearing deerskin and rabbit fur. Accomplished hunters, farmers, and fishermen, the Cherokee were known the continent over for their intricate and beautiful basketry and clay pottery. They also played a game called lacrosse, which survives to this day in countries around the world. The (C) Wampanoag tribe was found mainly in Massachusetts.

9. **Columbus first reached western hemisphere lands in what is now: (Easy) (Skill 1.3a)**

   A. Florida

   B. Bermuda

   C. Puerto Rico

   D. Bahamas

Answer: D. Bahamas

Christopher Columbus visited the Bahamas in 1492 and Puerto Rico in 1493 but never landed on either (B) Bermuda or (A) Florida.

10. **Which one of the following is *not* a reason why Europeans came to the New World? (Rigorous) (Skill 1.3b)**

    A. To find resources in order to increase wealth

    B. To establish trade

    C. To increase a ruler's power and importance

    D. To spread Christianity

Answer: B. To establish trade

The Europeans came to the New World for a number of reasons; often they came to find new natural resources to extract for manufacturing. The Portuguese, the Spanish, and the English were sent over to increase the monarch's power and spread influences such as religion (Christianity) and culture. Therefore, the only reason given that Europeans didn't come to the New World was to establish trade.

11. How many oceans cover Earth? *(Easy) (Skill 1.1b)*

   A. 3

   B. 4

   C. 5

   D. 6

Answer: C. 5

Oceans are the largest bodies of water on the planet. The five oceans of the earth are the Atlantic Ocean, one-half the size of the Pacific and separating North and South America from Africa and Europe; the Pacific Ocean, covering almost one-third of the entire surface of the earth and separating North and South America from Asia and Australia; the Indian Ocean, touching Africa, Asia, and Australia; and the ice-filled Arctic Ocean, extending from North America and Europe to the North Pole. The Southern Ocean stretches along Antarctica.

12. During the early years of colonization in New France, what commodity was the livelihood for many people, both in New France and in France? *(Easy) (Skill 1.3c)*

   A. Wampum

   B. Fish

   C. Gold

   D. Fur

Answer: D. Fur

French fur traders made friends with the friendly tribes of Indians, spending the winters with them getting the furs needed for trade. Most of the wealth for New France and its "Mother Country" was from the (D) fur trade, which provided a livelihood for many, many people. Manufacturers and workmen back in France, ship-owners and merchants, as well as the fur traders and their Indian allies, all benefited.

13. The middle colonies of the Americas were: *(Average) (Skill 1.3d)*

A. Maryland, Virginia, North Carolina

B. New York, New Jersey, Pennsylvania, Delaware

C. Rhode Island, Connecticut, New York, New Jersey

D. Vermont and New Hampshire

Answer: B. New York, New Jersey, Pennsylvania, Delaware

(A), (C) & (D). Maryland, Virginia, and North Carolina were Southern colonies, Rhode Island, Connecticut and New Hampshire were New England colonies and Vermont was not one of the 13 original colonies.

14.   Slavery arose in the southern colonies partly as a perceived economical way to: *(Average) (Skill 1.3d)*

A. Increase the owner's wealth through human beings used as a source of exchange

B. Cultivate large plantations of cotton, tobacco, rice, indigo, and other crops

C. Provide Africans with humanitarian aid, such as health care, Christianity, and literacy

D. Keep ships' holds full of cargo on two out of three legs of the "triangular trade" voyage

Answer: B. Cultivate large plantations of cotton, tobacco, rice, indigo, and other crops.

The southern states, with their smaller populations, were heavily dependent on slave labor as a means of being able to fulfill their role and remain competitive in the greater U.S. economy. (A) When slaves arrived in the South, the vast majority would become permanent fixtures on plantations, intended for work, not as a source of exchange. (C) While some slave owners instructed their slaves in Christianity and provided health care or some level of education, such attention was not their primary reason for owning slaves—a cheap and ready labor force was. (D) Whether or not ships' holds were full on two of three legs of the triangular journey was not the concern of Southerners as the final purchasers of slaves. Such details would have concerned the slave traders.

15. Which of the following was *not* a factor leading to the American Revolution? *(Rigorous) (Skill 1.4a)*

    A. The desire for an imperial state

    B. Belief in equality

    C. Belief in no taxation without representation

    D. The desire for freedom

Answer: A. The desire for an imperial state

The colonists had no desire for an (A) imperial state. They wanted equality, a representative government, and freedom.

16. France decided in 1777 to help the American colonies in their war against Britain. This decision was based on: *(Rigorous) (Skill 1.4a)*

    A. The naval victory of John Paul Jones over the British ship *Serapis*

    B. The survival of the terrible winter at Valley Forge

    C. The success of colonial guerilla fighters in the South

    D. The defeat of the British at Saratoga

Answer: D. The defeat of the British at Saratoga

The turning point in the Americans' favor occurred in 1777 with the (D) American victory at Saratoga. Because of this victory, the French decided to align themselves with the Americans against the British. With French warships blocking the entrance to Chesapeake Bay, British General Cornwallis, trapped at Yorktown, Virginia, surrendered in 1781 and the war was over.

17. The Bill of Rights was mostly written by: *(Average) (Skill 1.4b)*

    A. Thomas Jefferson

    B. James Madison

    C. George Washington

    D. Alexander Hamilton

Answer: B. James Madison

The Bill of Rights, along with the majority of the Constitution, was mostly written by James Madison. Thomas Jefferson wrote the Declaration of Independence. Washington and Hamilton were present at the Constitutional Convention of 1787 in Philadelphia, and they were advocates of federalism, or increasing the power of the federal government.

18. Which issue most divided the members of the nation's first two political parties? *(Rigorous) (Skill 1.5a)*

    A. The exact duties of each branch of government

    B. The outcome of the election of 1800

    C. The relative qualities of Hamilton and Jefferson

    D. The proper application of the Constitution

Answer: D. The proper application of the Constitution

The essential debate between the Federalists and Democratic-Republicans was the extent of the powers granted to the national government under the Constitution. The duties of each branch (A) were clear. Hamilton and Jefferson were leaders of the parties but not the cause of their debate (C). The parties had already formed by the time of the election of 1800 (B).

19. The Second Great Awakenings refers to:
(Easy)(Skill 1.5b)

A. Religious movements

B. Political movements

C. Military movements

D. Industrialization

Answer: A. Religious movement

The Second Great Awakening was a similar of religious zeal that moved through Georgia and the rest of the country in the early nineteenth century. Methodist and Baptist churches in particular saw huge growth. The Civil War cooled this revival in the North, but in the South the religious involvement was strengthened.

20. The area of the United States was effectively doubled through purchase of the Louisiana Territory under which President? *(Easy) (Skill 1.5b)*

A. John Adams

B. Thomas Jefferson

C. James Madison

D. James Monroe

Answer: B. Thomas Jefferson

(B) The Louisiana Purchase, an acquisition of territory from France in 1803 occurred under Thomas Jefferson. (A) John Adams was president from 1797 to 1801, before the purchase, and (C) James Madison after the Purchase, from 1809 to1817. (D) James Monroe was actually a signatory on the Purchase but did not become president until 1817.

21. Which one of the following was *not* a reason why the United States went to war with Great Britain in 1812? *(Rigorous) (Skill 1.5b)*

    A. Resentment over the sale, exploration, and settlement of the Louisiana Territory

    B. The westward movement of farmers because of the need for more land

    C. Canadian fur traders were agitating the northeastern Indians to fight American expansion

    D. The British navy continued to seize American ships on the high seas and force American seamen to serve aboard its ships

Answer: A. Resentment over the sale, exploration, and settlement of the Louisiana Territory

The United States went to war with Great Britain in 1812 for a number of reasons, including the expansion of settlers westward and the need for more land, the agitation of Indians by Canadian fur traders in eastern Canada, and the continued seizures of American ships by the British on the high seas. The War of 1812 is often considered to be the second American war for independence.

22.   Under the new Constitution, the most urgent of the many problems facing the new federal government was that of: *(Average) (Skill 1.5c)*

    A. Maintaining a strong army and navy

    B. Establishing a strong foreign policy

    C. Raising money to pay salaries and war debts

    D. Setting up courts, passing federal laws, and providing for law enforcement officers

Answer: C. Raising money to pay salaries and war debts

Maintaining strong military forces, establishment of a strong foreign policy, and setting up a justice system were important problems facing the United States under the newly ratified Constitution. However, the most important and pressing issue was how to raise money to pay salaries and war debts from the Revolutionary War. Alexander Hamilton, then Secretary of the Treasury, proposed increased tariffs and taxes on products such as liquor. This money would be used to pay off war debts and to pay for internal programs. Hamilton also proposed the idea of a national bank.

23. What was a major source of contention between American settlers in Texas and the Mexican government in the 1830s and 1840s? *(Rigorous) (Skill 1.6a)*

A. The Americans wished to retain slavery, which had been outlawed in Mexico

B. Cultural differences, including language and religion

C. Concern about the possible development of an American state within Mexico

D. All of the above were contentious issues between American settlers and the Mexican government

Answer: D All of the above were contentious issues between American settlers and the Mexican government.

With the influx of so many Americans and the liberal policies of the Mexican government, concern over the possible growth and development of an American state within Mexico grew. Settlement restrictions, cancellation of land grants, the forbidding of slavery, and increased military activity brought everything to a head. The language, the religion, the law, the customs, and the government of the two groups were totally different. A clash was bound to occur.

24. The right of the states to declare invalid any act of Congress that they felt was unjust was known as the: *(Average) (Skill 1.6a)*

A. Declaration of Independence

B. Missouri Compromise

C. Monroe Doctrine

D. Doctrine of Nullification

Answer: D. Doctrine of Nullification

(A) The Declaration of Independence declared the colonists' independence from England. (B) The Missouri Compromise stated that Missouri's constitution could not deny the protections and privileges to citizens that were guaranteed by the U.S. Constitution. The acceptance in 1820 of this second compromise opened the way for Missouri's statehood. (C) The Monroe Doctrine banned European incursion into the Americas. (D) The Doctrine of Nullification states that the states have the right to "nullify," declare invalid, any act of Congress they believed to be unjust or unconstitutional.

25. The belief that the United States should control all of North America was called: *(Easy) (Skill 1.6b)*

A. Westward Expansion

B. Pan Americanism

C. Manifest Destiny

D. Nationalism

Answer: C. Manifest Destiny

The belief that the United States should control all of North America was called (B) Manifest Destiny. This idea fueled much of the violence and aggression towards the Native Americans who already occupied the land. Manifest Destiny was certainly driven by sentiments of (D) nationalism and gave rise to (A) westward expansion.

26. The "Trail of Tears" relates to: *(Average) (Skill 1.6b)*

A. The removal of the Cherokees from their native lands to Oklahoma Territory

B. The revolt and subsequent migration of the Massachusetts Pilgrims under pressure from the Iroquois

C. The journey of the Nez Perce under Chief Joseph before their capture by the U.S. Army

D. The 1973 standoff between federal marshals and Native Americans at Wounded Knee, S.D.

Answer: A. The removal of the Cherokees from their native lands to Oklahoma Territory.

(B) There never was a revolt and migration of the Massachusetts Pilgrims under pressure from the Iroquois. (C) The 1877 journey of the Nez Perce under Chief Joseph was a strategically impressive attempt to retreat from an oncoming U.S. Army into Canada. (D) The 1973 Wounded Knee incident was the occupation of the town of Wounded Knee, South Dakota, by the American Indian Movement to call attention to issues of Native American civil rights. Their action led to a 71-day standoff with U.S. Marshals, which was eventually resolved peacefully.

27. **The tensions between the North and the South before the Civil War mostly stemmed from:** *(Rigorous) (Skill 1.7a)*

    A. Political differences

    B. Cultural differences

    C. Economic differences

    D. Historical differences

Answer C. Economic differences

The (C) economies of the North and the South diverged greatly during the early nineteenth century, as the North became more industrialized and the South relied more heavily on cash crops. These differences fueled greater divisions in politics, culture, and other factors over time.

28. **Of the following groups of states, which were slave states?** *(Rigorous) (Skill 1.7a)*

    A. Delaware, Maryland, Missouri

    B. California, Texas, Florida

    C. Illinois, Missouri, Kentucky

    D. Virginia, West Virginia, Indiana

Answer: A. Delaware, Maryland, Missouri.

(A) Delaware, Maryland and Missouri were all slave states at the time of the Civil War. (B) Florida and Texas were slave states, while California was a free state. (C) Kansas, Missouri, and Kentucky were all originally slave territories, and Missouri and Kentucky were admitted to the Union as such. However, Kansas's petition to join the union in 1858 was blocked in order to preserve the balance between slave and free states. Kansas was admitted as a free state in 1861. (D) Indiana was a free state.

29. What was one social effect of the expansion of the railroad during the nineteenth century? *(Rigorous) (Skill 1.8a)*

A. Increased immigration from Europe

B. Expanded trade between the eastern and western United States

C. The decline of labor unions

D. The establishment of standardized time zones

Answer: D. the establishment of standardized time zones

Technological developments can have significant social effects even as they shape economic and technological life. For example, the rise of the nationwide rail system during the late 1800s led to a shift from local time to large standardized time zones that permitted easier train scheduling.

30. What event sparked a great migration of people from all over the world to California? *(Easy) (Skill 1.8a)*

A. The birth of labor unions

B. California statehood

C. The invention of the automobile

D. The gold rush

Answer: D. The gold rush

The discovery of gold in California created a lust for gold that quickly brought immigrants from the eastern United States and many parts of the world. To be sure, there were struggles and conflicts, as well as the rise of nativism. Yet this vast migration of people from all parts of the world began the process that has created California's uniquely diverse culture.

31. **What technological development most influenced the growth of the American West?** *(Rigorous) (Skill 1.8a)*

    A. The steamboat

    B. The cotton gin

    C. The telegraph

    D. The railroad

Answer: D   the railroad

The American West grew greatly after the expansion of the (D) railroad during the mid-nineteenth century. The (A) steamboat had been an important transit development and the (B) cotton gin was an important industrial invention closer to the turn of the nineteenth century. The (C) telegraph eased long-distance communication but did not encourage settlement.

32. **The Industrial Revolution contributed directly to all of the following except:** *(Average) (Skill 1.8b)*

    A. Decline of the agricultural economy

    B. Urbanization

    C. Economic growth

    D. The Civil War

Answer: D. The Civil War

Although economic differences between the North and South contributed to tensions that led to the outbreak of the Civil War, industrialization was not a direct factor in the conflict. It did, however, encourage a shift to a manufacturing economy, growth of cities, and higher economic output.

33. **Increased immigration in the late 1800s led to all of the following except:** *(Rigorous)(Skill 1.8c)*

    A. The rise of political machines

    B. The growth of factories

    C. The construction of the transcontinental railroad

    D. The increase of the overall urban population

Answer: C. The construction of the transcontinental railroad

Although many immigrants worked on the transcontinental railroad in the West, its construction was not a result of the rise in immigration. Immigration contributed in a greater or lesser degree to all of the other changes.

34. **The American labor union movement started gaining new momentum:** *(Rigorous) (Skill 1.8d)*

    A. During the building of the railroads

    B. After 1865 with the growth of cities

    C. With the rise of industrial giants such as Carnegie and Vanderbilt

    D. During the war years of 1861–1865

Answer: B. After 1865 with the growth of cities

The American labor union movement had been around since the late eighteenth and early nineteenth centuries. The labor movement first began to experience persecution by employers in the early 1800s. The American labor movement remained relatively ineffective until after the Civil War. In 1866, the National Labor Union was formed, pushing such issues as the eight-hour workday and new policies of immigration. This gave rise to the Knights of Labor and eventually the American Federation of Labor (AFL) in the 1890s and the Industrial Workers of the World (IWW) in 1905. Therefore, it was the (B) period following the Civil War that empowered the labor movement in terms of numbers, militancy, and effectiveness.

35. Which of the following was *not* a factor in the United States' entry into World War I? *(Rigorous) (Skill 1.9b)*

    A. The closeness of the presidential election of 1916

    B. The German threat to sink all allied ships, including merchant ships

    C. The desire to preserve democracy as practiced in Britain and France as compared to the totalitarianism of Germany

    D. The sinking of the *Lusitania* and the *Sussex*

Answer: A. The closeness of the presidential election of 1916

President Woodrow Wilson was narrowly re-elected in 1916, but this was not a factor in the United States' entry into World War I. All the other answers were indeed factors.

36. The stock market crash of 1929 directly contributed to the beginning of: *(Average) (Skill 1.9d)*

    A. World War I

    B. The Marshall Plan

    C. The Great Depression

    D. The Second Industrial Revolution

Answer: C. The Great Depression

Along with increasing consumer debt, overproduction, poor lending practices, and declining farm prices, the stock market crash of 1929 was one of the main factors leading the (C) Great Depression of the 1930s.

37. **The international organization established to work for world peace at the end of the First World War was the:** *(Average) (Skill 1.9d)*

   A. League of Nations

   B. United Federation of Nations

   C. United Nations

   D. United World League

Answer: A. League of Nations

The international organization established to work for world peace at the end of the First World War was the (A) League of Nations. From the ashes of the failed League of Nations, the (C) United Nations, established following World War II, continues to be a major player in world affairs today.

38. **What Supreme Court ruling ended school segregation?** *(Average) (Skill 1.10c)*

   A. *Miranda v. Arizona*

   B. *Mapp v. Ohio*

   C. *Brown v. Board of Education*

   D. *Marbury v. Madison*

Answer: C. *Brown v. Board of Education*

In this landmark ruling, the Supreme Court struck down legalized segregation in public schools. *Miranda v. Arizona* (A) dealt with the rights of the accused; *Mapp v. Ohio* concerned how evidence was legally obtained; and *Marbury v. Madison* (D) established the precedent of judicial review.

39. In issuing an ultimatum for Soviet ships not to enter Cuban waters in October 1962, President John F. Kennedy, as part of his decision, used the provisions of the: *(Rigorous) (Skill 1.10b, 1.11a)*

    A. Monroe Doctrine

    B. Declaration of the Rights of Man

    C. Geneva Convention

    D. Truman Doctrine

Answer: A. Monroe Doctrine

(A) The Monroe Doctrine, initially formulated by Presidents James Monroe and John Quincy Adams and later enhanced by President Theodore Roosevelt, opposed European colonization or interference in the Americas, perceived any such attempts as a threat to U.S. security, and promised U.S. neutrality in conflicts between European powers and/or their already established colonies. (B) The Declaration of the Rights of Man, widely adapted in future declarations about international human rights, was formulated in France during the French Revolution and adopted by the National Constituent Assembly in 1789 as the premise of any future French constitution. (C) The Geneva Conventions (1864, 1929, and 1949, with later additions and amendments) established humanitarian and ethical standards for conduct during times of war and has been widely accepted as international law. (D) The Truman Doctrine (1947), formulated by President Harry Truman, provided for the support of Greece and Turkey as a means of protecting them from Soviet influence. It thereby began the Cold War, a period in which the United States sought to contain the Soviet Union by limiting its influence in other countries.

40. Which of the following developments is most closely associated with the Neolithic Age? *(Average) (Skill 2.1a)*

    A. Human use of fire

    B. First use of stone chipping instruments

    C. Domestication of plants

    D. Development of metallurgical alloys

Answer: C. Domestication of plants

The Neolithic Period also featured domesticated animals; food production; the arts of knitting, spinning, and weaving cloth; fires started through friction; house building rather than living in caves; the development of institutions including the family and religion; and a form of government or the origin of the state.

41. **China first became important during the same era as the rise of the:** *(Average) (Skill 2.1b)*

   A. Egyptians

   B. Japanese

   C. Greeks

   D. Maya

Answer: A. Egyptians

Both China and Egypt arose in ancient times. All of the other civilizations followed centuries later.

42. **Which ancient civilization is credited with being the first to develop irrigation techniques through the use of canals, dikes, and devices for raising water?** *(Average) (Skill 2.1b)*

   A. The Sumerians

   B. The Egyptians

   C. The Babylonians

   D. The Akkadians

Answer: A. The Sumerians

The ancient (A) Sumerians of the Fertile Crescent of Mesopotamia are credited with being the first to develop irrigation techniques through the use of canals, dikes, and devices for raising water. The (B) Egyptians also practiced controlled irrigation, but that was primarily through the use of the Nile's predictable flooding schedule. The (C) Babylonians were more noted for their revolutionary systems of law than their irrigation systems.

43. The politics of classical Athens is best described by which of the following? *(Average) (Skill 2.1c)*

    A. Limited democracy, including both slaves and free men

    B. One-man dictatorial rule

    C. Universal democracy among free owners of property

    D. Oligarchy with a few families controlling all decisions

Answer: C. Universal democracy among free owners of property.

Note the complete contrast between independent, freedom-loving Athens with its practice of pure democracy, i.e., direct, personal, active participation in government by qualified citizens, and the rigid, totalitarian, militaristic Sparta.

44. The first ancient civilization to introduce and practice monotheism was the: *(Easy) (Skill 2.1c)*

    A. Sumerians

    B. Hebrews

    C. Phoenicians

    D. Minoans

Answer: B. Hebrews

The Hebrews, also known as the ancient Israelites, instituted monotheism, the worship of one god. Judaism, the oldest of the eight major religions, was the first to teach and practice the belief in monotheism.

45. The principle of zero in mathematics is the discovery of the ancient civilization found in: *(Average) (Skill 2.1c)*

    A. Egypt

    B. Persia

    C. India

    D. Babylon

Answer: C. India

Although the (A) Egyptians practiced algebra and geometry, the (B) Persians developed an alphabet, and the (D) Babylonians developed Hammurabi's Code, which would come to be considered among the most important contributions of the Mesopotamian civilization, it was the (C) Indians that created the idea of zero in mathematics, drastically changing our ideas about numbers.

46. An early cultural group was so skillful in navigating on the seas that they were able to sail at night guided by stars. They were the: *(Average) (Skill 2.1c)*

    A. Greeks

    B. Persians

    C. Minoans

    D. Phoenicians

Answer: D. Phoenicians

Although the (A) Greeks were quite able sailors and developed a strong navy in their defeat of the (B) Persians at sea in the Battle of Marathon, it was the Eastern Mediterranean culture of the (D) Phoenicians that had first developed the astronomical skill of sailing at night with the stars as their guide. The (C) Minoans were an advanced early civilization on Crete, an island off the Greek coast; they were noted for their innovations in terms of sewage systems, toilets, and running water.

47. A historian might compare the governmental systems of the Roman Empire and the twentieth century United States with regard to which of the following commonalities? ? *(Average) (Skill 2.1c)*

   A. Totalitarianism

   B. Technological development

   C. Constitutional similarities

   D. Republican federalism

Answer: D. Republican federalism

(A) Totalitarianism is a form of government where citizens are completely subservient to the state. While this was sometimes the case during the reign of the Roman Empire, it was not common to 20th century America. (B) Technological development does not necessarily address similarities in governmental systems. (C) The Roman constitution applied to the republic of Rome but not directly to the empire as a whole. (D) Federalism is a type of governmental system where several separate states join under a common government. This describes both the United States and the Roman Empire and is the best answer.

48.   Development of a solar calendar, invention of the decimal system, and contributions to the development of geometry and astronomy are all the legacy of: *(Average) (Skill 2.1c)*

   A. The Babylonians

   B. The Persians

   C. The Sumerians

   D. The Egyptians

Answer: D. The Egyptians

The (A) Babylonians of ancient Mesopotamia flourished for a time under their great contribution of organized law and code, called Hammurabi's Code after the ruler Hammurabi. The fall of the Babylonians to the Persians in 539 B.C. made way for the warrior-driven Persian Empire that expanded from Pakistan to the Mediterranean Sea until its conquest by Alexander the Great in 331 B.C. The Sumerians of ancient Mesopotamia were most noted as one of the first civilizations and for their contribution towards written language, known as cuneiform. It was the (D) Egyptians who were the first true developers of a solar calendar and the decimal system and who made significant contributions to the development of geometry and astronomy

49. Chinese civilization is generally credited with the original development of which of the following sets of technologies: *(Average) (Skill 2.1d)*

A. Movable type and mass production of goods

B. Wool processing and domestication of the horse

C. Paper and gunpowder manufacture

D. Leather processing and modern timekeeping

Answer: C. Paper and gunpowder manufacture

(A) While China's Bi Sheng is credited with the earliest forms of movable type, mass production was spearheaded by America's Henry Ford in his campaign to create the first truly affordable automobile, the Model T Ford. (B) While wool has been processed in many ways in many cultures, production on a scale beyond cottage industries was not possible without the many advances made in England during the Industrial Revolution (18th century). Various theories exist about the domestication of the horse, with estimates ranging from 4600 BC to 2000 BC in Eurasia. Recent DNA evidence suggests that the horse may actually have been domesticated in different cultures at independent points. (C) The earliest mention of gunpowder appears in ninth-century Chinese documents. The earliest examples of paper made of wood pulp come from China and have been dated as early as the second century BC. (D) Leather processing and timekeeping have likewise seen different developments in different places at different times.

50. Which of these empires did *not* control Western Africa through powerful trading connections? *(Rigorous) (Skill 2.1d)*

   A. Ghana

   B. Mali

   C. Berber

   D. Songhai

Answer: C. Berber

51. During the Age of Exploration, who first desired to find a completely nautical route to Asia? *(Average)(Skill 2.2a)*

   A. The Portuguese

   B. The Spanish

   C. The English

   D. The Dutch

Answer: A. The Portuguese

Prince Henry of Portugal encouraged, supported, and financed the Portuguese seamen who led in the search for an all-water route to Asia.

52. The period of intellectual and artistic rebirth in Europe was called: *(Easy) (Skill 2.2a)*

A. Age of Exploration

B. Colonialism

C. Renaissance

D. Imperialism

Answer: C. Renaissance

The (A) Age of Exploration describes the time during which Europeans explored the New World. (B) Colonialism and (D) Imperialism are both types of foreign policy that dominated the world beginning during this time period, which was called the (C) Renaissance.

53. The ideas and innovations of the period of the Renaissance were spread throughout Europe mainly because of: *(Rigorous) (Skill 2.2a)*

A. Extensive exploration

B. Craft workers and their guilds

C. The invention of the printing press

D. Increased travel and trade

Answer: C. The invention of the printing press

The ideas and innovations of the Renaissance were spread throughout Europe for a number of reasons. While exploration, increased travel, and the spread of craft may have aided the spread of the Renaissance to small degrees, nothing was as important to the spread of ideas as Gutenberg's invention of the printing press in Germany.

54. The first explorer to reach India by sailing around the southern tip of Africa was: *(Average) (Skill 2.2a)*

   A. Amerigo Vespucci

   B. Vasco da Gama

   C. Ferdinand Magellan

   D. John Cabot

Answer: B. Vasco da Gama

(A) Amerigo Vespucci was the Italian explorer to first assert that the lands to the west of Africa and Europe were actually part of a new continent and thus the name "America" was derived from his own "Amerigo." (B) Portuguese Vasco da Gama built on the discoveries of previous explorers to finally round Africa's Cape of Good Hope and open a sea route for European trade with the east and the eventual Portuguese colonization of India. (C) Portuguese explorer Ferdinand Magellan, working for the Spanish crown, led the first successful expedition to circumnavigate the globe. Magellan himself actually died before the voyage was over, but his ship and eighteen crewmembers did return safely to Spain. (D) John Cabot was an Italian explorer working for the English crown and is thought to have been the first European to discover the North American continent (1497) since the Vikings.

55. Which of these was *not* a cause of the Protestant Revolution? *(Rigorous) (Skill 2.2a)*

   A. The rise of Calvinism

   B. The sale of religious offices

   C. The growth of nationalism

   D. The power of absolute monarchs

Answer: A. The rise of Calvinism

The rise of Calvinism was a result of the Protestant Revolution. All of the other factors were causes.

56. **Who is considered to be the most important figure in the spread of Protestantism across Switzerland?** *(Average) (Skill 2.2a)*

   A. Calvin

   B. Zwingli

   C. Munzer

   D. Leyden

Answer: A. Calvin

While (B) Huldreich Zwingli was the first to spread the Protestant Reformation in Switzerland around 1519, it was (A) John Calvin whose less radical approach to Protestantism really made the most impact in Switzerland. Calvin's ideas diverged from the Lutherans' ideas in the debate over the the sacrament of the "Lord's Supper," and his branch of Protestantism became known as Calvinism. Calvin certainly built on Zwingli's early influence, but he really made the religion widespread throughout Switzerland. (C) Thomas Munzer was a German Protestant reformer whose radical and revolutionary ideas about God's will to overthrow the ruling classes and his siding with the peasantry got him beheaded. Munzer has since been studied and admired by Marxists for his views on class. Leyden (or Leiden) was a founder of the University of Leyden, a Protestant place for study in the Netherlands.

57. **Bartholomeu Diaz discovered which cape near the southern tip of Africa became known as?** *(Average) (Skill 2.2a)*

   A. Cape Horn

   B. Cabo Bojador

   C. Cape of Good Hope

   D. Cape Hatteras

Answer: C. Cape of Good Hope

(A) Cape Horn is located at the southern tip of Chile, South America. It was discovered by Sir Francis Drake as he sailed around the globe in 1578. (B) Cajo Bojador, on the western coast of northern Africa, was first successfully navigated by a European, Portuguese Gil Eanes, in 1434. (D) Cape Hatteras is located on the U.S. Atlantic coast, in North Carolina.

58. Which of these rulers led classical India? *(Easy) (Skill 2.2a)*

    A. Akbar

    B. Asoka

    C. Genghis Khan

    D. Mansa Musa

Answer: B. Asoka

Akbar is considered to be ancient India's greatest ruler. He combined a drive for conquest with a magnetic personality and went so far as to invent his own religion, Dinillahi, a combination of Islam, Christianity, Zoroastrianism, and Hinduism. Asoka was an important ruler, as he was the first to fully unite India. Genghis Khan led the Mongols, and Mansa Musa ruled over West Africa.

59. What conclusion is best supported by the lengthy search for a Northwest Passage? *(Rigorous) (Skill 2.2a)*

    A. Europeans had a thirst for knowledge and exploration

    B. Europeans did not believe geographical information from native peoples

    C. Europeans wanted a water route to Asia

    D. Europeans had little interest in long-distance trade

Answer: C. Europeans wanted a water route to Asia

Europeans long sought the Northwest Passage in the hopes of finding an all-water route to Asia. Their efforts stemmed from economic motives (D), not those of pure knowledge (A), and did not discount the knowledge of native peoples (B).

60. **In Western Europe, the achievements of the Renaissance were unsurpassed and made these countries outstanding cultural centers on the continent. All of the following were accomplishments except: (Rigorous) (Skill 2.2a)**

   A. Invention of the printing press

   B. A rekindling of interest in the learning of classical Greece and Rome

   C. Growth in literature, philosophy, and art

   D Better military tactics

Answer: D. Better military tactics

Some of the most important developments during the Renaissance were Gutenberg's invention of the printing press in Germany and a reexamination of the ideas and philosophies of (B) classical Greece and Rome that eventually helped Renaissance thinkers to approach more modern ideas. Also important during the Renaissance was the (C) growth in literature (Petrarch, Boccaccio, Erasmus), philosophy (Machiavelli, More, Bacon) and art (Van Eyck, Giotto, da Vinci). Therefore, (D) improved military tactics is the only possible answer as it was clearly not a characteristic of the Renaissance in Western Europe.

61. **Which event most influenced the rise of the French Revolution? (Rigorous) (Skill 2.2b)**

   A. Industrial Revolution

   B. American Revolution

   C. Protestant Revolution

   D. Glorious Revolution

Answer: B. American Revolution

The success and democratic ideals of the American Revolution contributed to the French Revolution little over a decade later. The Industrial Revolution succeeded the French Revolution, and the others preceded it by a great number of years.

62. Colonial expansion by Western European powers in the 18th and 19th centuries was due primarily to: *(Average) (Skill 2.2b)*

A. Building and opening the Suez Canal

B. The Industrial Revolution

C. Marked improvements in transportation

D. Complete independence of all the Americas and loss of European domination and influence

Answer: B. The Industrial Revolution

Colonial expansion by Western European powers in the late 18th and 19th centuries was due primarily to the Industrial Revolution in Great Britain that spread across Europe and needed new natural resources and, therefore, new locations from which to extract the raw materials needed to feed the new industries.

63. Great Britain became the center of technological and industrial development during the nineteenth century chiefly on the basis of: *(Average) (Skill 2.2b)*

A. Central location relative to the population centers of Europe

B. Colonial conquests and military victories over European powers

C. Reliance on exterior sources of financing

D. Resources of coal and production of steel

Answer: D. Resources of coal and production of steel

Great Britain possessed a unique set of advantages in the 18th and 19th centuries, making it the perfect candidate for the technological advances of the Industrial Revolution. (A) Relative isolation from the population centers in Europe meant little to Great Britain, which benefited from its own relatively unified and large domestic market, enabling it to avoid the tariffs and inefficiencies of trading on the diverse (and complicated) continent. (B) Colonial conquests and military victories over European powers were fueled by Great Britain's industrial advances in transportation and weaponry, rather than being causes of them. (C) Reliance on exterior sources of funding: while Great Britain would enjoy an increasing influx of goods and capital from its colonies, the efficiency of its own domestic market consistently generated an impressive amount of capital for investment in the new technologies and industries of the age. (D) Great Britain's rich natural resources of coal and ore enabled steel production and, set alongside new factories in Britain's landscape, allowed the quick and efficient production of goods.

64. **It can be reasonably stated that the change in the United States from primarily an agricultural country into an industrial power was due to all of the following except:** *(Average) (Skill 2.2b)*

   A. Tariffs on foreign imports

   B. Millions of hardworking immigrants

   C. An increase in technological developments

   D. The change from steam to electricity for powering industrial machinery

Answer: A. Tariffs on foreign imports

It can be reasonably stated that the change in the United States from primarily an agricultural country into an industrial power was due, in a great degree, to three of the reasons listed above. It was a combination of millions of hard-working immigrants, an increase in technological developments, and the change from steam to electricity for powering industrial machinery. The only reason given that really had little effect was the tariffs on foreign imports.

65. **What was an immediate effect of the Russian Revolution?** *(Rigorous) (Skill 2.3a)*

   A. World War I began

   B. Russia left World War I

   C. The Cold War began

   D. Russia declared war on Germany in World War II

Answer: B. Russia left World War I

Not long after the Russian Revolution in 1917, the nation withdrew from World War I. The nation's involvement in the war had been one of the contributing factors to the outbreak of revolution. The other events followed much later.

66. **Of all the major causes of both World Wars I and II, the most significant one is considered to be:** *(Rigorous) (Skill 2.3a)*

   A. Extreme nationalism

   B. Military buildup and aggression

   C. Political unrest

   D. Agreements and alliances

Answer: A. Extreme nationalism

Although military buildup and aggression, political unrest, and agreements and alliances were all characteristic of the world climate before and during World War I and World War II, the most significant cause of both wars was extreme nationalism. Nationalism is the idea that the interests and needs of a particular nation are of the utmost and primary importance above all else. Some nationalist movements could be liberation movements while others were oppressive regimes; much depends on their degree of nationalism. The nationalism that sparked WWI included a rejection of German, Austro-Hungarian, and Ottoman imperialism by Serbs, Slavs, and others, culminating in the assassination of Archduke Ferdinand by a Serbian nationalist in 1914. Following WWI and the Treaty of Versailles, many Germans and others in the Central Alliance Nations, discontented with the concessions and reparations of the treaty, started a new form of nationalism, led by Adolf Hitler and the Nazi regime. Hitler's ideas were an example of extreme, oppressive nationalism combined with political, social, and economic scapegoating ,and were the primary cause of WWII.

67. The conflict between fascism and communism mostly stemmed from disagreements over:
(Rigorous) (Skill 2.3a)

A. The role of government

B. Control of the means of production

C. The importance of the military

D. The emphasis on national or international goals

Answer: D. The emphasis on national or international goals

Although the two ideologies forcefully opposed each other, they in fact shared many basic points. The largest difference was the focus on internal, nationalistic goals in the case of fascism and external internationalist goals in the case of communism.

68. Since World War II, population growth has mostly been a problem because of (Rigorous) (Skill 2.3a)

A. Inadequate technological development

B. Declining global health

C. Limited food supply

D. Decreasing literacy rates

Answer: C. Limited food supply

Global population rates have grown rapidly since the end of World War II, and the growth of the food supply has not kept pace, particularly in the developing world. This presents the biggest challenge to mass population growth.

69. The Cold War mostly stemmed from *(Rigorous) (Skill 2.3a)*

    A. Geographical and social issues

    B. Political and economic disagreements

    C. Eethical and intellectual divides

    D. Governmental and cultural splits

Answer: B. Political and economic disagreements

Although the United States and the Soviet Union had great social, ethical, intellectual, and cultural differences during the Cold War era, the main source of international tension was the nations' competing political and economic systems.

70. Increased _____ is both a cause and an effect of greater economic interdependence. *(Rigorous) (Skill 2.3b)*

    A. globalization

    B. consumer demand

    C. scarcity

    D. unemployment

Answer: A. globalization

As economies around the world become more interdependent, their relative on one another become increasingly linked. This (A) globalization both results from interdependence and makes it grew stronger.

71. **Which of these technological developments has had the least significant impact in the 21st century?** *(Rigorous) (Skill 2.3b)*

    A. Automobile

    B. Internet

    C. Cell phone

    D. E-mail

Answer: A. Automobile

The automobile was the driving factor of 20th century economic change. In the 21st century, technological shifts stemming from the Internet, e-mail, and cell phones have enacted change much more rapidly.

72. **Which force has *not* shaped changing world events in the 21st century? (Rigorous) (Skill 2.3b)**

    A. Communist expansion

    B. Global terrorism

    C. Religious extremism

    D. Arab democratic movements

Answer: A. Communist expansion

Although China—the world's most populous country—remains a communist nation, expansion of that political system has essentially halted. The other factors have emerged as major factors reshaping the global landscape.

73. What is *not* a purpose of government laws? *(Rigorous) (Skill 3.0a)*

A. Maintain order

B. Catch criminals

C. Keep people safe

D. Eestablish guidelines for behavior

Answer: B. Catch criminals

Rules and laws help establish (A) order and (D) guidelines for behavior that let people know how they should behave. This helps (C) keep people safe. When laws are broken, then law enforcement must (B) catch criminals, but the purpose of laws is not to create crime.

74. Who first suggested the idea of the "social contract"? *(Easy) (Skill 3.0b)*

A. Jean-Jacques Rousseau

B. John Locke

C. Niccolo Machiavelli

D. Thomas Hobbes

Answer: A. Jean-Jacques Rousseau

In his work of 1762, *The Social Contract*, (A) Jean- Jacques Rousseau described the "general will" leading to socialism. Niccolo Machiavelli (C) was the famous politician from Florence who disregarded the ideals of Christianity in favor of realistic power politics. Thomas Hobbes (D), whose most famous work was *Leviathan*, believed that a person's life was a constant, unceasing search for power and believed in the state's supremacy to combat this. (B) John Locke, whose book *Two Treatises of Government* has long been considered a founding document on the rights of people to rebel against an unjust government, was an important figure in the founding of the U.S. Constitution and on the general politics of the American colonies.

75. **Public administration, such as public officials in the areas of budgets, accounting, distribution of public funds, and personnel management would be a part of the field of:** *(Average) (Skill 3.0b)*

   A. Anthropology

   B. Sociology

   C. Law and taxation

   D. Political science and economics

Answer: D. Political science and economics

Public administration, such as public officials in the areas of budgets, accounting, distribution of public funds, and personnel management, would be parts of the fields of economics and political science. While political scientists would be concerned with public administration, economists would also be concerned with the distribution of public funds, budgets, and accounting and their effects on the economy.

76. **A political scientist might use all of the following except:** *(Rigorous) (Skill 3.0b)*

   A. An investigation of government documents

   B. A geological timeline

   C. Voting patterns

   D. Polling data

Answer: B A geological timeline

Political science is primarily concerned with the political and governmental activities of societies. (A) Government documents can provide information about the organization and activities of a government. (C) Voting patterns reveal the political behavior of individuals and groups. (D) Polling data can provide insight into the predominant political views of a group of people. (B) A geological timeline describes the changes in the physical features of Earth over time and would not be useful to a political scientist.

77. In the United States, checks and balances refers to: *(Average) (Skill 3.1a)*

    A. The ability of each branch of government to limit the actions of others

    B. The creation of a series of guaranteed rights

    C. The balance of power between the federal government and the states

    D. The recognition of minority rights alongside majority rule

Answer: A. The ability of each branch of government to limit the actions of others

The U.S. Constitution provides for limits of government power by creating three branches of government that have (A) the ability to limit each of the other branches. The Constitution also provides for a (B) Bill of Rights, (C) federalism, and (D) respect for minority rights.

78. In the Constitutional system of checks and balances, a primary "check" which accrues to the president is the power of: *(Average) (Skill 3.1a)*

    A. Executive privilege

    B. Approval of judges nominated by the Senate

    C. Veto of Congressional legislation

    D. Approval of judges nominated by the House of Representatives

Answer: **C**. Veto of Congressional legislation

The power to (C) veto congressional legislation is granted to the U.S. president in Article I of the Constitution, which states that all legislation passed by both houses of the Congress must be given to the president for approval. This is a primary check on the power of the Congress by the president. The Congress may override a presidential veto by a two-thirds majority vote of both houses, however. (A) Executive privilege refers to the privilege of the president to keep certain documents private. Answers (B) and (D) are incorrect, as Congress does not nominate judges. This is a presidential power.

79. **The term that best describes how the Supreme Court can block laws that may be unconstitutional from being enforced is:** *(Average) (Skill 3.1a)*

    A. Jurisprudence

    B. Judicial Review

    C. Exclusionary Rule

    D. Right of Petition

Answer: B. Judicial Review

(A) Jurisprudence is the study of the development and origin of law. (B) Judicial review is the term that best describes how the Supreme Court can block the enforcement of laws that it deems as unconstitutional as set forth in *Marbury v. Madison*. The (C) "exclusionary rule" is a reference to the Fourth Amendment of the Constitution and says that evidence gathered in an illegal manner or search must be thrown out and excluded from evidence. There is nothing called the (D) "Right of Petition", however the Petition of Right is a reference to a statement of civil liberties sent by the English Parliament to Charles I in 1628.

80. **Constitutions are formally changed by:** *(Average) (Skill 3.1a)*

    A. Amendments

    B. Court decisions

    C. Laws

    D. Referendums

Answer: A. Amendments

Both the U.S. constitutions and state constitutions are formally changed, or amended, by (A) amendments. (B) Court decisions, (C) laws, and (D) referendums may informally influence how constitutions are interpreted.

81. **Collectively, the first ten Amendments to the Constitution are known as the:** *(Easy) (Skill 3.1a)*

   A. Articles of Confederation

   B. Mayflower Compact

   C. Bill of Rights

   D. Declaration of the Rights of Man

Answer: C. Bill of Rights

The (A) Articles of Confederation was the document under which the thirteen colonies of the American Revolution came together and was the first governing document of the United States. The (B) Mayflower Compact was an agreement signed by several of the Pilgrims aboard the Mayflower before establishing their colony at Plymouth in 1620. The (D) Declaration of the Rights of Man was the French document adopted after the French Revolution in 1789. The first ten amendments of the US Constitution, spelling out the limitations of the federal government, are referred to as (C) the Bill of Rights.

82. **Why is the system of government in the United States referred to as a federal system?** *(Easy) (Skill 3.1b)*

   A. There are different levels of government

   B. There is one central authority in which all governmental power is vested

   C. The national government cannot operate except with the consent of the governed

   D. Elections are held at stated periodic times, rather than as called by the head of the government

Answer: A. There are different levels of government

(A) The United States is composed of fifty states, each responsible for its own affairs but united under a federal government. (B) A centralized system is the opposite of a federal system. (C) That national government cannot operate except with the consent of the governed is a founding principle of American politics. It is not a political system like federalism. A centralized democracy could still be consensual but would not be federal. (D) This is a description of electoral procedure, not a political system like federalism

83. Which branch is responsible for carrying out the laws of the country? *(Easy) (Skill 3.1b)*

A. Judicial

B. Executive

C. Legislative

D. Supreme Court

Answer: B. Executive

In the United States, the three branches of the federal government mentioned earlier, the **executive**, the **legislative**, and the **judicial**, divide up their powers thus: Article II of the Constitution created the (B) executive branch of the government, headed by the president, who leads the country, recommends new laws, and can veto bills passed by the legislative branch. As the chief of state, the president is responsible for carrying out the laws of the country and the treaties and declarations of war passed by the legislative branch.

84. Which of the following is *not* a branch of government? *(Rigorous) (Skill 3.1b)*

A. Executive branch

B. Federal branch

C. Legislative branch

D. Judicial branch

Answer: B. Federal branch

The three branches of U.S. government are (A) the executive branch, (C) the legislative branch, and (D) the judicial branch. The (B) federal government is a level of government, rather than a branch.

85. The _____ branch of government is made up of the House of Representatives and the Senate. *(Average) (Skill 3.1b)*

   A. Judicial

   B. Executive

   C. Legislative

   D. Supreme Court

Answer: C. Legislative

In the United States, the three branches of the federal government mentioned earlier, the **executive**, the **legislative**, and the **judicial**, divide up their powers thus: Article I of the Constitution established the (C) legislative, or law-making, branch of the government called the Congress. It is made up of two houses, the House of Representatives and the Senate.

86. Which one of the following is *not* a function or responsibility of the U.S. political parties? *(Rigorous) (Skill 3.1e)*

   A. Conducting elections or the voting process

   B. Obtaining funds needed for election campaigns

   C. Choosing candidates to run for public office

   D. Making voters aware of issues and other public affairs information

Answer: A. Conducting elections or the voting process

The U.S. political parties have numerous functions and responsibilities. Among them are (B) obtaining funds needed for election campaigns, (C) choosing the candidates to run for office, and (D) making voters aware of the issues. The political parties, however, do not (A) conduct elections or the voting process, as that would be an obvious conflict of interest.

87. Which of the following are *not* local governments in the United States? *(Rigorous) (Skill 3.1e)*

   A. Cities

   B. Townships

   C. School boards

   D. All of these are forms of local government

Answer: **D**. All of these are forms of local government

Citizens wishing to engage in the political process to a greater degree have several paths open, such as participating in local government. Counties, states, and sometimes neighborhoods are governed by locally elected boards or councils that meet publicly.

88. The head of state of a monarchy might be called a: *(Easy) (Skill 3.2a)*

   A. President

   B. King

   C. Prime minister

   D. Dictator

Answer: B. King

A monarchy is a form of government headed by an absolute, hereditary ruler, such as (B) a king (or a queen). The presidential system is headed by (A) a president, while the parliamentary system is typically led by (C) a prime minister. (D) Dictators rule over tyrannies and dictatorships.

89. _____is the effort to create, by dictatorial means, a viable national society in which competing interests are to be adjusted to each other by being entirely subordinated to the service of the state although it will tolerate some private ownership of the means of production. *(Average) (Skill 3.2a)*

A. Dictatorship

B. Parliamentary system

C. Anarchism

D. Fascism

Answer: D. Fascism

(A) A dictatorship is rule by an individual or small group of individuals (oligarchy) that centralizes all political control in itself and enforces its will with a terrorist police force. (B) A parliamentary system is a system of government with a legislature, usually involving a multiplicity of political parties and often coalition politics. There is division between the head of state and head of government. The head of government is usually known as a prime minister, who is also usually the head of the largest party. The head of government and the cabinet usually both sit and vote in the parliament. (C) Anarchism is a political movement believing in the elimination of all government and its replacement by a cooperative community of individuals. (D) Fascism is a belief as well as a political system, opposed ideologically to communism, though similar in basic structure, with a one-party state, centralized political control, and a repressive police system. Fascism tolerates private ownership of the means of production, though it maintains tight overall control.

90. **The movement of cultural ideas or materials between populations is known as: (Rigorous) (Skill 5.1)**

   A. Adaptation

   B. Innovation

   C. Acculturalization

   D. Cultural diffusion

Answer: D. Cultural diffusion

(A) Adaptation is the process that individuals and societies go through in changing their behavior and organization to cope with social, economic, and environmental pressures. (B) Innovation is the introduction of new ways of performing work or organizing societies; it can spur drastic changes in a culture. (C) Acculturation is an exchange or adoption of cultural features when two cultures come into regular direct contact. (D) Cultural diffusion is the movement of cultural ideas or materials between populations independent of the movement of those populations.

91. **Absolute location is identified by:** *(Average) (Skill 4.0a)*

   A. Direction

   B. Latitude and longitude

   C. City and state

   D. Regional characteristics

Answer: B. Latitude and longitude

Absolute location is the description of a place's geographic location using lines of (B) latitude and longitude. Relative location describes a place using (A) direction from other places, while a place's (C) city and state and (D) regional characteristics are still other ways to describe it geographically.

92. **All of these are examples of human-environment interaction except:** *(Rigorous) (Skill 4.0b)*

   A.   Agriculture

   B.   Map-making

   C.   Mining

   D.   Building suburbs

Answer: B. Map-making

Human-environment interaction describes ways that people adapt to and use the land, such as (A) farming, (B) mining, and (D) building communities such as suburbs. (B) Map-making does not fall under this category.

93. **The influence of physical characteristics on how people live is part of which theme of geography?** *(Rigorous) (Skill 4.0b)*

   A.   Regions

   B.   Location

   C.   Movement

   D.   Human-environment interaction

Answer: D. human-environment interaction

The five themes of geography describe places and people's interaction with those places in various ways. The concept of how the land influences people's lives is part of the theme of (D) human-environment interaction.

94. Relief maps can be depicted in different ways. One way is the use of: *(Easy) (Skill 4.1a)*

A. Great-Circle Route

B. Opisometer

C. Meridians

D. Contour Lines

Answer: D. Contour Lines

A (A) great circle is any circle that cuts a sphere, such as the globe, into two equal parts. Because of distortion, most maps do not show great-circle routes as straight lines. A method for measuring curvilinear map distances is to use a mechanical device called (B) an opisometer. This device uses a small rotating wheel that records the distance traveled. The recorded distance is measured by this device in either centimeters or inches. (C) Meridians, or lines of longitude, are the determining factor in separating time zones and determining time around the world. (D) The way to show relief is by using contour lines. These lines connect all points of a land surface which are the same height surrounding the particular area of land.

95. Meridians, or lines of longitude, not only help in pinpointing locations, but are also used for: *(Average) (Skill 4.1b)*

A. Measuring distance from the poles

B. Determining direction of ocean currents

C. Determining the time around the world

D. Measuring distance to the equator

Answer: C. Determining the time around the world

Meridians, or lines of longitude, are the determining factor in separating time zones and determining time around the world.

96. **The study of spatial patterns would be used by people in the field of:** *(Easy) (Skill 4.1c)*

    A. Political science

    B. Anthropology

    C. Geography

    D. Sociology

Answer: C. Geography

(C) Geography is the discipline within social science that most concerns itself with the study of "spatial relationships and interaction". (B) Anthropology is the study of human culture and the way in which people of different cultures live. The artifacts created by people of a certain culture can provide information about the behaviors and beliefs of that culture. (D) Sociology, and (A) political science are more likely to study behaviors and institutions directly than through individual artifacts created by a specific culture.

97. **Which of these is the best example of a thematic map?** *(Average) (Skill 4.1c)*

    A. A map showing election results

    B. A map showing rivers

    C. A map showing state capitals

    D. A map showing landforms

Answer: A. A map showing election results

Thematic maps show collection information such as election results. Physical maps depict physical features such as rivers and landforms. State capitals would appear on a political map.

98. What information might a map key best show? *(Average) (Skill 4.1d)*

A. Population density

B. Map distortion

C. Boundary location

D. Cardinal direction

Answer: A. Population density

Map keys give information needed for reading a map, such as the meaning of shading and symbols. Distortion is inherent in mapmaking. Boundaries are typically shown without need for a map key. Cardinal direction is shown on a compass rose.

99. A physical geographer would be concerned with which of the following groups of terms? *(Average) (Skill 4.2a)*

A. Landform, biome, precipitation

B. Scarcity, goods, services

C. Nation, state, administrative subdivision

D. Cause and effect, innovation, exploration

Answer: A. Landform, biome, precipitation.

(A) Landform, biome, and precipitation are all terms used in the study of geography. A landform is a physical feature of Earth, such as a hill or valley. A biome is a large community of plants or animals, such as a forest. Precipitation is the moisture that falls to earth as rain or snow. (B) Scarcity, goods, and services are terms encountered in economics. (C) Nation, state, and administrative subdivision are terms used in political science. (D) Cause and effect, innovation, and exploration are terms in developmental psychology.

100. Which of these is *not* a division of human geography? *(Rigorous) (Skill 4.3a)*

A. Cultural geography

B. Economic geography

C. Physical geography

D. Population geography

Answer: C. Physical geography

Human geography is the study of how people interact with the world. Physical geography examines landforms and physical features. Thus, all of the disciplines listed except for (C) fall under the domain of human geography.

101. Which question might a cultural geographer ask? *(Rigorous) (Skill 4.3a)*

A. What is the highest point in this nation?

B. How does religion shape this region?

C. Which political system is used in this country?

D. What level of economic development has this region reached?

Answer: B. How does religion shape this region?

Cultural geographers study issues relating to culture such as religion, language, and ethnicity. A physical geographer would consider characteristics such as highest points; a political geographer, government systems; and an economic geographer, levels of economic development.

102. How do deltas most shape human activity? *(Rigorous) (Skill 4.4a)*

    A. By providing adequate farmland

    B. By discouraging settlement

    C. By offering drinking water supplies

    D. By serving as natural borders between countries

Answer: A. By providing adequate farmland

River deltas, such as Egypt's famed Nile Valley delta, are among the world's finest farming areas. Although they may offer drinking water or serve as borders, that is not their most important geographical function. Deltas do not typically discourage settlement as less hospitable areas might.

103. Which of the following is not a river? *(Rigorous) (Skill 4.4a)*

    A. Yangtze

    B. Rio Grande

    C. Arctic

    D. Ganges

Answer: C. Arctic

A) The Yangtze and (D) the Gangesare important rivers in Asia. The (B) Rio Grande, in North America, forms part of the border between the United States and Mexico. The (C) Artic is an ocean.

104. The basic unit of study in geography is: *(Easy) (Skill 4.4a)*

    A. The region

    B. A country

    C. One mile

    D. A culture

Answer: A. The region

A basic unit of geographic study is the region, an area on the earth's surface that is defined by certain unifying characteristics. The unifying characteristics may be physical, human, or cultural. In addition to studying the unifying characteristics of a region, geographers study how a region changes over time.

105. An economist might engage in which of the following activities? *(Rigorous) (Skill 5.0a)*

    A. An observation of the historical effects of a nation's banking practices

    B. The application of a statistical test to a series of data

    C. Introduction of an experimental factor into a specified population to measure the effect of the factor

    D. An economist might engage in all of these

Answer: D An economist might engage in all of these

Economists use statistical analysis of economic data and controlled experimentation, as well as historical research, in their field of social science.

106. Economics is best described as: *(Average) (Skill 5.0b)*

    A. The study of how money is used in different societies

    B. The study of how different political systems produce goods and services

    C. The study of how human beings use limited resources to supply their necessities and wants

    D. The study of how human beings have developed trading practices through the years

Answer: C. The study of how human beings use limited resources to supply their necessities and wants

(A) How money is used in different societies might be of interest to a sociologist or anthropologist. (B) The study of how different political systems produce goods and services is a topic of study that could be included under the field of political science. (D) The study of historical trading practices could fall under the study of history. Only (C) is the best general description of the social science of economics as a whole.

107. In order to achieve efficiency, two conditions must be fulfilled: *(Average) (Skill 5.0c)*

    A. Low unemployment and low inflation

    B. Full employment and full production

    C. Full employment and stable monetary supply

    D. Access to resources and full production

Answer: B. Full employment and full production

In order to achieve efficiency, two conditions must be fulfilled: full employment and full production. Full employment refers to having all resources employed. Idle resources result in lower levels of output. The other condition, full production, means that resources should be employed in their most productive capacity.

108. Capitalism and communism are alike in that they are both: *(Average)* *(Skill 5.0d)*

    A. Organic systems

    B. Political systems

    C. Centrally planned systems

    D. Economic systems

Answer: D. Economic systems

While economic and (B) political systems are often closely connected, capitalism and communism are primarily (D) economic systems. Capitalism is a system of economics that allows the open market to determine the relative value of goods and services. Communism is an economic system where the market is planned by a central state. While communism is a (C) centrally planned system, this is not true of capitalism. (A) Organic systems are studied in biology, a natural science.

109. Which of the following is *not* a significant influence within the free enterprise system? *(Rigorous)* *(Skill 5.0d)*

    A. Government planning

    B. Markets

    C. Entrepreneurs

    D. Innovation

Answer: A. Government planning

The free enterprise system is driven by the demands of the free (B) market, and relies on the (D) innovations of (C) entrepreneurs. It has little involvement from (A) the government.

110. In a command economy: *(Average) (Skill 5.0d)*

    A. The open market determines how much of a good is produced and distributed

    B. The government determines how much of a good is produced and distributed

    C. Individuals produce and consume a specified good as commanded by their needs

    D. The open market determines the demand for a good, and then the government produces and distributes the good

Answer: B. The government determines how much of a good is produced and distributed.

A command economy is where (B) the government determines how much of a good is produced and distributed, as was the case in the Soviet Union and is still the case in Cuba and North Korea. A command economy is the opposite of a market economy, where (A) the open market determines how much of a good is produced and distributed.

111. One method of trade restriction used by some nations is: *(Easy) (Skill 5.0e)*

    A. Limited treaties

    B. Floating exchange rate

    C. Bill of exchange

    D. Import quotas

Answer: D. Import quotas

One method of trade restriction used by some nations is (D) import quotas. The amounts of goods imported are regulated in an effort to protect domestic enterprise and limit foreign competition. Both the United States and Japan, two of the world's most industrialized nations have import quotas to protect domestic industries.

112. The interaction of supply and demand most affect: *(Rigorous) (Skill 5.0g)*

   A. Scarcity

   B. Prices

   C. Production

   D. Entrepreneurship

Answer: B. Prices

As levels of supply and demand diverge, (B) prices may rise or fall significantly until they reach equilibrium. Levels of supply are influenced by the relative (A) scarcity of the resources needed to provide a good or service and (C) the amount producers are willing to supply.

113. What is a major difference between monopolistic competition and perfect competition? *(Rigorous) (Skill 5.1a)*

   A. Perfect competition has many consumers and suppliers, while monopolistic competition does not

   B. Perfect competition provides identical products, while monopolistic competition provides similar, but not identical, products

   C. Entry to perfect competition is difficult, while entry to monopolistic competition is relatively easy

   D. Monopolistic competition has many consumers and suppliers, while perfect competition does not

Answer: B. Perfect competition provides identical products, while monopolistic competition provides similar, but not, identical products.

Perfect competition is the most competitive of all market structures. For the most part, perfect competition is a theoretical extreme. Products are homogenous in this market structure. The numerous firms sell a product identical to that sold by all other firms in the industry. There are a large number of buyers and a large number of sellers, and no one buyer or seller is large enough to affect market price. The price is thus determined entirely by supply and demand. The opposite of perfect competition is a monopoly, a market structure in which only one seller sells a unique product for which there are no substitutes. The firm is the only supplier of the good, so the firm can control the price

114. Of the following, the best example of an oligopoly in the United States is: *(Average) (Skill 5.1a)*

A. Automobile industry

B. Food services

C. Cleaning services

D. Clothing manufacturing

Answer: A. Automobile industry

An **oligopoly** is a market structure in which there are a few sellers of products that may be either homogeneous, such as steel, or heterogeneous, such as automobiles. In contrast, numerous companies exist to provide food, cleaning services, or clothing.

115. Savings most contributes to the growth of the economy by (Rigorous) (Skill 5.1b)

A. Decreasing consumer spending

B. Increasing the overall money supply

C. Providing funds for investment

D. Encouraging inflation

Answer: C. Providing funds for investment

By putting money in banks, people make it available for (C) further investment. The other options do not help cause economic growth.

116. The _____ is a monetary measure of the economy's output during a specified time period and is used by all nations to measure and compare national production. *(Easy) (Skill 5.2a)*

   A. float rate

   B. gross domestic product (GDP)

   C. unemployment rate

   D. national output

Answer: B. Gross Domestic Product (GDP)

The GDP is a monetary measure of the economy's output during a specified time period and is used by all nations to measure and compare national production. Tabulating the economy's output can be measured in two ways, both of which give the same result: the expenditures approach and the incomes approach. Basically, what is spent on the national output by each sector of the economy is equal to what is earned producing the national output by each of the factors of production. The two methods have to be equal.

117. Inflation is the result of the economy _____? *(Average) (Skill 5.2c)*

   A. expanding too slowly

   B. remaining stable

   C. expanding too quickly

   D. expanding in conjunction with the unemployment rate

Answer: C. expanding too quickly

Inflation is caused by the economy expanding too quickly. There is excess aggregate demand that is fueling the inflation. This is a situation where the appropriate governmental action is to slow down the economy. The government will implement contractionary monetary and fiscal policies that result in less spending to end the inflation..

118. As a sociologist, you would be most likely to observe: *(Average) (Skill 6.0a)*

A. The effects of an earthquake on farmland

B. The behavior of rats in sensory-deprivation experiments

C. The change over time in Babylonian obelisk styles

D. The behavior of human beings in television focus groups

Answer: D. The behavior of human beings in television focus groups

Predominant beliefs and attitudes within human society are studied in the field of sociology. (A) The effects of an earthquake on farmland might be studied by a geographer. (B) The behavior of rats in an experiment falls under the field of behavioral psychology. (C) Changes in Babylonian obelisk styles might interest a historian. None of these answers fits easily within the definition of sociology. (D) A focus group, where people are asked to discuss their reactions to a certain product or topic, would be the most likely method for a sociologist of observing and discovering attitudes among a selected group.

119. All of the following are basic institutions around which societies are organized except: *(Rigorous) (Skill 6.2a)*

A. Education

B. Religion

C. Corporation

D. Family

Answer: C . Corporation

Sociologists have identified important institutions around which societies organize themselves, including (A) schools, (B) belief systems, and (D) family structure that share cultural and social values. Although economic institutions play important roles in societies, the (C) corporation is too narrow to qualify as a major institution on its own.

120. **Populations are usually measured by all of the following except:**
     (Rigorous) (Skill 6.3a)

     A. People's jobs

     B. People's education levels

     C. People's interaction with the natural environment

     D. People's relative health levels

Answer: C. People's interaction with the natural environment

Populations are typically measured on quantifiable statistical data, such as education attainment (B), jobs (A), or life spans (D). Information such as interaction with the natural environment is not a demographic measure.

121. **Which term best relates to the naturally occurring attitude that people, for the most part, are most comfortable with others like themselves?**
     (Average) (Skill 6.4a)

     A. Pluralism

     B. Discrimination

     C. Ethnocentrism

     D. Racial Bias

Answer: C. Ethnocentrism

Psychologists have suggested that (C) ethnocentrism is a naturally occurring attitude. For the large part, people are most comfortable among other people who share their same upbringing, language, and cultural background and are likely to judge other cultural behaviors as alien or foreign. (A) Cultural pluralism is the simultaneous existence of several cultures and ethnic groups, with each afforded the protection and ability to observe their cultural institutions. It is also sometimes called multiculturalism. (B) Prejudice, or racial bias, is the act of pre-judging something or someone without firsthand experience. It often involves making judgments based on stereotypes or the automatic rejection of a behavior or practice that seems unusual or foreign. (B) Discrimination takes place when a person or group acts out of prejudice to harm or deny privileges to another.

122. The native metaphysical outlook of Japan, usually characterized as a religion, is: *(Rigorous) (Skill 6.4b)*

A. Daoism

B. Shinto

C. Nichiren Shoju

D. Shaolin

Answer: B. Shinto

(A) Daoism is a religious tradition sourced in China. (B) Shinto is the system of rituals and beliefs honoring the deities and spirits believed to be native to the landscape and inhabitants of Japan. (C) Nichiren Shoju is a strand of Nichiren Buddhism, a tradition started by a Japanese Buddhist monk, Nichiren. (D) The Shaolin temple (originally built in 497 AD) is the Chinese Buddhist monastery considered to be the source of Zen Buddhism and its subsequent martial arts.

123. The world religion which includes a caste system is: *(Easy) (Skill 6.4b)*

A. Buddhism

B. Hinduism

C. Sikhism

D. Jainism

Answer: B. Hinduism

(A) Buddhism, (C) Sikhism, and (D) Jainism all rose out of protest against Hinduism and its practices of sacrifice and the caste system. Under the caste system, people were born into castes that would determine their class for life including who they could marry, what jobs they could perform, and their overall quality of life.

124. What concept calls for mutual respect between ethnic groups and cultures, allowing them to exist together and perpetuate their cultures? *(Average) (Skill 6.4d)*

    A. Syllogism

    B. Conformance

    C. Discrimination

    D. Cultural pluralism

Answer: D. Cultural pluralism

(C) Discrimination takes place when a person or group acts out of prejudice to harm or deny privileges to another. Discrimination takes place between all races and ethnic groups and between men and women at all levels. It can occur between individuals or groups. (D) Cultural pluralism is the simultaneous existence of several cultures and ethnic groups, with each afforded the protection and ability to observe their cultural institutions. It is also sometimes called multiculturalism.

125. Which of the following is *not* one of the four broad areas affecting modern social problems? *(Rigorous) (Skill 6.5a)*

    A. Assimilation

    B. Environment

    C. Education

    D. Health

Answer: A. Assimilation

The list of major social problems facing the world is long, with each culture approaching them based on their own values and beliefs. Four broad areas where social problems are affecting the world are the global economy, the environment, education, and health. Assimilation is state of adopting another culture entirely as one's own.

CPSIA information can be obtained at www.ICGtesting.com
Printed in the USA
BVOW051414080513

320234BV00003B/136/P